The Sound Structure of English

The Sound Structure of English provides a clear introduction to English phonetics and phonology. Tailored to suit the needs of individual, one-term course modules, it assumes no prior knowledge of the subject, and presents the basic facts in a straightforward manner, making it the ideal text for beginners. Students are guided step-by-step through the main concepts and techniques of phonetic and phonological analysis, aided by concise chapter summaries, suggestions for further reading and a comprehensive glossary of all the terms introduced. Each chapter is accompanied by an engaging set of exercises and discussion questions, encouraging students to consolidate and develop their learning, and providing essential self-study material. The book is accompanied by a companion website, which helps readers to work through specified in-chapter problems, suggests answers to end-of-chapter exercises, and contains links to other sites of interest to those working on English sound-structure. Providing the essential knowledge and skills for those embarking on the study of English sounds, it is set to become the leading introduction to the field.

CHRIS McCULLY is a writer and independent scholar who teaches part-time at the Rijksuniversiteit, Groningen. His recent publications include *Generative Theory and Corpus Studies* (edited with Bermúdez-Otero, Denison and Hogg, 2000) and *The Earliest English* (with Sharon Hilles, 2005).

Cambridge Introductions to the English Language

Cambridge Introductions to the English Language is a series of accessible undergraduate textbooks on the key topics encountered in the study of the English language. Tailored to suit the needs of individual taught course modules, each book is written by an author with extensive experience of teaching the topic to undergraduates. The books assume no prior subject knowledge and present the basic facts in a clear and straightforward manner, making them ideal for beginners. They are designed to be maximally reader-friendly, with chapter summaries, glossaries and suggestions for further reading. Extensive exercises and discussion questions are included, encouraging students to consolidate and develop their learning, and providing essential homework material. A website accompanies each book, featuring solutions to the exercises and useful additional resources. Set to become the leading introductions to the field, books in this series provide the essential knowledge and skills for those embarking on English Language Studies.

Books in the series
The Sound Structure of English Chris McCully
Old English Jeremy J. Smith

The Sound Structure of English

An Introduction

Chris McCully

CAMBRIDGE
UNIVERSITY PRESS

CAMBRIDGE UNIVERSITY PRESS
Cambridge, New York, Melbourne, Madrid, Cape Town, Singapore, São Paulo, Delhi

Cambridge University Press
The Edinburgh Building, Cambridge CB2 8RU, UK

Published in the United States of America by Cambridge University Press, New York

www.cambridge.org
Information on this title: www.cambridge.org/9780521615495

First published 2009

Printed in the United Kingdom at the University Press, Cambridge

A catalogue record for this publication is available from the British Library

Library of Congress Cataloguing in Publication data
McCully, C. B.
The sound structure of English : an introduction / Chris McCully.
   p.   cm. – (Cambridge introductions to the English language)
Includes bibliographical references and index.
ISBN 978-0-521-85036-0
1. English language – Phonology.   2. English language – Phonetics.   3. English language –
Phonetic transcriptions.   I. Title.   II. Series.
PE1133.M36   2009
421′.5–dc22

                2008049136

ISBN 978-0-521-85036-0 hardback
ISBN 978-0-521-61549-5 paperback

Cambridge University Press has no responsibility for
the persistence or accuracy of URLs for external or
third-party internet websites referred to in this book,
and does not guarantee that any content on such
websites is, or will remain, accurate or appropriate.

Contents

Figures

Acknowledgements

This book wouldn't exist had it not been for the kind and constructive comments of three anonymous readers for Cambridge University Press, who assessed the preliminary proposal(s) for the work. In that CUP context, Helen Barton has given positive and encouraging feedback at every stage of the writing process, and I am most grateful for that. I am also more than grateful for the work of Alex Bellem, CUP's copy-editor. I would also like to thank Heinz Giegerich, of the Department of English Language, University of Edinburgh, for his influential role in helping me develop this textbook. He has throughout offered me the best kind of criticism. I would also like to thank Monika Schmid, of the Rijksuniversiteit Groningen, for making her graphic summaries of English vowel distribution available to me. My greatest debt, however, is to the students in Manchester, Amsterdam, Groningen and elsewhere, who have not only functioned as the recipients of some of this work, but who have also occasionally saved me from authorial errors and slips, and who for more than twenty years have endured my washing machines (vowel trapezia), chamber pots, and other dubious metaphors and analogies. Occasionally these same students even endured my singing. I don't suppose I shall ever be forgiven. Never mind. On we go.

CBMcC
Usquert
October 2008

A note on using this book

In what follows you'll find a book of eleven chapters, whose contents are detailed above. Throughout each chapter I've set what are intended to be thought-provoking questions. Each question appears in **bold** font and in boxed text. Sometimes I've begun to answer such questions in the text that follows them, but more usually I've not answered them within the covers of this book. You will, however, find that such questions are useful to discuss in seminars, or even outside classes. You'll also find a fuller set of answers in the web pages that accompany the book. You will need to open the following URL: http://www.cambridge.org/9780521615495.

Similarly, at the end of each chapter you'll find a set of more formal exercises. These are labelled e.g. **exercise 1a**, **exercise 3d** and so on. These also appear in bold font, and in text boxes. Again, I have sometimes offered commentary, but more often I've placed a discussion of them in the relevant web pages.

Although the book can be used as a stand-alone textbook *you won't get the best out of it unless and until you access the web pages that complement it.*

You'll also find a glossary in the apparatus which concludes the book. The glossary contains all those terms which, on their first appearance in the text, are set in **bold** font. In the glossary I've given brief (and, I hope, uncontroversial) definitions to these terms, and have also, where relevant, included a page or section reference detailing where those terms appear in this book. There's also a full index, again in the concluding apparatus, so you shouldn't get lost.

CHAPTER 1

Introduction

In this chapter …

In this chapter we explore a system for thinking about, and then describing, English speech sounds. We will see that there are important differences between the usual written system of English and how the system of sounds is structured – so many differences, in fact, that the familiar written system of English could never be used as a transcription of either the structure that lies behind speech or the occurrence of English speech sounds themselves. As we'll see, in order to work systematically with the sounds of English we need to analyse both *the structure that lies behind speech* (we call this *phonology*) and the nature and occurrence of speech sounds themselves (we call this *phonetics*).

Here, too, we begin to look at some of the principles that govern phonology: the *distribution* of sounds, and how they *contrast*. We draw an analogy between this system and the system, or timetable, of trains, and see that to study phonology is to study part of the 'timetable of language'.

1.1 Written and spoken English

It's critical for our purposes to distinguish between the *written* and the *spoken* systems of English. Although it contains significant clues as to how English was once pronounced, English spelling is unreliable as a guide to recent and present-day pronunciation, so much so that George Bernard Shaw once suggested that the familiar word *fish* should be spelled as <ghoti> – <gh> from *enough*, <o> from *women*, and <ti> from words such as *motion*. Consider also the vowel sound (or sounds) one produces in words such as <oar>. For many speakers of English, particularly those who don't typically pronounce the final *r* of <oar>, the vowel represented by the written symbols <oa> is also found in words such as <auk>, <ought>, <sure> and <ford>, where it's represented by the *written* symbols <au>, <ou>, <ure> and <or>.

> The above paragraph introduces a useful convention: when we analyse English, it's convenient to refer to *written* (or *common alphabetic*) *forms* by inserting them within angled brackets, < ... >. When we come to analyse the *sounds* of English, we will insert these into different brackets, either / ... / or [...], depending on the kind of transcription of sound we are making (see below, 1.6 and 1.7).

We're usually so familiar with the written form of English that it can mislead us into making wrong assumptions about the sound system. The word <school>, for example, conventionally begins with three common alphabetic symbols, <s+c+h>, but in terms of *sounds*, the word actually begins with two **consonants** (roughly, and just for the moment, an 's' sound and a 'k' sound). Similarly, the word <shore> begins with two symbols, <s+h>, but only one consonant in speech (a kind of 'sh' sound – for the relevant symbol, see chapter 2). And again, for many (though by no means all) speakers of English, the final <r> of words such as <oar>, <ear>, <car> isn't pronounced; for many (though by no means all) speakers of English the final <g> of words like <king>, <song>, <fishing> isn't pronounced. In your studies, as analysts of the English language and its many different varieties, **it's always important to distinguish very carefully between the written and the spoken forms of English.**

> Can you construct other, possibly unusual combinations of letters which 'spell' English words, e.g. <ghoti> = 'fish', <aughturnun> = 'afternoon' (<aught> from <dr*aught*>, <ur> from <aub*ur*n>, <un> from <l*un*-atic>)?

1.2 More on written and spoken English: the primacy of speech

Although it's not the primary object of attention here, the written system of English doesn't lack interest. Studying the physical shapes of the letters, analysing how and why such letter shapes differ from each other, and working out how the alphabet developed, is to study **graphology** and its history. The earliest English alphabets were in fact modified forms of alphabetic shapes used for written Latin, but also incorporated some characters (symbols) inherited from the Germanic **runic** alphabet. (For a brief introduction to runes, see Graddol *et al.* 1996: 42 or Crystal 1995: 9 – though it's worth pointing out that the runic alphabet was itself a special adaptation of Greek and Latin symbols.) It's also the case that many present-day English spellings give us significant clues to the spoken histories of the words in question. It's reasonable to suppose, for example, that written vowel shapes like <ea> were, at some point in the history of English, pronounced differently from vowel shapes written as <ee>. That is, <meat> was once pronounced differently from <meet>, despite the fact that in many present-day varieties of English these words are **homophones**. (Homophones are words that sound identical, despite differences in spelling: other examples in my own variety of spoken English are <sea> and <see>, <site> and <sight>.) So spellings can be and often are used by linguists as important evidence bearing on how a language's sound system has developed, and how its history may be reconstructed.

There's another reason why analysing and transcribing speech is an activity properly distinct from the analysis of written language. Human beings learn to speak long before they can write (even assuming they ever learn to write). Speech is for many of us the primary, and certainly the most overt, mode of human communication, while writing systems usually begin life as an attempt to capture speech sounds, implying that speech is a primary medium, while writing is derived from it.

Writing is usually very much more conservative than speech. The English language is incessantly, though often imperceptibly, changing, and these changes often show up first in speech, rather than in the written system. (Many changes never reach the written system at all.) For example, in the last forty years there has been a definite shift in how the vowel shape represented by <a> is pronounced in some prestige varieties of British English (BrE, and on the abbreviation, see the boxed text below) in words like <cat>, <hand>, or the first – and, in BrE, stressed – syllable of <garage>.

I will be using some abbreviations in this book. 'British English' will be abbreviated as 'BrE', and 'General American' – a variety that typically includes the pronunciation of 'r' after vowels and finally in a word (*fourth, door*) – as 'GA'. I will explain abbreviations, and any special symbols used here, in boxed text as we work.

Such a shift in pronunciation isn't at all represented in changed spellings: the spellings of the words affected have remained constant. This means that often enough, students of language look to speech, not writing, when they are thinking through how languages have changed over time.

How many other pairs of homophones can you find in your own variety of spoken English?

The reason these points are being made now is that many students beginning their study of the sound structure of English are so accustomed to thinking of the written system of the language as in some sense 'primary' that they may make faulty generalisations about the sound structure of the language they speak. For example, try the following exercise. Construct a list of ten English words – preferably, words comprising one and only one syllable – that begin with:

- one consonant
- two consonants
- three consonants

This simple exercise contains the word 'consonant'. The term implies something spoken ('con+sonant' = 'sounding together'). The list of words beginning with one consonant generally presents no problem: **monosyllables** (i.e. words of just one syllable) such as *dog, cat, house, sit, pin, tar* and *cup* make their appearance. But with the list of words that begin with two consonants, problems arise – and they're almost invariably problems stemming from the fact that you are still thinking in terms of the *written system* of English. 'Words that begin with two consonants? Well … How about *ship?*' The difficulty there is that <ship> certainly appears to begin with two written consonant shapes, but in terms of the *sound structure* of the language, the word actually begins with just *one* consonant. The following lists make this point clear:

Words only *appearing* to begin with two consonants
ship   (graphic <sh> represents *one* speech sound)
chase   (graphic <ch> ditto)
thigh   (graphic <th> ditto)

there   (graphic <th> ditto)
phone   (graphic <ph> ditto)

Words only *appearing* to end with two consonants
fish   (graphic <sh> represents *one* speech sound)
bath   (graphic <th> ditto)
Bach   (proper name: graphic <ch> ditto)
graph   (graphic <ph> ditto)

Things get more complicated if we ask about words that begin and/or end with three consonants. 'Three consonants at the beginning … Well, what about *school*?' The problem is that the word *school* appears to begin with *three* written consonant shapes (<s>, <c> and <h>), whereas in terms of the word's sound structure, *only two* consonants are present. The following lists emphasise this pseudo-problem:

Words only *appearing* to begin with three consonants
school   (graphic <sch> represents *two* speech sounds)
phrase   (graphic <phr> ditto)
shrew   (graphic <shr> ditto)
sphere   (graphic <sph> ditto)

Words only *appearing* to end with three consonants
graphs   (graphic <phs> represents *two* speech sounds)
laughs   (graphic <ghs> ditto)
baths   (graphic <ths> ditto)

The point bears repeating: from the beginning of our study of the sound structure of English we need to distinguish carefully between the written and spoken systems of the language. Our familiarity with the written system can sometimes mislead us into making wrong generalisations about the sound structure of the language, or into constructing transcriptions of sound which are inappropriate. Notice that we're not saying that familiar graphic conventions – the conventions of written English – are 'wrong'. We're just saying that the familiar written system of English doesn't offer us the *symbolic consistency* or the *adequacy* we need in order to describe and transcribe the *system* that underlies the way we speak our varieties of English.

1.3 Speech as a system

In the paragraphs above we've begun to use the word *system* – the 'system of writing', the 'sound system of English'. What allows us to make the claim that the sound structure of present-day English is a 'system'?

As we'll see, speech sounds are themselves organised within the overall structure of the English language: certain speech sounds **contrast** with other speech sounds, and such contrasts are meaningful. In many spoken varieties of English, for example, there's a perceptible *spoken* difference between a vowel like that represented by the <i> of <sit>, and one like that represented by the <ea> of <seat>, the <e> of <met> and the <ee> of <meet>. <sit> and <met> contain **short vowels** (we'll define the term 'short' more precisely later, see in particular chapters 9–10), while <seat> and <meet> contain **long vowels**. The difference in length is a *meaningful* contrast.

Speech sounds also tend to behave *predictably*. For example, the speech sounds corresponding to the beginning of the written word <pray> form the beginning of a well-structured syllable (about which you can read more in chapter 6), but the speech sounds corresponding to *<rpay> (see boxed text below) do not.

The asterisk occurring before a particular linguistic form indicates a form that isn't merely non-occurring, but deviant. For instance, the made-up word <brip> doesn't appear to occur in any variety of English, *even though it is well formed* in terms of its sound structure. Its non-occurrence is merely an accidental gap. On the other hand, *<rpay> is ill-formed: a 'p' simply cannot follow an 'r' in order to begin an English word. Such an ordering would violate the underlying principles of how English speech sounds are ordered.

Similarly, the speech sounds corresponding to <grinds> form a well-structured syllable, but those corresponding to *<rgidns> do not; <blue> is fine, but *<lbue> isn't. If you're asked why the asterisked forms are deviant or otherwise unacceptable, you might reply that they're 'difficult to say' or 'impossible to pronounce'. There's a reason for that difficulty or impossibility: there are *principles* operative within the spoken system of English that determine which speech sounds can co-occur with other speech sounds. Knowing those principles is part of our wider (and usually tacit) knowledge of the structure of the English language. Analysis of *spoken* English can reveal a great deal about what those principles are, and how they might be formulated and studied.

By observing your own variety of spoken English, how much data could you amass to support the claim that your use of that spoken system was largely *systematic*?

1.4 *Accent* and *dialect*

Another reason why we might want to study the sounds of English systematically is so that we can analyse the richness of English **accents**. We need to discriminate between the terms *accent* and **dialect**. *Accent* refers to features, patterns and phenomena belonging to variations in *speech*. For example, three speakers of English from different parts of the world may all pronounce the same word – say, the word spelled <path> – rather differently: a speaker of a Northern variety of British English (a speaker from, say, Leeds) may characteristically pronounce the word with a short vowel, a speaker of Southern Standard British English may pronounce it with a long vowel, and a speaker who has learned English as a second language may pronounce the final 'th' sound rather like some variety of 't'. These variations are variations of *accent*. Professional linguists are interested in precisely these variations, and in answering questions about them. Why do they occur? Where did these variations originate? How historically stable are they? Linguists are *not* interested in making personal judgements about the 'correctness' or otherwise of particular English accents. Like it or not, *every* user of English 'speaks with an accent'. Questioning *why* those accents exist, and asking *how* they are patterned, are the proper concerns of linguists. In this field of study, as in any other science, value judgements are irrelevant.

If the term *accent* refers to spoken features of English, then *dialect* refers to variations that include accent, but also include features of syntax and vocabulary. (In linguistics the word for 'vocabulary', or our 'mental dictionary' of meaningful words, word parts and phrases, is **lexicon**.)

To make this clearer, consider the following sentence (in linguistics, such a sentence is called a **substitution frame**) and fill in the indicated gap with a demonstrative pronoun – a word such as 'those' or 'them':

He caught the pike between_____weeds

(A pike is a predatory freshwater fish.) Clearly, you could insert the word *those* into the frame. But for many speakers of English, you could also insert *them* ('them weeds'). For other speakers, you could insert the form *dey* (and such speakers would also tend to use the form *de* for the definite article – *de pike*). Such variations do not just involve pronunciation, they also involve **grammar** – in this instance, the system of pronoun forms. As such, the variations (including accent, but also embracing other syntactic features of English) belong to the study of *dialect*. They are *dialectal variations*. (Note: please distinguish between the term *dialectal* and the term *dialectical*. This last term belongs properly to philosophy, rather than to linguistics.)

Other examples of dialectal variation: for many speakers of English, *I need this plug mending* is a perfectly usual structure – but not for speakers of some varieties of Scots English, for whom *I need this plug mended* would be normative. This difference, a syntactic difference involving the inflectional **morphology** (roughly, the word-building) of verb forms, is dialectal. Or again, I could refer to an acquaintance *raising her little finger*, while you might normatively refer to her *raising her pinkie*. The difference, between *little finger* and *pinkie*, is a variation that is said to be *lexical* (involving the lexicon, the 'mental dictionary' of a speaker).

Every English speaker uses some form of dialect. By historical accident, political choice, or societal pressure (or perhaps all three), the particular dialect used may have become some kind of *standard* form of English, a prestige form, a form taught and transmitted ('Don't say *them* weeds, Christopher! Say *those* …'). But – and uncomfortably for self-appointed guardians of the 'purity of the English language' – 'standard' forms of English are themselves dialects, and for dialect speakers, whether they be from Somerset, Scotland or Singapore, their native dialect is a perfect communicative medium, neither better nor worse than other dialects. Just as they attempt to study accents with scientific detachment and impartiality, so linguists bring the same analytical detachment to the study of dialect. The questions that interest the linguist are: How did this dialect originate? How has it changed over time? What factors have caused it to change? What is the relationship between spoken and written forms of this particular dialect?

What *accent* of English do you think you use? Would your immediate circle of friends and family agree that you use that form of accent? (Try asking them.) What *dialectal features* can you find in your own variety of English?

1.5 More on systems and structure

I've talked about structures and systems, and about how the spoken system of English is rather different from the written. But what sort of object *is* the sound structure of English? How can we study it? What does it mean, 'making generalisations about' the behaviour of certain items within that system?

To help understand the word 'structure', and what it entails in this kind of linguistic study, I'm going to introduce an analogy. The analogy is between the behaviour of sounds, and the behaviour of trains. The analogy isn't my own; it's a reworking of an analogy constructed by the Swiss linguist Ferdinand de Saussure in the early years of the twentieth century (Saussure 1983: 107). Here goes.

For many years I took a morning train to work. The train was the 07.52 from Greenfield to Manchester. Sometimes this train arrived with two yellow carriages, sometimes with four blue ones. Sometimes the train arrived, and subsequently departed, late. Sometimes it didn't arrive at all.

Now, whatever the physical appearance of the train, and however late it was, this didn't alter the fact that the train itself was still the 07.52 from Greenfield to Manchester.

The point is this. The identity of the train I took to work depended on its place in the *timetable*, and that timetable is a *structure*. Even when the 07.52 was late, cancelled, or varied in colour it was still, always, the 07.52, whose identity was guaranteed by the timetable of trains – specifically, by the fact that the 07.52 behaved in a certain way (it travelled from Greenfield to Manchester, not to Blackpool, Bolton or Paris), and by the fact that this train *wasn't*, and could never be, the 08.05 or the 08.15.

When we start to think about how the sounds of English or any other language 'work', we have to understand that these speech sounds operate in terms of a *structure*. Whatever the physical, or acoustic, properties of a sound (for example, whether the sound represented by the symbol 'g' is pronounced loudly or softly, spoken, whispered, or sung), this doesn't alter the fact that in English we still understand it as that particular sound.

How can we prove, or infer, the existence of a linguistic structure? We can infer the timetable (or structure) of the running of trains by looking at their physical arrival and departure, and similarly, when we start thinking abut the sound structure of English, we can infer a great deal from the physical nature and distribution of the speech sounds themselves – that is, whether a particular sound can begin a syllable, or end a syllable, or both, or whether it can occur after 's' in the beginning of a syllable, or not … and so on. However, while the railway timetable represents the underlying structure of the running of trains, it doesn't tell us whether the trains are red or yellow. These are part of the physical characteristics of the trains themselves, and not part of the underlying timetable or structure. And when a linguist thinks about structure, he or she is thinking *primarily about the system, rather than the actual physical implementation of that system.*

Because it's useful to have a term for that kind of thinking, let's use one: the sound structure of a language is the **phonology** of that language, and the physical manifestation of the actual sounds is the **phonetics** of that language.

1.6 **Phonetic observation and phonological generalisation**

From 1.5 it follows that there are different kinds of way in which we could study the sound structure of English. We could focus on the physical characteristics, and acoustic properties, of various sounds (this would be a largely phonetic focus). Or we could study the relatedness (or lack of relatedness) of particular sounds, as these occurred as part of the structure of English, and we could also study how these same sounds, or classes of sounds, were distributed within the syllable, i.e. which consonants, for example, could function as **pre-vocalic** (occurring before vowels), or **post-vocalic** (occurring after vowels); which consonants could occur after the speech sound 's'; which consonants were of apparently restricted distribution, and so on. If we studied the sound structure of English in this way, we would be thinking *phonologically*.

The prime focus of this book is on (English) phonology. But there's a problem here: to get a secure phonological generalisation, we must also take into account some phonetic, that is, acoustic, detail. Why? Precisely because we can make phonological *inferences* from that detail.

To give further definition to the material we've started to think about, try an experiment. This involves the speech sound which is invariably written as <p> – the 'p' you get in English monosyllables such as *pin*, *spin* or *nip*.

First, hold the open palm of your right/left hand about 5cm from your mouth. Now pronounce the monosyllable *pin*, clearly and distinctly. No need to shout or whisper, just say the word clearly, and without undue emphasis. As you utter the 'p' of *pin*, do you feel anything on your open palm?

You should feel a definite puff of air as you pronounce the syllable-initial consonant. This is because the English speech sound represented (so far) by 'p' is produced, when it occurs at the beginning of words like *pin* or *path*, with a rapid explosive release of air (on the precise mechanism involved, see chapter 2). Such a puff of air, occurring in this environment (initially, in a stressed syllable), is known as *plosion* or *aspiration*.

Next, and while holding your open palm in the same position, utter the monosyllable *nip*, and notice what happens when you pronounce the 'p'. This time, was there the same puff of air on your open palm? I doubt it. In fact, in many varieties of English, particularly in quick or casual speech, the 'p' sound that occurs finally in a syllable is accompanied by no explosive release of air at all.

> Last, and still holding your open palm in the same position, clearly utter the monosyllable *spin*. As you do so, *listen* very carefully to what happens when the 'p' sound of *spin* is uttered. As you do this part of the exercise, you should find not only that the 'p' of *spin* has less explosive release than the 'p' of *pin*, but also that where it occurs after 's' and before a vowel, our apparently innocuous 'p' begins to sound something like a 'b'.

If we're observing the acoustic, measurable differences in the kinds of explosive release involved in the production of 'p' in the words *pin*, *nip* and *spin* then clearly we're dealing with observations that are largely *phonetic* in character.

'Fine – but what's that got to do with phonology?'

> Take the same exercise two stages further. This time, hold your opened, downward-facing palm parallel to the floor, but place it 2–3 cm immediately below your mouth. Now utter the words *tun*, *nut*, and *stun*. Notice what happens when you pronounce the 't' in each respective word.
>
> In *tun*, 't' has a rapid explosive release, just like the 'p' of *pin*.
>
> In *nut*, 't' has much less plosion (if any), just like the 'p' of *nip*.
>
> And in *stun*, 't' has less plosion than in *tun*, and also begins to sound like a 'd' (compare the behaviour of 'p' in *spin*).
>
> For the last stage of this exercise, keep your downward-facing, opened palm in the same position as it was for the *tun-nut-stun* exercise, but this time, pronounce the monosyllables *kin*, *nick* and *skin*. What phonetic observations can you make about the behaviour of the 'k' sound?

The 'k' behaves just like its predecessors 'p' and 't': it's accompanied by strong plosion when it occurs initially in the syllable; it has almost no plosion (and perhaps none at all) when it occurs syllable-finally; and after 's' and before a vowel, the 'k' has less plosion than when it occurs in absolute or sole syllable-initial position, *and* in this position – after 's' and before a vowel – this 'k' sounds suspiciously like a 'g'.

Observing and/or measuring plosion is a matter of acoustic phonetics. On the other hand, we can *infer* from the above exercise that (1) the speech sounds 'p, t, k' have identical patterns of *distribution* within the syllable, i.e. they can occur pre-vocalically (before a vowel), post-vocalically (after a vowel), and after 's', *and* that (2) in the same environments, each of these apparently different sounds seems to behave in exactly the same way. These last are *phonological*, not phonetic, observations. Among other things,

11

these observations strongly suggest that 'p, t, k' appear in the same contexts to behave in the same way as each other, and therefore may form a particular kind of 'class' of sounds (see further chapters 7 and 11, where we look at the notion of classes of sound in more detail).

1.7 Transcription types

Suppose that we're vitally interested in transcribing the acoustic differences there are in the production of 'p' where this occurs in *pin*, *nip* and *spin*. Because each variety of 'p' shows acoustic differences, we can indicate this in a *phonetic transcription*. A 'p' sound with maximal plosion, for example, we could represent by the symbol [pʰ]. A 'p' sound that had no plosion whatsoever (*nip*), we could represent using the symbol [p̚]. And a 'p' sound that had only weak plosion, and had acquired other features – when, say, 'p' occurs after 's', and before a vowel (*spin*) – we might symbolise as [b̥]. These are symbols which indicate the quality of the sound which actually occurs in speech: they are *phonetic symbols* and are therefore used in *phonetic transcriptions*.

It looks as if we're dealing with three separate symbols, each with some kind of diacritic mark, to represent three predictably occurring manifestations of 'p'. In purely *phonetic* terms we might want to make transcriptions such as the following:

Graphic shape	Phonetic transcription
\<pin\>	[pʰɪn]
\<nip\>	[nɪp̚]
\<spin\>	[sb̥ɪn]

> I'm using the International Phonetic Association (IPA) symbol [ɪ] to indicate the relevant vowel. You'll find out much more about this symbol, and its potential contrast with /i:/ (compare the pronunciation of *nip* and *neap*, *sit* and *seat*), in chapters 5–7, but particularly in chapters 8 and 9.

From a *phonological* point of view, though, we're not so much interested in the acoustic character of the respectively different 'p' varieties, as in the *distribution* of 'p': in the fact that 'p, t, k' appear to *function*, in some way, as a class of sounds; and in the fact that the 'p' sound can make meaningful *contrasts* with 't' or 'k' (compare the words *pin*, *tin* and *kin*, and see 2.1 on the important issue of **contrastiveness**). For a phonologist the precise phonetic character of the sound(s) is of less ultimate interest than the fact that *analytically, there is one, underlying, sound /p/ (or /t/, or /k/) – a sound* *which, nevertheless, has contextually determined realisations.* These 'underlying sounds' are parts of the structure that lies behind speech, parts of the timetable of language. They are **phonemes**, and are used in making **phonemic transcriptions**.

To a phonologist, therefore, transcriptions such as the following are appropriate:

Graphic shape	**Phonemic transcription**
<pin>	/pɪn/
<nip>	/nɪp/
<spin>	/spɪn/

Notice the differences between the phonetic transcriptions and their phonemic analogues. ('Phonemic' is used merely as a synonym for 'phonological'.)

- The phonetic transcriptions are 'narrow' (they symbolise the acoustic character of the sounds in question) while the phonemic transcriptions are 'broad' (they transcribe the sounds in question by symbolising their underlying character, not their precise phonetic properties).
- Phonemic transcriptions represent, or symbolise, the underlying form of speech sounds; phonetic ones describe, or symbolise, how they actually sound when spoken.
- Phonemic transcriptions work at the level of *system*; phonetic transcriptions work at the level of *event* (the actual spoken sound).
- Phonemic transcriptions contain more simple romanic characters than phonetic transcriptions, and the simplest phonemic transcriptions contain no diacritics or other marks; phonetic transcriptions may contain diacritic and other marks, and may make use of fewer romanic characters.
- The phonetic transcriptions appear in square brackets […], while the phonemic ones appear in slant brackets / … / The brackets appear at the beginning and end of whatever string of sound it is you wish to transcribe, whether this be a single speech sound, or a whole sentence or paragraph.

These last are universal, and important, conventions

You may think that phonemic transcriptions are in some sense simpler than phonetic ones. After all, there are fewer of those awkward and hard-to-remember diacritic marks in phonemic transcriptions. But the simplicity or otherwise of a given transcription is a matter of point of view. To a phonologist, even the simplest of phonemic transcriptions is full of detail and interest, because it contains information about the distinctiveness, the contrastiveness, and to some extent the distribution, of the underlying speech sounds of that variety of whichever language is being transcribed.

I've begun to use the term *contrastive*. Since contrastiveness is one of the keys to English phonology – indeed to phonology in general – it's time now to look at that notion in more detail, and to find out why contrastiveness is so important in defining the English consonant system. That's the topic of the next chapter.

Exercises

After each of the chapters of this book you'll find a section of exercises. It's important to complete *all* the exercises before moving on to read the next chapter. You'll find further commentary and notes on each exercise in the web pages that accompany this book. Generally, the exercises you are set will be of two types: there will be practical exercises, and theoretical ones.

For some of the practical exercises it will be helpful if you have some pieces of equipment. For example, a small hand mirror is useful, so that you can observe what's happening in your mouth (which linguists know as the 'oral cavity') when you produce certain sounds. A spatula is also handy, so you can touch parts of the oral cavity that would otherwise be beyond the reach of your index finger. A bottle of mouthwash, too, can help you to think through questions such as 'What happens in, and to, the organs of speech when I gargle?'

For the theoretical exercises, all you have to bring is an open mind.

Let's begin here with a practical question.

Exercise 1a   **You'll find two diagrams below, reprinted from Giegerich's 1992** *English phonology*. **The first diagram shows the organs of speech. We'll return to these diagrams in chapter 2, so there's no need for the moment to get hung up on the various technical names shown there. You might be interested to note, though, that in diagram 1.2 the** *lungs* **are included. After all, if I asked you to gesture towards 'where speech sounds are produced' you'd probably in the first instance point to your mouth. But the lungs are included in the second diagram because it's important for us to think about the** *airstream mechanisms* **which human beings use to produce speech sounds. Particular modifications of the airstream, as we'll see, engender particular sounds, or classes of sound. So in studying these diagrams, try to form what is at this stage merely a general impression of all the organs of speech. Notice also that the oral cavity (see the paragraph below) appears in a hatched box in diagram 1.2.**

The second diagram introduces one of the stars of the piece, the *oral cavity*. **Again, since this diagram will reappear in chapter 2 there's no need to get hung up on terminology, or worry about terms such as 'alveolar ridge', 'velum' and so forth. We are going to need these descriptive terms, but for**

The Organs of Speech

1-nasal cavity

2-lips

3-teeth

4-alveolar ridge

5-hard palate

6-velum (soft palate)

7-uvula

8-apex (tip) of tongue

9-blade (front) of tongue

10-dorsum (back) of tongue

11-oral cavity

12-pharynx

13-epiglottis

14-larynx

15-vocal cords

16-trachea

17-oesophagus

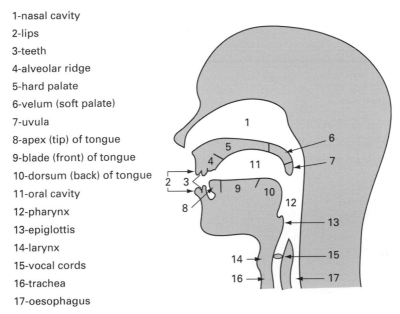

Figure 1.1 The organs of speech

now all that's important is that you begin to form a general picture of how the oral cavity is structured. Lips, teeth, alveolar ridge, hard palate, soft palate … all of these *places of articulation* are crucially involved in the production of many speech sounds of English. Notice too the size and shape of the *nasal cavity*, and the size and position of the tongue.

For the practical exercise, what I'd like you to do is to think of English consonants. At this point I'm going to assume simply that you have some intuitive idea about what consonants are. You need again to be careful to distinguish between consonants proper to the sound structure of English, and written shapes. For example, there are certain speech sounds which are written as 'consonants', but which are sometimes graphic representations of *vowels*:

Graphic shape	*Problem shape*	*Speech sound*
<sky>	<y>	<y> represents a vowel
<you>	<y>	represents a consonant
<now>	<w>	represents (part of) a vowel
<walk>	<w>	represents a consonant

With this caution in mind, think of *at least six* speech sounds which you judge to be unambiguously part of the consonant system of your own variety of English. Note down the words in which these consonants occur, and note

15

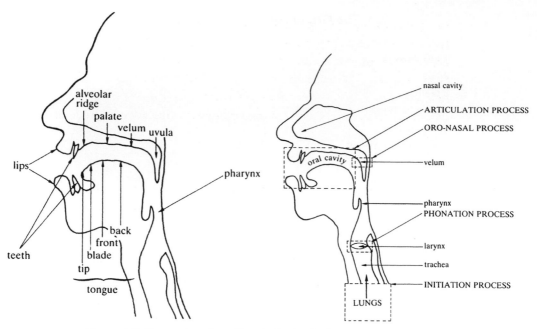

Figure 1.2 The oral cavity, with principal articulators

also how these consonant shapes are *distributed* (do they, for example, typically occur at the beginnings of words and syllables, or at the ends, or both?).

You might have constructed a list like this: 'The "p" of *pit*: occurs at the beginning of a word/syllable; can also occur at the end, as in the syllable *nip*. The "t" of *tip*: occurs at the beginning of a word/syllable; can also occur at the end, as in the syllable *pit*. The "k" of *kin*: occurs at the beginning of a word/syllable; also occurs syllable-finally, as in *nick*. The "n" of *kin*: occurs syllable-finally; can also occur syllable-initially, as in *nick …* '

Try to find at least six of these consonants.

Now turn back to Figure 1.2. For each of the six consonants you've selected, work out *where* in the oral cavity the sounds are produced. For example, in the production of 'p' the lips are pretty clearly the relevant organs of speech, the active articulators. In the production of 't', clearly there's some sort of contact between (the tip of) the tongue and the alveolar ridge. (We will look more at the precise nature of that contact in the next chapter.) In the production of 'n', again there seems to be some sort of contact between (the tip of) the tongue and the alveolar ridge …

… And so on. There's no need to be particularly specific at this stage. I'm setting you this exercise so you can begin thinking now not only about the idea that speech sounds behave in *structured* ways, but also because we need to be able to *classify* them and their behaviour. Working out *where* a given speech sound, particularly a consonantal sound, is produced – the 'place of articulation' of that consonant sound – is an important sub-part of classification. Of course, there are several other ways we can classify the behaviour of English consonants – we need, for example, to be able to state unambiguously *how* the relevant sounds are produced and also to show *how they are distributed*.

Now for a theoretical question.

Exercise 1b The work of the linguist Ferdinand de Saussure has already been mentioned. Apart from drawing a clever and useful analogy between language structure and train timetables, Saussure also, and famously, drew another analogy, between language and chess. 'A game of chess', he wrote (1983: 87), 'is like an artificial form of what languages present in a natural form.'

Think about the sound structure of English (note: sound *structure*, not simply 'the sounds of English'; *phonology*, not simply *phonetics*). In what ways could you analogise the principles that lie behind the sound structure of English with a game of chess? If you don't know the rules of chess, try to analogise the rules that lie behind the behaviour of English speech sounds with the rules of any other game.

Exercise 1c Here's a set of twenty-one nonsense words. Some words are well formed in terms of their *phonotactics* (literally, their 'sound-touching', the way in which particular segments precede and/or follow each other). Others are not only difficult to say, but would be quite impossible to judge as well formed because their structures violate the underlying principles of phonological well-formedness. For each word, judge whether (a) it's well formed but happens – accidentally, one might say – not to occur in English, or (b) whether it violates well-formedness principles. Try to say *why* you have judged each word as (a) or (b). (That's the tricky part of the exercise.) Here's the word list:

bron	nreb	flig	lgop	prug	nbat
fnak	tikn	besr	hift	stlif	fusps
grtup	bgr	stib	stw	woh	stripm
puj	tlw	frk			

I've set this exercise because completing it will help to make explicit, and/or consolidate, your tacit knowledge of the phonotactic principles that lie behind the distribution of the English consonant system – the topic of the next chapter. (You'll find more about the distribution of English consonants in 4.1 – but are strongly advised not to skip 3.1–3.3.)

Key terms introduced in this chapter
(see also the **glossary** at the end of this book)
accent
articulation
aspiration
consonant
contrast(ive)
dialect
grammar
graphology
homophone
lexicon
long vowel
monosyllable
morphology
phonetics
phonology
plosion
post-vocalic
pre-vocalic
runic
short vowel
substitution frame

Further reading

Clark, John and Colin Yallop. 1990. *An introduction to phonetics and phonology*. Oxford: Blackwell. Chapter 1.

Giegerich, Heinz J. 1992. *English phonology: an introduction*. Cambridge University Press. Chapter 1.

McMahon, April. 2002. *An introduction to English phonology*. Edinburgh University Press. Chapter 1.

Saussure, Ferdinand de. 1983. *Course in general linguistics*. Translated and with notes by Roy Harris. [First edition of Saussure 1916.] London: Duckworth.

CHAPTER 2

Consonants (1): contrastiveness

In this chapter …

In this chapter we begin to look at how *contrast* can be put to formal use in identifying what entities function as the underlying consonant sounds of English. We see that certain speech sounds – consonants – contrast with each other when they appear in certain positions of words and/or syllables (an example would be /pɪn/ and /tɪn/). From the contrast we can infer that these sounds are reliably parts of the *system* of English sounds.

We shall also observe that there are certain sounds one can make that are *not* part of the system of English sounds. They are not, precisely because they don't contrast with other consonant sounds in the same environments: they are just 'noise'. Of course, such noises – 'tut-tut' and so forth – may have important societal functions (e.g. to indicate (dis)approval), but nevertheless they are not part of English phonology.

At the end of the chapter we begin to do further work on contrastiveness and we'll notice how important the notion of 'minimal pair' is in diagnosing how many English consonants there might be. We construct several minimal pair tests, and these will net twenty-four consonants for us to consider. In chapters 3–4 we shall further examine how English consonants might be *classified* using features of production and perception such as *voice*, *place* and *manner*.

2.1 Contrastiveness (and similarity)

Because contrastiveness lies at the heart of phonology, it's worth saying something at the outset about this important topic – and by necessary extension, about similarity, too.

How do we recognise anything as having a discrete identity? We do so partly because certain physical characteristics of that thing allow us to identify it as *differing from* adjacent things. On the desk where I'm writing, for example, there's a diary, a manila folder, a coffee mug, an unused ashtray full of coins, a dictaphone and a book. I recognise these things as distinct entities because each is physically different from the items surrounding it. So physically different are these items, in fact, that I could find that dictaphone in the dark, or distinguish the manila folder from the diary, the diary from the book.

There's another important way in which I can recognise these items as distinct. Each item on my desk has a particular *function*. The coffee mug, for example, has the function of containing hot beverages. Similarly, the manila folder has a function distinct from the diary. Both are there, in a general way, to help me work, and contain 'stuff I've written'; furthermore, both structures are comprised of a cover and some inside leaves of paper, but the function of the manila folder is to hold the final draft of a pamphlet of poems, while the function of the diary is to hold appointments, addresses and reminders. So between the manila folder and the diary there is both a *physical* difference and a *functional* one.

Let's think about *similarity* for a moment. When we say two (or more) things are similar, what are we implying?

> **Consider the structure that is a box of matches, including its contents.**
> **If I said to you 'All the matches in this box are similar', what allows me**
> **to make this claim?**

First, all the matches in the box share – or better, appear to share – certain physical properties. The matches themselves are in fact sufficiently alike, have sufficient properties in common, to allow us to identify them as 'the same'. But they are also similar *because they function in the same way*. So if *contrast* works on two axes, the physical and the functional, so does *similarity*.

Interestingly, items often only *appear* to be 'the same'. Consider all the matches in the box again. They're all around 3cm long, all are wooden, and all have a red-painted combustible head. These similarities, plus the presumed similarity of the function of each match, are quite sufficient for us to say 'These are matches'.

Physically, though, each match in the box (we're still talking about the same hypothetical matchbox, the same hypothetical matches) will be different from every other match. The differences may be so small that we could only detect them by examining each individual match under a microscope, but they would undoubtedly be there. This match, for example, is 3.00007cm long, and that one is 3.00006 cm. This one has a splinter of wood near its base, that one doesn't. And so on. Physically, each match is unique, and its uniqueness could be, if we wished, experimentally verifiable. *Nevertheless, and because all the matches in the box share certain physical characteristics as well as the same function, we say 'These are all matches, they belong to the class of things that is "match", and could be nothing but "match" ...'*

What has all this got to do with the sound structure of English?

When we think about the consonant **segments** of English (by 'segments' I can be taken to mean simply 'sounds' here, though I explain the term segment in more detail below, and shall revisit the term throughout the book), we think about segments that not only have *physical* properties in common, or which are different from one another because they do *not* share certain physical properties, but which also have similar, or have different, *functions* within the overall system of English sound structure.

Consider again the monosyllable *pin*. Focus just on the /p/ consonant with which the syllable begins. Now say the same monosyllable repeatedly: 'pin ... pin ... pin ... pin'. You think that with each repetition you are saying 'the same word'. And in one sense, you are: all these 'pin's have sufficient properties in common for you and me to hear them as 'the same'. Among these properties is our shared knowledge that /p/ has a range of particular functions within the system of English: it can occur initially in the syllable, or it can occur after /s/ (*spit, splay*); it can occur syllable-finally (*nip*), and so on. This identifiable range of functions is sufficient for us to recognise your repeated pronunciations of this monosyllable as 'the same'.

Yet in another respect your repetitions aren't the same. On each repetition of the same syllable there will be experimentally verifiable differences in pronunciation: differences in the extent and degree of plosion of /p/; differences in quality of the vowel; differences in the degree of **voicing** (see the end of this chapter, and the beginning of the next), or even the length, of the concluding consonant phoneme /n/; differences, each time, in the air pressure issuing from the lungs ...

As the linguist April McMahon has wisely written: 'In linguistic terms, it's not just that I say *tomahto* and you say *tomayto*; it's that I say *tomahto* and *tomahto* and *tomahto*, and the three utterances are subtly different, but we both think I said the same thing three times' (2002: 3).

And so, when a student of language says, for example, 'The speech sounds /b/ and /p/ are contrastive', they're claiming the following:

- There is a *physical difference* in the *production* and *perception* of the respective speech sounds. (This is a *phonetic* matter.)
- The difference is *meaningful at a structural level*. In the two syllables /bɪn/ and /pɪn/, for example, the *contrast* of sounds (/b/ and /p/) allows us to perceive a difference in *meaning*: a *pin* isn't a *bin*.
- Sounds showing such meaningful contrasts are *phonemes* – underlying, and functional, units of the sound structure of language.
- Phonemes are parts of the underlying structure of a given language (in the present case, English).

2.2 Consonants, vowels, segments, letters ... and noise

In your variety of English, as in mine, what we produce as speakers isn't, of course, merely wilful, random noise. No adult speaker of *any* language, in fact, appears to use the whole repertoire of speech sounds available. The phonology of any language is a *selection*.

> You'll probably be aware – or you're coming to be aware – that on a daily basis you make many sounds that are *not* parts of the phonology of your variety of English. Can you give any examples of such sounds?

Examples might be the sound of disapproval you make when you 'tut-tut', or the gasp of astonishment you make when confronted with another wonderful November morning, or the sound you make largely through your lips (i.e. the lips are the active articulators) when you're perishing cold ('brrrrr!'), or the trilling you make with your tongue when you're trying to imitate the sound of helicopter rotors for a child.

Such sounds are not parts of your phonology, though they certainly have a range of interesting, possibly mimetic, and certainly social, functions. And why aren't they parts of your phonology? They don't *contrast* with any other speech sounds. Unlike, say, the phonemes /b/ and /p/, these mimetic and/or social noises aren't *distributed* in any meaningful way, or with any predictability. For instance, we could say absolutely reliably about the phoneme /b/ that it can occur in initial position in a syllable (*bin, bend*); that it doesn't occur after /s/; that it can occur as the first of a pair of syllable-initial consonants, but not as the second *(blue* is okay, **lbue* isn't); that it can occur on its own in the closing position of a syllable (*nib, blub*), and so on.

But we couldn't make any of the same claims about 'brrr!' or 'tut! tut!', or a gasp of astonishment.

Then again, the general *absence* of 'brrr!' or 'tut! tut!' or a gasp of astonishment from our inventory of English phonemes shouldn't be taken to mean that these sounds can't function as parts of the phonology of other languages. And it's also worth remembering that human infants seem at first to explore the *whole* repertoire of speech sounds available to them. It's only somewhat later that they learn the principles of selection and distribution that make up the phoneme inventory of their variety of English. In some ways, your phoneme inventory can be interestingly analysed as a selection from the possibilities allowed by universal phonetics. (We'll look again at the term and concept 'universal', and its application in linguistics, in chapter 11.)

So far, I've written rather loosely about 'speech sounds', 'consonants' and 'phonemes'; in one place above I have even referred to '(consonant) segments'. In the next paragraphs I'd like to refine these notions.

First, the term 'speech sounds' is a cover term for both the phonemes of the language, and their predictable phonetic instantiations (see also the next section of text). As such, the term 'speech sounds' doesn't really have very much to tell us. In fact, since phonemes are abstract and underlying in nature, they're possibly better viewed as counters in a language game rather than as 'sounds'. This is why, when talking of the sound structure of a language, analysts invariably speak of *phonemes* rather than of 'speech sounds'.

Second, as we'll see, principles of contrastiveness oblige us to distinguish *consonant* phonemes from *vowel* phonemes. For example, how are the lexical monosyllables *pin*, *pen* and *pan* distinguishable? They have different vowels, certainly – but the key point is that these differences are contrastive, functional. They allow us to make the claim that these vowel shapes, *because* they contrast in this way, are parts of the phonology of English.

Third, it's wearisome always to type 'consonants and vowels' – sometimes it's convenient to have a cover term that allows us to refer to individual consonants, or individual vowel shapes. We can't use the cover term 'speech sounds', for the reasons sketched above, and so occasionally in this book I will use the term *segments* – one or more vowel segments, one or more consonant segments. As I use the term here, *segment* refers to one underlying unit, one meaningful, contrastive shape, in the phonology of English. (I shall also say something more about the notion of segment in chapter 11, where segments are described as being the expressions of bundles of internal *features*.) Thus, in the transcription /pɪn/ there is, intuitively, *one* syllable, composed of *three* segments – the /p/, the medial vowel and the /n/.

Notice that as I am defining them, segments are very different from *letters*. The term 'letters' refers to graphic shapes familiar from the deployment of the normal written English alphabet. In the written version of the syllable <thin>, for instance, there are *four* letter shapes (<t+h+i+n>). But if we look at a phonemic transcription of the word – /θɪn/ – we see that there are *three* segments, an initial consonant, a vowel, and a concluding consonant.

It's usually a cardinal principle of any kind of analysis to be consistent and accurate in your use of terminology. Further, it's always a good idea to:

- delimit the object(s) to be studied – a 'what' question
- think through how the object(s) to be studied *can* be studied – a 'how' question

There's a further pay-off. These apparently cautious preliminaries allow us to pose, and then partly answer, a somewhat surprising question. This question is answered in the next section of text.

2.3 More on consonants, contrastiveness and function

You'll remember from exercise 1a that one or more diagrams of the human **vocal tract** are waiting for exploration, together with their accompanying technical terms. It's tempting at this stage of our work to jump straight into those diagrams and that terminology, since both will eventually help us to answer the question 'What are the consonants of my variety of English?' I'd prefer, though, to continue for a while longer in terms of the ideas I was stressing through the introductory chapter, and which have also appeared in 2.1–2. Those ideas focus on *contrastiveness* and on *functionality* (the idea that certain consonants have a function within English sound structure). Taking those ideas as a prompt, what we can do is begin to establish a basic consonant **inventory** for most varieties of English *without immediate reference to any phonetic terminology whatsoever*. That is, we're going to put contrastiveness and function first, and not phonetics.

Immediately below, you'll find a phonological substitution frame. There's an underscore in the first (left-hand) slot of the frame. What I'd like you to do is insert a consonant (that is, one single consonant) in that position, so that the result is a well-formed English monosyllable – the sort of monosyllable whose range of meanings you could look up in a dictionary. To give you the general idea, I've inserted the first viable consonant for you (although to alert readers this insertion won't come as much of a surprise):

Substitution frame 1   /__ɪn/
Insertion   /p/   /pɪn/   'pin'

Other consonants you could insert would be /b/ ('bin'), /t/ ('tin'), /d/ ('din'), /k/ ('kin'), /s/ ('sin') and /f/ ('fin'), like this:

Substitution frame 1		/__ɪn/	
Insertion	/p/	/pɪn/	'pin'
	/b/	/bɪn/	'bin'
	/t/	/tɪn/	'tin'
	/d/	/dɪn/	'din'
	/k/	/kɪn/	'kin'
	/s/	/sɪn/	'sin'
	/f/	/fɪn/	'fin'

This simple exercise has already yielded seven consonants of English – seven contrastive, functional speech sounds. You might notice, too, just how close these phonemic transcriptions are to their alphabetic cousins.

Some of you will have spotted this already, but there are two or three further, single consonants that can be inserted into our substitution frame. The snag is that such single consonants are written alphabetically as two letter shapes, and so therefore you might not immediately think of them as 'single consonants'. What are they?

They are the consonants symbolised alphabetically by <ch> (<chin>), by <sh> (<shin>), and by <th> (<thin>).

> **We've got a small problem, in that we can't just redeploy the familiar alphabetic symbols to indicate the relevant consonant phonemes. Can you work out why not?**

The reason is that if we were to use <th> as a phonemic symbol then we'd run the risk of confusion and ambiguity in the notation for our emerging consonant inventory. For example, <th> stands alphabetically for the consonant that begins the syllable <thin>, but it also stands alphabetically for the consonant that begins the syllable <then>, and this last <th> has a different spoken quality to the <th> of <thin>. Therefore, we need a separate, distinctive symbol, a symbol that will indicate precisely which <th> is being deployed and analysed. For the single consonant that begins the syllable <thin> we'll use the International Phonetic Association (IPA) symbol /θ/ – and with that, we can add /θɪn/ to our list.

> The **International Phonetic Association** was inaugurated in 1886. As explained in their pamphlet 'The Principles of the International Phonetic Association' (1979 reprint of the 1949 text), '[t]he idea of establishing a phonetic alphabet was first put forward by Otto

> Jespersen ….in … 1886….[A]fter consultations extending over more
> than two years the first version of the International Phonetic Alphabet
> was drawn up'. Although the founding principles of the IPA have been
> modified over the past 100 years, they are still worth studying. You can
> find them in the Association's pamphlet. You'll also find the IPA chart of
> consonants in the appendix of this book (p. 212). Once you've read this
> chapter, done the concluding exercises and studied the IPA chart, you'll
> be in a stronger position to understand how the English consonant
> system is a *selection* from the range of possible consonants as these are
> found distributed among the world's languages.

We also need special, dedicated symbols for the 'sh' of shin' and the 'ch' of
'chin'. As with the case of 'th', we can't simply redeploy the familiar alphabetic letter shapes as symbols for phonemes; therefore we'll use the IPA
symbols /ʃ/ (for the 'sh' that appears in 'shin') and /ʧ/ (for the 'ch' of
'chin'). Accordingly, we'll add these to our developing list:

Substitution frame 1		/__ɪn/	
Insertion	/p/	/pɪn/	'pin'
	/b/	/bɪn/	'bin'
	/t/	/tɪn/	'tin'
	/d/	/dɪn/	'din'
	/k/	/kɪn/	'kin'
	/s/	/sɪn/	'sin'
	/f/	/fɪn/	'fin'
	/θ/	/θɪn/	'thin'
	/ʃ/	/ʃɪn/	'shin'
	/ʧ/	/ʧɪn/	'chin'

> The first seven consonant symbols in our list are simple to write in
> longhand: they're exactly like their alphabetic equivalents. The last three
> symbols (/θ/, /ʃ/ and /ʧ/) though, will be unfamiliar, and they need to be
> practised, so that those reading the transcriptions you will eventually make
> will be able to judge your work as accurate or otherwise. Make sure the
> long, squirly /ʃ/ symbol ('sh') is kept absolutely distinct from the written
> <s> symbol. You may also like to practise making the single consonant
> symbol /ʧ/. If you're drawing this last in longhand, it helps to think of the
> symbolic shape as a single consonant if you ensure the crossbar and tail of
> the 't' touch, but don't intersect with, the downstroke of the 'ʃ'.
>
> If you are working on your PC, Doulos SIL is one of the clearest fonts
> you can use, and you can download it from various sources for free (try
> www.sil.org).

> So far we only have a small list of consonants, ten in all. Of course you'll have noticed that there are several other consonants of English that haven't yet figured in our work. Can you work out what these other consonants are? And can you work out why the existence of these consonants couldn't have been deduced from the above exercise and its substitution frame?

Intuitively, some of the 'missing' consonants are segments like /n/, /m/, /z/, /h/, /v/, /g/ – and others, which I'll discuss in a moment. The reason the existence of such consonants hasn't (and can't have) been deduced so far is that if you insert the relevant consonants into our substitution frame, then the insertion doesn't yield meaningful English syllables. Try it:

Substitution frame 1
Insertion

	/__ɪn/	
/m/	/mɪn/	'min'?
/n/	/nɪn/	'nin'?
/z/	/zɪn/	'zin'?
/h/	/hɪn/	'hin'?
/v/	/vɪn/	'vin'?
/g/	/gɪn/	'gin'?

(Note: 'gin' – the drink – doesn't begin with the same consonant as e.g. *gun*. For the relevant consonant – the initial segment in the syllable *gin* – see below.)

I've queried these syllables, rather than marking them as deviant with an asterisk. After all, there's *nothing structurally ill formed about such syllables*. Intuitively, again, it looks very much as if /m/ can stand on its own at the beginning of a stressed English monosyllable (*min* is apparently non-occurring, but *mint* is fine). So can /n/ (*nin* is non-occurring, but *nine* or *nip* are fine). So can /z/ (*zin* might be non-occurring, but *zip* or *zest* are fine), and /v/ (*vin* doesn't occur, but *veal* does). And, yes, /h/, too, looks as if it can begin English syllables perfectly readily: *hin* may be non-occurring, but *hint* is fine.

All that our exercise so far reveals is that it's probably unlikely that we could ever deduce the existence of *all* English consonants from a mere one substitution frame. So where do we go from here? We construct another, or possibly two or three (or four …), substitution frame(s) which will yield incontrovertible evidence that these other consonants are parts of the system of English, i.e. that they are phonemes.

A second frame we might construct is the following:

Substitution frame 2
Insertion

	/__ɪp/	
/n/	/nɪp/	'nip'
/z/	/zɪp/	'zip'
/h/	/hɪp/	'hip'

Frame 2 nets us three further consonants, at least – but not /m/ (since *mip* is non-occurring). We could with ease construct another frame to establish the contrast between /f/ and /v/, and thereby prove that /v/ is a consonant phoneme:

Substitution frame 3	/__at/		
Insertion			
/f/	/fat/	'fat'
/v/	/vat/	'vat'

(On the vowel phoneme /a/, see chapter 8, especially 8.1.)

To rectify the glitch on /m/, and also to include /g/, we can construct another substitution frame:

Substitution frame 4	/__et/		
Insertion			
/n/	/net/	'net'
/m/	/met/	'met'
/g/	/get/	'get'

What we've done is use the *distribution* and the *contrastive potential* of English consonants to guide us in constructing a *phonemic inventory*: that is, we've found out that certain sounds are consonants in English because they have a functional difference from one another – they signify a difference in meaning between two words.

There are still some consonants unaccounted for by what we've done so far. These are /w/ (*win*); /j/ (which represents the initial consonant found in words such as *yawn* or *yacht*); /l/ (*lad*); the consonant /ŋ/, which is a symbol for the 'ng' sound found in some varieties of English in words such as *sing*; and the speech sound usually represented by the graphic shape <r>, which for the time being, and not quite accurately, we can think of as phonemic '/r/'. Another consonant whose existence we haven't yet noted is symbolised /ʒ/. This is the post-vocalic sound you find in loanwords such as *rouge* or *beige*, or occurring inter-vocalically (between vowels) in words such as *measure*. And lastly, there's the consonant you find both initially and finally in words such as *judge*. This is symbolised /dʒ/.

To establish the existence of these consonants, we're going to construct more substitution frames, but in doing so we're also going to refine the procedure and give it a name.

2.4 Minimal pairs

Consider again the pair *pin* and *bin*. Each term in this pair is suspiciously similar to its counterpart, and indeed, the /_ɪn/ part of each term is identical.

The syllables differ *minimally*, in that the initial consonants /b/ and /p/ are contrastive.

A linguist would call such a pair a **minimal pair**, and the construction of minimal pairs – the sort of thing we've been doing for the past few pages – is an important discovery procedure in establishing the phonology of a language. A useful definition of minimal pairs, and the 'minimal pair' test, comes in Crystal (1991: 219):

minimal pair (test) One of the DISCOVERY PROCEDURES used in PHONOLOGY to determine which sounds belong to the same class, or PHONEME. Two WORDS which differ in meaning only when one sound is changed are referred to as a 'minimal pair', e.g. *pin* v. *bin*, *cot* v. *cut*, and linguists or native speakers who make these judgements are said to be carrying out a 'minimal pair test'. A group of words differentiated by each having only one sound different from all others, e.g. *big*, *pig*, *rig* ... is sometimes called a 'minimal set'.

In the substitution frames we constructed, we were establishing minimal sets, or minimal pairs.

> To establish the existence of the consonant segments /w/ (*win*), /j/, /r/, /l/, /ŋ/, /ʒ/ and /dʒ/, what do we do? Precisely: we construct minimal-pair tests. Try it.

- /w/: /pɪn/ and /wɪn/ form a straightforward minimal pair.
- /j/: /jɪn/ contrasts with /wɪn/, or /pɪn/, but 'yin' is a somewhat odd (loan) word in English, since it exists only in e.g. 'yin and yang'. But we could construct the minimal pair /jɪp/ and /nɪp/ (the 'yips' are an unfortunate golfing condition), or /jet/ ('yet') and /net/.
- /r/ and /l/: a perfect minimal pair would be /rɪp/ and /lɪp/.
- /ŋ/: notice that this consonant cannot apparently begin syllables in English (*/ŋɪp/ or */ŋet/ are ill formed), but can readily end them. A good minimal pair would be /sɪn/ and /sɪŋ/, *sing*.
- /ʒ/, too, has a restricted distribution, in that it can't apparently begin syllables in English (though it can in other languages). But it readily occurs between vowels (*measure*) or, occasionally, syllable-finally (*beige*, *rouge*). A minimal pair that would establish /ʒ/ as part of the English consonant system would be *beige* and *baize*.
- /dʒ/ has no such restricted distribution. It occurs initially (*judge*) and finally (*judge* again, or *edge*). Indeed, had we thought of it then, our very first substitution frame could have established the existence of this one for us: /pɪn/ contrasts minimally with /dʒɪn/, *gin*.

There's one further English consonant that we've so far barely noticed, and that is the 'th' sound you find in syllable-initial position in words such as *then* or *there*, or syllable-finally in *bathe*. We already have one 'th' sound in our inventory – remember /θɪn/, *thin*? – but the 'th' of *then* or *there* is different from the 'th' of *thin*, so it looks like we need another symbol to represent this new consonant. Further, the minimal pair *men* and *then* clearly establishes the existence of this second 'th' sound. We're going to use the IPA symbol /ð/ for the 'th' sound you find in *then* or *bathe*.

Here's the list of consonants established by our minimal-pair tests:

English consonants, first inventory

/p/	/pɪn/	'pin' (contrasts with *bin*, frame 1)
/b/	/bɪn/	'bin' (contrasts with *pin*)
/t/	/tɪn/	'tin' (contrasts with *pin*)
/d/	/dɪn/	'din' (contrasts with *pin*)
/k/	/kɪn/	'kin' (contrasts with *pin*)
/s/	/sɪn/	'sin' (contrasts with *pin*)
/f/	/fɪn/	'fin' (contrasts with *pin*)
/θ/	/θɪn/	'thin' (contrasts with *pin*)
/ʃ/	/ʃɪn/	'shin' (contrasts with *pin*)
/ʧ/	/ʧɪn/	'chin' (contrasts with *pin*)
/n/	/nɪp/	'nip' (contrasts with *zip*, frame 2)
/z/	/zɪp/	'zip' (contrasts with *nip*)
/h/	/hɪp/	'hip' (contrasts with *nip*)
/v/	/vat/	'vat' (contrasts with *fat*, frame 3)
/m/	/met/	'met' (contrasts with *net*, frame 4)
/g/	/get/	'get' (contrasts with *met*, frame 4)
/w/	/wɪn/	'win' (contrasts with *pin*)
/j/	/jet/	'yet' (contrasts with *net*)
/r/	/rɪp/	'rip' (contrasts with *nip*)
/l/	/lɪp/	'lip' (contrasts with *rip*)
/ŋ/	/sɪŋ/	'sing' (contrasts with *sin*)
/ʒ/	/beɪʒ/	'beige' (contrasts with *baize*)
/ʤ/	/ʤɪn/	'gin' (contrasts with *pin*)
/ð/	/ðen/	'then' (contrasts with *men*)

Such a list looks pretty unsystematic. We've established the existence of twenty-four consonants, true, and done so using an empirically verifiable test (the minimal-pair test), but the list as it stands looks full of randomness and afterthoughts.

You may be surprised that there are twenty-four consonant phonemes. Many of us think that there are 'twenty-six letters in the English alphabet' – but of course that's somewhat crude, merely alphabetic thinking (and those twenty-six letter shapes also include letter shapes corresponding to vowels). In developing our list, we needed two symbols, for example, for the different kinds of 'g' (the /g/ of *get, gun* and the /ʤ/ of e.g. *age*), two symbols for the different kinds of 'th', symbols for 'sh' and '(t)ch', and a special symbol for 'ng' as this occurs in some varieties of English.

What surprises me is that the consonant inventory of most varieties of English is so *small*, so impoverished. Many other languages, for instance, find a structural place for what are known as ejectives, or clicks, or bilabial trills, among others (on the range of speech sounds possible in human language, see Ladefoged and Maddieson 1996), but these don't usually (or even at all) figure as part of English phonology.

Let's return to our as-yet-unsystematic list. We can be more systematic if we return to the diagrams of the vocal tract we introduced, but didn't discuss, in exercise 1a. We can use the articulators found in the vocal tract to help *classify* our list of consonants, and identify further patterns of behaviour among the items contained in the list. In particular, we can appeal to certain *features* of articulation, notably:

(a)   whether consonants are **voiced** or **voiceless**,
(b)   **how** consonants are produced (the **manner of articulation**), and
(c)   **where** consonants are produced (the **place of articulation**).

Using such diagnostics – voicing, place, and manner – helps us to *classify* English consonants. This seems a solid procedure: first, identify what entities are parts of a system (a 'what' question) and then, second, see how such entities can be classified (a 'how' question). Classification of English consonants is the topic of the next chapter.

Exercises

Exercise 2a   You're ready to attempt some *simple phonemic transcription.* Remember that simple phonemic transcriptions are transcriptions of underlying structure. They use some romanic characters (that is, a subset of romanic characters) drawn from the IPA. There are few (or no) diacritic characters in a simple phonemic transcription, and no capital letters. Furthermore, each *whole transcription* is cast within slant brackets / ... / at the beginning and end of the stretch of language you wish to transcribe, whether this is a word, a phrase, a sentence, or a longer stretch of discourse.

At this point in our work we can't make extended transcriptions, largely because we have only, so far, encountered the short vowels /ɪ/ (*pit* etc) and /e/ (*get* etc), with just a glance at the vowel /a/. I have used one or the other of these vowels /ɪ/ or /e/ in all the words below, so you will find nothing unfamiliar there.

In what follows, make a *simple phonemic transcription* of the following words and phrases as you would expect to use and hear them in your own variety of English. I've completed the first three transcriptions for you. If you encounter difficulties (and you may – consider for instance the final consonant of *pinch*, and whether my transcription is accurate for your usage), simply note them down separately. It may also help to jot down (i) your date and place of birth, and (ii) what variety of English you *think* you speak, before proceeding with the exercise:

chin /tʃɪn/	*chest* /tʃest/	*pinch* /pɪnʃ/
shin	*shed*	*edge*
edging	*fishing*	*win*
whin	*winning*	*pending*
prince	*prints*	*brittle*
meddle	*tipple*	*bringing*
in which	*string*	

Exercise 2b   You need a tape recorder, dictaphone or other recording device for this one.

First, record yourself reading back the words in the list in exercise 2a, then play it back. Try to listen critically to your own accent: is it what you *think* it is? (A supplementary question here, too: to what extent do you feel self-conscious when you hear recordings of yourself speaking? And if you do feel self-conscious (many people do, including me), why might that be?

Second, record someone else – someone you know well, a close friend or family member – reading back the same words. What accent do they have? What accent do they think they have? How self-conscious do *they* feel when they hear their own speech played back to them?

Exercise 2c   This exercise anticipates work we'll be doing in the next chapter. To begin, produce a long-drawn-out 'hissing s' (the phoneme /s/). Stop. Now produce a long-drawn-out 'buzzing z' (the phoneme /z/). Stop. Repeat the exercise, but this time, move without stopping from long-drawn-out /s/ to long-drawn-out /z/. As you switch from phoneme to phoneme, do any of the articulators in your oral cavity change shape – i.e. does the tongue move? Do the lips move? Or not? If not, how would you account for the fact that there is definitely both a functional and an acoustic difference between /s/ and /z/?

Exercise 2d   **Repeat exercise 2c, but this time using the phonemes /f/ and /v/. Ask yourself the same questions.**

Exercise 2e   **In this chapter we've made a great deal of use of the procedure that employs minimal pairs to detect which phonemes exist in English. Can you think of any other way in which the sound structure of your variety of English might be reliably – that is, scientifically – analysed?**

Key terms introduced in this chapter
features
inventory
manner of articulation
place of articulation
segments
vocal tract
voice

Further reading

Ladefoged, Peter and Ian Maddieson. 1996. *The sounds of the world's languages*. Oxford: Blackwell.
McMahon, April. 2002. *An introduction to English phonology*. Edinburgh University Press. Chapters 1–3.

CHAPTER 3

Consonants (2): classification

In this chapter …

In this chapter we build on the work we introduced in chapter 2, and look at how English consonants might be more rigorously classified. To introduce the classification we shall analyse the parameters of *voice*, *manner of articulation*, and last, *place of articulation*. For every consonant, then, we will be able to show that it has a three-way classification: (i) whether it's voiced or voiceless; (ii) *how* it's produced (i.e. whether it's a stop, or a fricative, and so on); and (iii) *where* it's produced.

    After a discussion of these diagnostics we shall make a table of English consonant phonemes, which will appear together with their terms of classification.

3.1 Voice

Before we turn back to the diagram of the vocal tract, please repeat the small experiment you conducted – that you *should* have conducted – as part of the exercises you found at the end of the previous chapter.

> Put your thumb and index (or second) finger lightly on either side of your Adam's apple – the cartilaginous structure below your chin, on the front part of your neck. This physical structure is usually more prominent in men than in women, but women readers will have no trouble in distinguishing it.
>
> With your fingers lightly in place, utter a continuous 'zzzz' sound. Do you feel anything under your fingers? You should feel a vibration, a buzz, inside the Adam's apple. If this vibration isn't immediately tangible, try uttering a continuous 'ssss' sound, and then switch from 'ssss' to 'zzzz', then back from 'zzzz' to 'ssss' again. You should feel vibration under your fingers when you utter the continuous 'zzzz', but not when you utter 'ssss'.

Now try the same exercise again, but this time switch from a continuous 'ffff' to 'vvvv', and then from 'vvvv' to 'ffff'. You should once more feel vibration under your fingers as you produce 'vvvv', but not when you produce 'ffff'.

What you've just done is identify, and gain empirical evidence for, a feature of articulation that linguists call **voicing**.

The Adam's apple is physiologically present because in that part of the vocal tract, within the **larynx**, the **vocal folds** (or *vocal cords*) are to be found, and the external musculature of the Adam's apple protects the structure inside from damage.

Of these places of articulation, Gimson writes as follows (1994: 10–11):

The larynx is a casing, formed of cartilage and muscle, situated in the upper part of the trachea [the windpipe: McC]. Its forward portion is prominent in the neck below the chin and is commonly called the 'Adam's apple'. Housed within this structure from back to front are the vocal folds, two folds of ligament and elastic tissue which may be brought together or parted by the rotation of the arytenoid cartilages ... through muscular action ... The opening between the folds is known as the GLOTTIS ...

The action of the vocal folds which is most characteristically a function of speech consists in their role as a vibrator set in motion by lung air – the production of voice, or phonation; this vocal-fold vibration is a normal feature of all vowels or of such a consonant as [z] compared with voiceless [s]. In order to achieve the effect of voice, the vocal folds are brought

35

sufficiently close together that they vibrate when subjected to air pressure from the lungs ...

It's precisely the feature of *voicing* that allows us to distinguish between pairs of consonants that are otherwise pronounced in the same way. In the exercise you've just completed, for example, you've observed the difference between 'ssss' and 'zzzz' (/s/ and /z/), and 'ffff' and 'vvvv' (/f/ and /v/). There are also other pairs of consonant phonemes where both segments are produced identically, but differ only in the presence or absence of the feature of voicing.

> Can you work out what such pairs of consonants are? It might help to begin to make a list, something like the following. I've helped you by filling in the first terms.

Pairs of consonants

Voiceless	Voiced
/s/	/z/
/f/	/v/
...?	

Several candidate pairs come to mind. Perhaps the first to examine is a voiced/voiceless pair that's easily susceptible to the same 'Adam's apple' test we applied to /s/ and /z/. How about the pair of 'th' phonemes? These are symbolised /θ/ (voiceless, as in *thin*) and /ð/ (voiced, as in *then*). If you conduct the 'Adam's apple' test on this pair, then clearly they're contrastive, differing only in the presence or absence of voicing. You could conduct the same test, with the same result, on the pair /ʃ/ and /ʒ/. Or think of the minimal pair *chin* and *gin* (/tʃɪn/ and /dʒɪn/). Here again we have a pair of consonants that seem to be produced in the same way, using the same active articulators, but which differ only in terms of voicing. You might not immediately have spotted this pair as a candidate, since the 'Adam's apple' test doesn't work quite so obviously on consonants that are produced using a complete or partial stoppage of the air-stream, but the principle is good. So let's add all these to our list of consonant pairs:

Pairs of consonants

Voiceless	Voiced
/s/	/z/
/f/	/v/
/θ/	/ð/
/ʃ/	/ʒ/
/tʃ/	/dʒ/

And there are several other pairs: /p/ and /b/; /t/ and /d/; /k/ and /g/:

Pairs of consonants

Voiceless	Voiced
/s/	/z/
/f/	/v/
/θ/	/ð/
/ʃ/	/ʒ/
/ʧ/	/ʤ/
/p/	/b/
/t/	/d/
/k/	/g/

In all, these contrasts help to sort sixteen of our list of twenty-four consonant phonemes into voiceless/voiced pairs. Theoretically it's possible to conceive of a language that organised its whole consonant system in terms of such oppositions, but that doesn't happen in English. You might like to look at the consonants that do *not* fall neatly into voiceless/voiced pairs, and try to work out what they have in common, as well as how they differ.

The consonants that *don't* fall into voiceless/voiced pairs are:

/h/	/hɪp/	'hip'
/n/	/nɪp/	'nip'
/m/	/met/	'met'
/ŋ/	/sɪŋ/	'sing'
/r/	/rɪp/	'rip'
/l/	/lɪp/	'lip'
/j/	/jet/	'yet'
/w/	/wɪn/	'win'

These are indubitably consonants, and have been exhaustively established as such via their function in minimal pairs and sets. And yet they're all voiced, with the exception of /h/ (which has no voiced partner). So what gives this group of consonants their identity? What differentiates them and allows them to be consonant phonemes of English?

3.2 Manner

To answer this last question we can't appeal to voicing or voicelessness. Instead, we have to refer to (at least) one other feature of pronunciation, and that is their *manner* of articulation – *how* (in addition to voicing or voice-lessness) they are pronounced.

I've set the list at the end of 3.1 in a particular way, with /h/ at the top and /j/ and /w/ at the bottom, for a reason. Here it is.

Conduct the 'Adam's apple' test on the /h/ that occurs in the syllable /hɪp/. It may help to produce the /h/ lengthened (you'll sound as if you're hoarse). Clearly, this initial /h/ is voiceless (if you utter the whole syllable *hip* slowly, you'll feel that voicing begins on the vowel), but if you repeat the exercise, concentrating again just on /h/, you should feel a slight contraction in the muscles below your fingers, because when /h/ is produced, the vocal folds are stiffened so that the airflow is turbulent. When any consonant is produced with such friction, whether this takes place in the glottis or elsewhere in the oral cavity (tongue and teeth (/θ/ and /ð/), lips and teeth (/f/ and /v/) are obvious examples), they are said to belong to a class of sounds known as **fricatives**. Fricatives are very 'consonant-like' consonants, precisely because they are produced with this overt modification of the airstream (friction). And because it's perceived as such a consonant-like consonant, I've put /h/ at the top of the last list.

The next three consonants – /n/, /m/ and /ŋ/ – also have things in common. They are all voiced (try conducting the 'Adam's apple' test on 'nnnn', 'mmmm'), but you won't feel any turbulence in the airstream when such sounds are produced, so these sounds aren't fricatives. And /n/ and /m/ (and less certainly, /ŋ/) have other things in common: they are voiced; they can function as syllabic peaks in certain environments (*button, chasm*, where the boldened part of the word is a syllable in its own right); and they seem to be unlike /p/ or /s/, /f/ or /g/, which involve some momentary stoppage or friction in the oral cavity, and can *never* function as syllabic. That is, what we're going call the **nasal** consonants – (/n/, /m/, /ŋ/) – are less 'consonant-like' (though they're still consonants), and perhaps more vowel-like, than many of their relatives in the English consonant phoneme inventory.

The same general remarks hold good for /l/ and /r/. These are both voiced, both are produced without friction, and both can function as syllabic peaks (consider *bottle* or GA *butter*). That is, these are indubitably consonants, but behave unlike some other consonants, or groups of consonants, within the entire set.

And for /j/ and /w/? Try producing a long-drawn-out articulation of the /j/ you find beginning the syllables *yes* or *yet*: /jjjj/ ... You'll notice that /j/ has much in common with the vowel /ɪ/. (Although I'll revisit this later, notice how /j/, like /ɪ/, can be pronounced with spreading of the lips, and with the body of the tongue raised and to the front of the oral cavity.) If you conduct the same experiment with a long-drawn-out /w/ (try the initial consonant of *wet*: /wwww/), you'll find that the consonant /w/ has much in common with the vowel alphabetically symbolised as <u> or <oo>. Therefore, even though they are truly consonants, /j/ and /w/ are among the least consonant-like, and most vowel-like, of consonants.

The foregoing has taken us some way from discussing the *manner of articulation* of the various consonants, but it's useful in that it hints at the fact that our erstwhile indiscriminate list of consonant phonemes can be subclassified in certain ways, and suggests that certain pairs or even groups of consonants may, beyond voicing, have features of articulation (and/or distribution) in common.

Let's return to the *manner of articulation*.

Take the pair /p/ and /b/, voiceless and voiced respectively. You'll remember from the introductory chapter that when we produce the /p/ of a stressed syllable like *pin* the /p/ was aspirated (accompanied in production by a puff of air). Why? Because the egressive airstream issuing from the lungs is briefly *stopped* in the oral cavity – in the case of /p/ and /b/, stopped by closed lips. As /p/ is pronounced, the lips part, and the pent-up air is released explosively. For this reason, phonemes such as /p/ and /b/ are classified as **plosives** (or simply, as **stops**). If we also take voicing into account, we can arrive at a succinct, but still partial, description of these two consonants, like this:

Classifying consonants

Consonant	Voice	Manner
/p/	–	plosive
/b/	+	plosive

We can do exactly the same with another pair of plosives, /t/ and /d/. Here the egressive airstream is stopped not by closure of the lips, but by the fact that the tip or blade of the tongue is momentarily pressed onto the bony structure immediately behind the top teeth, and then released. The same principle operates with the pair of consonants /k/ and /g/, although in this instance the oral cavity is momentarily sealed by the body and back of the tongue pressing momentarily against the soft palate, or *velum*.

That is, /p/ and /b/, /t/ and /d/, /k/ and /g/ are all *plosives*; this is their *manner of articulation*:

Classifying consonants

Consonant	Voice	Manner
/p/	–	plosive
/b/	+	plosive
/t/	–	plosive
/d/	+	plosive
/k/	–	plosive
/g/	+	plosive

Even so, subclassifying consonants in terms of voicing and manner isn't quite enough to distinguish one consonant phoneme from another. In the above list, for instance, /p/, /t/ and /k/ are all voiceless plosives. We need one other diagnostic tool in order to distinguish them unambiguously, and that is the *place of articulation*.

3.3 Place

Here we can return at last to the diagram of the vocal tract I asked you to study, but not to explore, at the end of the introductory chapter. The diagram of the vocal tract is repeated here for convenience:

> Before we match English consonants to their appropriate places of articulation, it might help to try another small experiment. Purse your lips into an 'O' shape (don't actually close your lips), and breathe normally. On an out-breath, lightly flick your middle finger against your right cheek, and at the same time, modify the 'O' shape of your lips into an 'OR' shape, into an 'AH' shape, and then back again. What do you hear?

You should hear that the resonance of the sounds produced by this exercise changes. That's because the oral cavity is basically a hollow shape which, when you breathe out, is filled with air. If by muscular action you change the shape that's filled by air, then of course the resonance of the sounds produced will alter. And so, since the production of consonants involves more or less radical change in the shape and nature of the egressive (out-breathing) air-stream flowing through the vocal tract, we can regard consonants as a

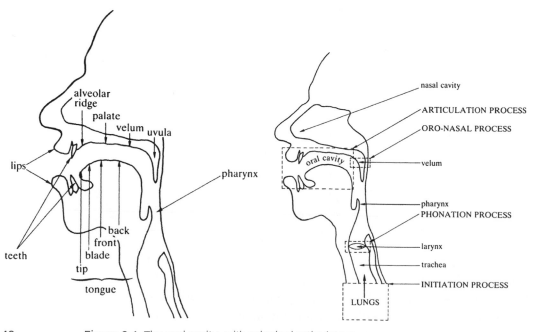

Figure 3.1 The oral cavity, with principal articulators

specific subset of the range of potential sounds generated by muscular activity in, and surrounding, the vocal tract.

Another experiment. Have the diagram of the vocal tract open in front of you. You will need an index finger for this one.

- First, feel your lips (technically, the *labia*). Notice their relative size, and their softness and pliability. The lips can of course be parted, or held together. If they are held together, one effect is to momentarily block the egressive airstream flowing into the oral cavity from the lungs. If the lips are subsequently parted, the result is a rapid, explosive release of air (note the form of the term: 'ex-plosive'). We have already noted the existence of (at least) two consonants for which plosion is a feature of pronunciation. These are /p/ and /b/. They are *bilabial* consonants – *bi*-labial since *both* lips are the active articulators:

Classifying consonants

Consonant	Voice	Manner	Place
/p/	–	plosive	bilabial
/b/	+	plosive	bilabial

- Behind your lips you'll feel your teeth (technically, the *dentes*). We have already encountered consonants which are produced either by the inter-action of the lips and teeth (/f/ and /v/) or the tongue and teeth (/θ/ and /ð/) – that is, it is precisely the form of such interaction that produces a distinc-tive modification to the egressive airstream sufficient for us to produce and perceive these consonants. In the case of /f/ and /v/, the fricatives (a term introduced in the previous section), both the bottom lip and the upper teeth are the active articulators, and in the case of /θ/ and /ð/, the (tip of the) tongue and both upper and lower teeth. The first two sounds are said to be **labio-dental**; the second two are said to be simply **dental**:

Classifying consonants

Consonant	Voice	Manner	Place
/p/	–	plosive	bilabial
/b/	+	plosive	bilabial
/f/	–	fricative	labio-dental
/v/	+	fricative	labio-dental
/θ/	–	fricative	dental
/ð/	+	fricative	dental

> **Note**
> In what follows you'll find the other consonants in the inventory of English discussed under bullet points. At the end of the discussion of each bullet point I shall *not* repeat the list of consonants, but I *do*

> expect you to add items, or pairs of items, to the list as we go along. The entire list of English consonants (including one or two items that might not be part of your own variety of English), subclassified into Voice–Manner–Place, may be found at the end of this section of text.

- On the upper part of the oral cavity, immediately behind your upper teeth, you'll find a small, bony ridge. This important place of articulation is known as the **alveolar ridge**. (It's very easy to feel with your index finger. Notice its prominence, and its extent.) Now consider the articulation of the consonants /t/ and /d/, remembering that so far we have no way of distinguishing them from /p/ and /b/ (i.e. they are all voiced/voiceless plosives). If you think about the production of /t/ and /d/, you'll find that the airstream is modified once again by stoppage: the tip of the tongue lies on the alveolar ridge, and the sides of the tongue are sealed against the upper teeth. However, the stoppage may be modified if the tip of the tongue is momentarily retracted from the alveolar ridge. The result is a rapid, explosive release of air. And therefore, /t/ and /d/ may confidently be classified as *alveolar plosives*.

- Another small experiment, this time involving /s/. Produce the consonant /t/, but don't explode it. You'll feel air-pressure building up in the oral cavity (you'll feel the pressure distinctly behind your upper teeth). Now release the pressure by retracting the tip of your tongue from its present position on the alveolar ridge. The result will be a sound that you might hear as 'ts'. Produce the sound again, but this time extend the production of the 's'. Note the position of your tongue relative to the alveolar ridge. It's held just back of the ridge, and the air is forced through the millimetric gap there, with resulting *friction*. We can use precisely these features of production to help subclassify /s/ and /z/ (and so distinguish them from /f/ and /v/ and other fricatives). That is, they are *alveolar fricatives*.

- There's another pair of consonants that is produced using the alveolar ridge as one of the articulators. (Can you think what it is?) Before we identify the relevant pair, and again using your finger, explore the upper part of the oral cavity, the part behind the alveolar ridge. You'll feel this as a hard, bony structure, like the top of an oral cavern. This is the **hard palate** (or just the *palate*).

  Now consider the consonants /ʧ/ and /ʤ/. As the transcription symbols imply, these consonants begin with the (tip of the) tongue sealing the oral cavity by contact with alveolar ridge. That is, there is a stop component to the phoneme. But the air-release of /ʧ/ isn't quite like 'ts'. Instead, the tip and front part of the tongue remain high in the oral cavity, and the blade of the tongue remains sufficiently high for the escaping air to be squeezed through the millimetric gap between tongue (blade) and the hard palate. That is, while the phoneme begins with a(n alveolar) stop component, its air release is fricative, and palatal. Therefore, we can specify the place of articulation for /ʧ/ and /ʤ/ as **palato-alveolar**. There's no way of avoiding what seems to be clumsiness in the nomenclature: phonetically, both the alveolar ridge and the hard palate are critically involved in the production of the respective sounds. And there's a further point we should make. We can't call /ʧ/ and /ʤ/ simply 'stops', because they have a crucial, fricative air-release. Nor can we call them simply 'fricatives' (because their articulation also critically involves plosion). We seem to need, therefore, a new name for such sounds. Let's use one. They're **affricates**.

- Now you've classified /ʧ/ and /ʤ/ it should be relatively easy for you to classify /ʃ/ and /ʒ/. These have no plosive component, and so they are … ? Right: they're *palatal fricatives*.

- If you now, using the same clean index finger, explore the top of the oral cavity back of the hard palate, you'll encounter soft, sensitive tissue. This is the *soft palate*, or **velum**. A candidate pair of consonants whose place of articulation is the velum are /k/ and /g/. In production of these, notice how it is the back of the tongue that is arched towards the velum and seals off the oral cavity (you can actually feel this with your finger, if you produce an unexploded /k/ or /g/). Once the tongue momentarily lowers, and the seal is broken, then the result is an explosive release of pent-up air. /k/ and /g/ are, therefore, *velar plosives*.

- This still leaves /n/, /m/ and /ŋ/ unaccounted for (as it does /h/, /r/, /l/, /j/ and /w/, which I'll discuss under the next two bullet points). To consider /n/, /m/ and /ŋ/, look again at the diagram of the vocal tract given above. You'll see that at the back of the velum there is a space which allows egressive air access to the nasal cavity. Although we are unconscious of its potential for movement, the velum can actually be raised (thereby blocking off air access into the nasal cavity), or lowered (allowing egressive air into the nasal cavity, and from there out through the nostrils). In normal breathing, too, the velum is lowered, so that ingressive air can find its way into the trachea and from there into the lungs.

What happens if you have a heavy cold? The nasal cavity is filled with phlegm – blocked. Under that unfortunate circumstance, how do the consonants /n/ and /m/ sound? Try producing the phrase *cold in my nose* as if you did indeed have a heavy cold, and the result is something that sounds, transliterated, like *cold id by doze*. If the nasal cavity is sealed, therefore, /n/ is produced like /d/, and /m/ like /b/. There's a good reason for that: /n/ is a consonant where the air-escape is *nasal*, and where, at the same time, the tip of the tongue touches the alveolar ridge. Because of this alveolar gesture, if the nasal cavity is sealed when we try to produce /n/, we hear the result as an alveolar *and oral* (i.e. non-nasal) stop – the speech sound we've already analysed as /d/. Again, if we try to produce the nasal /m/ orally (if the nasal cavity is sealed), the result is somewhat like /b/, the bilabial plosive.

We can, therefore, confidently classify the *manner* of articulation of /n/, /m/, and /ŋ/, too, as *nasal*. Further, since they are produced with either an alveolar gesture (/n/), a bilabial one (/m/), or a velar one (/ŋ/), we can further say that these nasals involve, like their oral plosive counterparts, some *stoppage* in the oral cavity, i.e. they are **stops**.

● Now to /l/ and /r/. Both /l/ and /r/ are voiced. In the case of /l/, where is the tongue when the sound is produced (try producing *lip*, /lɪp/)? The tip of the tongue rests on the alveolar ridge, but the sides of the blade of the tongue are retracted away from the upper teeth, so that air may escape *laterally*. A useful contrast and minimal pair that you might consider here is that between /lɪp/ and /dɪp/. With /d/, the sides of the tongue are sealed against the upper teeth, and there is no lateral air escape. We can, therefore, classify /l/ as a voiced, **lateral** alveolar.

/r/ is more problematic, largely because it's a consonant whose phonetic implementation varies widely between language varieties; Gimson (1994: 187) notes that '[t]here are more phonetic variants of the /r/ phoneme than of any other English consonant'. For older speakers born and raised in parts of the north of England, for example, the sound may even be **uvular** – produced in an area of the vocal tract behind and below the velum – and involve frication. For other speakers, such as those speaking some varieties of Scots English, the sound may be an alveolar **trill** (= intermittent closure, in the form of one articulator acting on another). In other varieties, such as the varieties of Indian English, the sound may be a **tap**. In my own variety, which is standard Northern British English, if I produce /r/ in a word such as /rɪp/, the tongue is raised, and the front and tip of the tongue are held just behind the alveolar ridge. There's no actual contact with the alveolar ridge, nor is there any friction (compare the production of /s/ in e.g. /sɪp/). So in my variety, /r/ is voiced, and may be characterised as *post-alveolar* (this phoneme is properly – if we are strictly following the IPA – symbolised as /ɹ/, and you can read more about /r/, /ɹ/ etc in chapter 11). That still leaves the problem, though, of its manner of production.

Because in my variety /r/ has certain vowel-like characteristics (e.g. it can function as syllabic), I'm provisionally going to classify the sound as an **approximant**. In theory it would have been entirely possible to classify /l/ as an approximant, too (cf. Gimson 1994: 182ff.), but the characteristic air-escape mechanism of /l/ is so overtly lateral as to make the term 'lateral' easily mnemonic. *Approximant* may be taken to mean 'somewhat vowel-like, but with general distributional features characteristic of true consonants'. Crystal adds a further helpful note on the term *approximant*: 'The term is based on the ARTICULATIONS involved, in that one articulator approaches another [e.g. in the case of /r/, tip of tongue approaches alveolar ridge: McC], but the degree of narrowing involved does not produce audible friction' (1991: 23).

With some misgivings, therefore, I shall for the time being classify /r/ as a voiced, post-alveolar approximant (and continue, for the time being, to notate it as /r/). We'll return to /r/ in chapters 10 and 11.

- This leaves /j/ and /w/. Rather like /r/, these consonants have several vowel-like features (we've already pointed some of these out). There is no particular friction involved in the production of the sounds, nor stoppage, nor nasality. Yet the sounds are distributed like true consonants, in that they may begin syllables (/jet/, *yet*, /wet/, *wet*), or function as the second consonant in syllable openings containing two consonants (/bj ... / in *beauty*, /sw ... / in e.g. /swet/, *sweat*). So as with the case of /r/, I'm going to classify both /j/ and /w/ as *approximants*. In the case of /j/, the body of the tongue is raised, and approaches the hard palate, yet no contact or frication takes place. And in the case of /w/, there is raising of the body and back of the tongue towards the velum (though no contact or friction takes place there), and simultaneously, there is lip-rounding.

  /j/, therefore, can be classified as a *palatal approximant*, and /w/ as a *labio-velar approximant*.

- All of which leaves just /h/ to classify – and *one* other consonant which you may, or may not, have as part of your own phonemic inventory. I'll come to that in a moment, but first, to /h/.

  Look again at the diagram of the vocal tract. Now produce /h/ as this occurs in words such as /hɪp/, *hip* or /hed/, *head*. Where is /h/ produced? How would you classify it in terms of voicing, and manner of production?

  /h/ is a voiceless, **glottal** fricative. You can actually feel the muscular contraction involved in the frication if you apply the 'Adam's apple' test to a slow pronunciation of *hip, head*.

- There's one other consonant that's part of the inventory of millions of English speakers, though it's no longer part of standard varieties within England among my generation of speakers, or those younger than fifty. (The consonant is only sporadically present in my own *idiolect*, that is, my particular implementation of standard Northern British English, and then only under certain geographical or social circumstances.)

To identify the consonant involved, consider the following question. In your own variety, are the words *wit* and *whit* homophones? Or *witch* and *which*? Or *win* and *whin*?

If, for you, these words are *not* homophones then it's likely that you produce the *first* of each pair with syllable-initial /w/ (/wɪt/, /wɪtʃ/, /wɪn/). This will be true for many speakers of Irish English, Scots English, and some varieties of American. For the second word of each pair, such speakers will have a sound that contrasts with /w/, but which nevertheless has some phonetic similarities with /w/. For this new sound we can't, of course, simply redeploy the symbol /w/ (or transcribe */wh/). We need a new symbol to capture syllable-initial 'wh' in those varieties for which the contrast between *wit* and *whit*, or *wine* and *whine*, is phonemic, i.e. where those are minimal pairs. We shall use the IPA symbol /ʍ/ for this new consonant:

win	/wɪn/
whin	/ʍɪn/
witch	/wɪtʃ/
which	/ʍɪtʃ/

/ʍ/ may be classified as a voiceless labio-velar fricative.

Here's the list of all the consonants we have discussed. I'll refine the ordering in chapter 4, but I'll add no new consonants to the list, nor change the terms of subclassification:

Consonant phonemes: an inventory and diagnostic			
Consonant	Voice	Manner	Place
/p/	–	plosive	bilabial
/b/	+	plosive	bilabial
/f/	–	fricative	labio-dental
/v/	+	fricative	labio-dental
/θ/	–	fricative	dental
/ð/	+	fricative	dental
/t/	–	plosive	alveolar
/d/	+	plosive	alveolar
/s/	–	fricative	alveolar
/z/	+	fricative	alveolar
/tʃ/	–	affricate	palato-alveolar
/dʒ/	+	affricate	palato-alveolar
/ʃ/	–	fricative	palatal
/ʒ/	+	fricative	palatal

/k/	–	plosive	velar
/g/	+	plosive	velar
/n/	+	nasal (stop)	alveolar
/m/	+	nasal (stop)	bilabial
/ŋ/	+	nasal (stop)	velar
/l/	+	lateral (approximant)	alveolar
/r/	+	approximant	post-alveolar
/j/	+	approximant	palatal
/w/	+	approximant	labio-velar
/h/	–	fricative	glottal
/ʍ/	–	fricative	labio-velar

Remarks on the list of consonant symbols

There are several unfamiliar symbols here, and you'll need to practise drawing them. Particular attention should be given to the affricates, to the palatal fricatives, to /ŋ/, to the dental fricatives, and to /ʍ/. If this last consonant is part of your own phonemic inventory, make sure that if you're transcribing in longhand this symbol is kept carefully distinct from that for /m/.

If you're working from a PC, Doulos SIL is a font that contains all the symbols you need. All the SIL IPA fonts may be downloaded free from www.sil.org.

There's no substitute for practice.

I also advise a further exercise. If you're working on your own, cover up the Voice–Manner–Place columns with a slip of paper and see how well you can memorise these features.

Another good exercise is to cover up the left-hand list of consonant symbols themselves and, working simply from the Voice–Manner–Place features, identify the consonant symbols described by the features.

A final exercise. Throughout this chapter I've given many examples of words (syllables) in which all of these consonants appear. Instead of merely trusting me to have done a thorough job, find your own examples. If you do this, pay careful attention to the *distribution* of the consonant or consonants you're thinking about: does a particular consonant, for example, characteristically begin syllables, or occur between vowels, but not end syllables (this would be the case with /h/, or /w/, or /ʍ/)? Does the consonant you're studying occur relatively freely within words? Does the consonant you're studying occur after other consonants in the opening of syllables and words? Or not?

> These last questions are posed because in starting to think about the distribution of English consonant phonemes we are anticipating the next chapter, 4, which is, as you might expect, about the *distribution* of the English consonants.

Exercises

Exercise 3a   This is an exercise concerning what we have symbolised so far as /r/. There's no need at this stage to make transcriptions, but study the following list of words, pronounce each one as neutrally and normally as possible, and note where, and to what extent, /r/ is present in your variety of English:

rip	*reap*	*ripe*
bring	*pray*	*try*
hard	*burp*	*blurt*
fear	*lure*	*fair*

Now study – and pronounce – the following list of words and phrases, and once again, note the presence or absence of /r/:

fairies	*fear is*
car	*car is*
Armada	*Armada is*
never	*never in*
beater in	*beta in*

What can you observe about the distribution and deployment of /r/, as this occurs in your own variety of English? If you detect an /r/ in your pronunciation of e.g. *–mada is* or *beta in*, where might this /r/ come from? (Note: this problem will be revisited in chapters 10 and 11.)

Exercise 3b   More transcription. Study the following list of words and phrases, and then make a *simple phonemic* transcription of them. Your transcription should reflect the structure underlying your own accent. Remember that transcriptions of this kind *do not contain capital letters, nor marks of punctuation, nor diacritic marks*. They have the now-familiar slash mark ('/') at the beginning and end of the word or phrase being transcribed, *not* after each phoneme. In what follows I shall again use the very restricted set of vowels we've mentioned in this book to date, so there's no need to learn new symbols for the transcription of vowels: the vowel in each case will be either /ɪ/ (as in the word *bid* or *pitch*) or /e/ (as in

bed or *bet*). If you encounter difficulties (and you may), then simply make
a note of them, and bear them in mind as you read the next chapter.
Here's the list (I've again completed the first couple of problems for you):

wedding	/wedɪŋ/
intent	/ɪntent/
Yes!	
when it's wet	
betting	
it's jelly	
This gin is red!	
any wrecked men	
this pitch end	
Is Fred dead, then?	
Is Chris willing?	
mend his knitting	

Exercise 3c   The list of consonants above seems simple enough, but there are some
difficult conceptual problems still lurking within it. To anticipate one of
these problems, make a further list. On the new list, state for each consonant
whether it can occur at the beginnings of words/syllables, and whether it can
occur at the end. You'll find that many of the consonants can readily occur in
both positions (an example would be /t/, which can occur readily in word-
initial position – *tin* – and equally readily in word-final position – *nit*). But
some consonants can't and don't. What are they?

Key terms introduced in this chapter
affricate
alveolar ridge
approximant
bilabial
dental
fricative
hard palate
labio-dental
larynx
lateral
nasal
palato-alveolar
plosive
stop
trill

uvular
velum
vocal folds

Further reading

Gimson, A. C. 1994. *Gimson's pronunciation of English*. 5th edition, revised by
    Alan Cruttenden. London: Arnold. This is quite advanced, but chapters 3 and 10
    (which last focusses wholly on consonants) will be most useful.

CHAPTER 4

Consonants (3): distribution

In this chapter …

In this chapter we look at material that allows us to conceptualise the formal differences between phonology and phonetics. One construct that allows us to think about that difference quite precisely is that of the allophone. Allophones are parts of the 'events' of speech: they are manifestations of the underlying system. Moreover, allophones occur in predictable environments and therefore have places within syllables reserved exclusively for them. We shall sum up this exclusivity by claiming that allophones occur in *complementary distribution*.

Because it seems to be part of the possible manifestations of underlying /t/ we also look at the *glottal stop*, and will judge whether this can be analysed as 'an allophone of /t/' or not. (As we'll see – it can't; it's not.)

The chapter closes with a brief recap on the work we've done on the consonant system of English to date.

4.1 Consonant distribution and intuitions about syllables

By 'distribution' we mean the ways in which consonant segments may be distributed within well-formed English syllables – how they occur, and what kinds of segments they can co-occur with. It must be admitted that at this stage in our work we only have an intuitive notion of what a syllable is, but nevertheless I've found in my teaching that such an intuitive awareness is quite sufficient on which to base preliminary judgements about how English consonants are distributed. And in fact exercise 1c relied critically on your intuitions as to the well-formedness or otherwise of English syllables.

To prove you have an accurate intuitive awareness of English syllables, answer the following: how many syllables does a word such as *mud* have? How many syllables does a word such as *happy* or *phoneme* have? How many syllables does a word such as *transcription* have?

Answers? One; two; and three. Further, if I ask you to judge the well-formedness of a syllable such as **gtrub* you'd say 'impossible in English', and you'd be right. You'd know intuitively that *gtr* can't begin a well-formed English syllable. If, on the other hand, I asked you to judge the well-formedness of *trub* you'd probably say: 'Well, the syllable's OK – there are after all English syllables that can begin with *tr* (*true*, *trip*), as well as syllables that can end with *ub* (*blub*, *grub*) – but the word doesn't occur in my English. It's well-formed, yes – but accidentally, as it were, there's no such word.'

That's what I mean by 'intuition'. It's precisely that set of structured hunches that we're going to use to work through how English consonants are distributed within well-formed syllables.

First, look again at the inventory and diagnostic of English consonants above. How many of these consonants can stand alone at the beginning of syllables to make well-formed English words?

The answer is 'all of them – except /ʒ/ and /ŋ/'. /ʒ/ can occur fairly readily at the *ends* of well-formed syllables (as in the loanwords *beige* and *rouge*), or it can occur inter-vocalically (*leisure, pleasure*), but it can't stand on its own at the beginning of English syllables – there's no /ʒɪn/ or /ʒen/ (though such syllables may be completely OK in other languages). Similarly, in several varieties of English /ŋ/ can readily occur at the ends of syllables (*tang, sing*), or between vowels (*singing, clanging*) – but there's no /ŋɪn/ or /ŋet/.

So of our consonant inventory, all items can freely stand on their own at the beginnings of syllables … except two, which are said to have a *restricted distribution*.

Here I'm going to introduce some new terminology to help us discuss distributional facts within the syllable. Consider again the well-formed

English syllable /pɪn/, *pin*. Like many other well-formed English monosyllables, it begins with a single consonant, has a (short) vowel medially, and closes with a single consonant.

The consonant or consonants that begin a syllable I shall call the **onset** of that syllable. The vowel or vowels standing at the heart of the syllable I shall call the **nucleus**. And the consonant or consonants standing at the end of the syllable I shall call the **coda**. So the well-formedness of /pɪn/ can be imagined like this:

(1)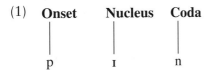

When we asked above 'what consonants can stand on their own to make well-formed beginnings to syllables?' we were actually asking ourselves to make judgements about well-formed *onsets*. Our generalisation so far is that **all consonants bar /ʒ/ and /ŋ/ can be well-formed single-segment onsets.**

> Let's make the well-formedness, or otherwise, of syllable onsets somewhat more analytically tricky. If there are *two* consonants present in the onset of a well-formed syllable, what can these two consonants be? And what can they not be? You might like to make two lists, for well-formed and non-well-formed syllables. Work top to bottom from the consonant inventory list already given and give examples of your own. You can use the alphabetic system of English for your examples if necessary.

Your lists might look something like this (but notice that the following list is by no means complete; see also exercise 4d):

Distribution of English consonants

Well-formed two-consonant onsets		Ill-formed (or non-occurring) two-consonant onsets	
/pl/	*play*	/lp/	Example: *<lpay>
/pr/	*pray*	/rp/	Example: *<rpay>
/br/	*brown, bride*	/rb/	Example: *<rbit>
/bl/	*blue*	/lb/	Example: *<lbue>
/fr/	*free*	/rf/	Example: *<rfee>
/fl/	*flee*	/lf/	Example: *<lfee>
/vr/	*ʔvroom*	/rv/	Example: *<rvoom>
(/vl/ non-occurring?)		/lv/	Example: *<lvoom>
/θr/	*three*	/rθ/	Example: *<rthee>

53

(/θl/ non-occurring?)		/lθ/	Example: *\<lthee>
(/ð/ doesn't seem to occur with a following consonant in a well-formed onset)			
/tr/	*try*	/rt/	Example: *\<rty>
(/tl/ non-occurring?)		/lt/	Example: *\<lty>
/dr/	*dry*	/rd/	Example: *\<rdy>
/sp/	*spin*	/ps/	Example: *\<psin>
/st/	*step*	/ts/	Example: *\<tsep>
/sk/	*skin*	/ks/	Example: *\<ksin>
/sf/	*sphere*	/fs/	Example: *\<fsin>
/sn/	*snow*	/ns/	Example: *\<nsow>
/sm/	*smooth*	/ms/	Example: *\<msooth>

The last six lines above involve what we call *sC clusters* (C = any consonant), e.g. /sp/, /st/ and so forth. However, sC clusters behave very oddly in terms of English syllable structure, as we'll see later (chapter 6), and we can't at this point base any secure generalisations on them. In the examples beginning with /p, b, f, v, θ, t, d/, though, it does look as though there's a generalisation we can make: it's usually fine for these segments to be followed, in a two-consonant onset, by /l/ or /r/ – although the example ?\<vroom> is dubious, /θ/ may be followed by /r/ but not /l/, and /ð/ doesn't appear to co-occur with a following consonant in any well-formed onset (though it's fine on its own: \<then>, \<they>).

I'll continue working in this way – analysing the distribution of consonants in both the onset and the coda of syllables – when we look more rigorously at the structure of the syllable itself in chapter 7 and later chapters, and I've set a further exercise on this topic at the end of this chapter. What I'd like to emphasise is that this last piece of work helps us to understand the English consonant system because consonants are *distributed in characteristic ways*, i.e. there's a *reason* why, in a two-consonant onset, /p/ or /b/ may so readily be followed by /r/ or /l/ (but not by /s/ or /v/ or /ʤ/). That reason has ultimately to do with how 'consonant-like' or 'vowel-like' our consonant segments actually are, and that's an issue we began to track when we considered e.g. /w/, /r/ and /j/ (the *approximants*). You may also like to ask yourself now about why it is that, say, /pj/ (\<pew>) and /pr/ (\<pray>) are well-formed, two-consonant onsets, but /pw/ is not; about why /tr/ is OK (\<try>) but /tl/ is not. The answer is in the *place of articulation*, one of the topics we covered in the last chapter. In general, it turns out that consonants in a two-segment onset *cannot share the same place of articulation*: /p/ is bi*labial*, so it's comfortably followed by /l/ (alveolar) or /r/ (post-alveolar), but not by /w/ (*labio*-velar), or /m/ (bi*labial*). /t/ is alveolar, so it's comfortably followed by /r/ (post-alveolar) but not by /l/ (alveolar) – <trip> is fine, but *<tlip> isn't.

There's a final reason why I asked us to think about the distribution of consonants within well-formed syllables. It's because distributional factors of this kind help us to understand the *phonetic implementation of underlying consonant phonemes* – that is, it helps us to begin to understand **allophony**. That's the topic of the next section.

4.2 A first look at allophones

The alert reader will recall from 1.6 that there are underlying consonant phonemes which have contextually determined realisations. Examples given in 1.6 included the phonemes /p/, /t/ and /k/. These may have phonetic realisations which are strongly aspirated when they occur at the beginning of stressed syllables, are not aspirated when they occur finally in syllables, and which have yet another kind of realisation when they occur after /s/ in an onset.

I introduced these data back in 1.6 in order to emphasise the difference between *underlying* structure (phonology) and the *acoustic implementation of that underlying structure* (phonetics). In this section I want to take that difference one stage further. That in turn means looking at some phonetics.

The phonetic details we're going to analyse here help us to infer something valuable about the behaviour of phonemes – specifically, it can show us that consonant phonemes fall into **classes**. We *infer* the existence of those classes by finding out what the signal of speech can tell us about the underlying structure.

If you think about the phoneme /p/ and its contextually determined, phonetic realisations it's helpful to think about the matter diagrammatically, like this:

(2) **Underlying phoneme**

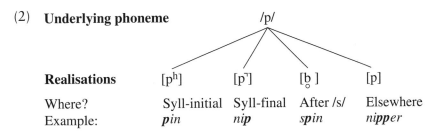

Realisations	[pʰ]	[p˺]	[b̥]	[p]
Where?	Syll-initial	Syll-final	After /s/	Elsewhere
Example:	*p*in	ni*p*	s*p*in	ni*pp*er

There's some more detail we'd need to include in order to be wholly accurate. For instance, this behaviour occurs in *stressed* syllables, and it occurs *within words*: /p/ doesn't have the realisation [b̥], for example, when it occurs after /s/ *when this is part of the coda of a preceding syllable* (as in the phrase *nice pin*). You'll also have noticed that I have included the realisation [p] – that realisation of underlying /p/ that occurs in positions that aren't syllable-initial, aren't syllable-final, and aren't immediately after

/s/. (We could call this [p] 'common or garden [p]' if you'll forgive the expression – which, of course, you won't.) Typically, this variety of underlying /p/ will show up between vowels – as in *nipper*, or *typical* – where the vowel to which /p/ is an onset is unstressed (the final syllable of *nipper*, the penultimate syllable of *typical*).

The point is this – these phonetic realisations of underlying /p/ depend crucially on *context*: [pʰ] has an exclusive place reserved for it, and that place is 'initial in a stressed syllable'. Similarly with the other realisations: *they can occur in that environment and nowhere else*. Therefore, these realisations are *predictable*.

Predictable realisations of underlying phonemes are called **allophones**. The varieties of /p/ we've just looked at, for instance, are all allophones of /p/. We could take the diagram above and substitute the word *allophones* for 'realisations' – and we'd be absolutely right to do so.

If we now turn to the other voiceless plosives, /t/ and /k/, we can see that they function in terms of their allophony in exactly the same way as /p/:

(3)

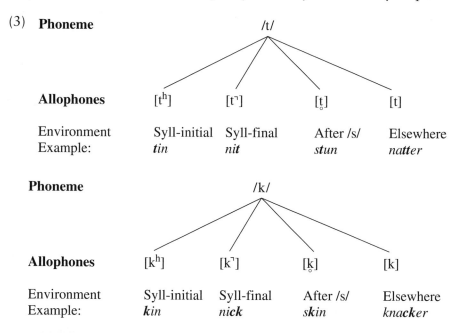

Phoneme		/t/		
Allophones	[tʰ]	[t˺]	[t̥]	[t]
Environment	Syll-initial	Syll-final	After /s/	Elsewhere
Example:	*tin*	*nit*	*stun*	*natter*

Phoneme		/k/		
Allophones	[kʰ]	[k˺]	[k̥]	[k]
Environment	Syll-initial	Syll-final	After /s/	Elsewhere
Example:	*kin*	*nick*	*skin*	*knacker*

If we think about the voiceless plosives of English in this way, we can infer that precisely *because* of this behaviour, the segments in question – the underlying phonemes – together form a *class*.

'Yes,' you might say, 'but the terminology we've learned – calling all these phonemes "voiceless plosives" – suggests that they're a natural class anyway. So why do we need other terminology?'

What we're thinking about isn't just a terminological matter. Allophones can tell us a great deal about phonological structure. These structural inferences help us to understand that underlying phonemes can sometimes behave, *qua* allophony, in ways that wouldn't be predictable from their place of articulation.

An important characteristic of allophones is that they are in **complementary distribution** with one another. This means that each allophone of a given phoneme has an exclusive place, an environment, reserved for it – as we've seen, the allophone [kʰ] of the phoneme /k/ appears syllable-initially *and nowhere else*, while the allophone [k̚] may appear syllable-finally *and nowhere else*.

Phonemes, on the other hand, are in **contrastive distribution** with one another, meaning that two phonemes can appear in exactly the same position within a syllable, but there create a contrast between two words, as we saw with the minimal pair tests.

Allophones do not create contrast. For example, if you say [b̥ɪn] or even [pɪn] when you mean [pʰɪn], your interlocutor will either ask 'What did you say?' or accuse you of sounding ... a bit weird. On the other hand, if you say [kʰɪn] (the realisation of /kɪn/) when you actually mean /pɪn/, you risk being totally misunderstood.

I've illustrated the basic principles behind the distinction between phonemes and allophones with reference simply to the class of oral stops. There are many other underlying consonant phonemes that have particular allophones associated with them, but at this stage in our work I'm not going to give further analysis, nor further lists. We will however, return to the matter of the relationship between underlying (phonemic) and surface (phonetic) structure in chapter 11.

4.3 A note on the glottal stop

There's one realisation of underlying /t/ (and to a lesser extent, the other oral plosives) that occurs relatively frequently, but which is nevertheless *not* an allophone of /t/.

> **Can you work out what this realisation of /t/ might be? If it helps, consider the following words and phrases (pronounce them if necessary, or get a friend or colleague to pronounce them):** *get, get at, getting; hat, hatchet, hat shop; ought, ought to.*

The realisation of /t/ that occurs in these examples is, in many varieties of English, the *glottal stop*. As Gimson explains it (1994: 154), the closure of the airstream that is involved in the production of the glottal stop may be described as follows:

the obstruction to the airstream is caused by the closure of the vocal folds ... The air pressure below the glottis is released by sudden separation of the vocal folds. The compression stage of its articulation consists of silence, its presence being perceived auditorily by the sudden cessation of the previous sound or by the sudden onset (often with an accompanying strong breath effort) of the following sound. The plosive is voiceless …

The glottal stop is distributed very widely. Not only is it a feature of prestige varieties of **British English** (BrE), but it occurs in **General American** (GA), and is also, in regional varieties of BrE, distributed in exclusive ways – ways typical of these varieties.

Despite – or perhaps because of – its wide distribution, the glottal stop is a target for prescriptivists, those laying down 'rules' for 'proper' or 'correct' spoken English.

In the examples above, underlying /t/ might be realised as a glottal stop when the underlying sound occurs: (i) in absolute finality in the syllable (*get*, *at*, *ought*); (ii) where it occurs between vowels (*getting*); and (iii) where it occurs finally in a syllable, where that syllable is followed by another syllable beginning with a consonant (*hatchet*).

That distribution is actually enough to tell us that the glottal stop *can't* be an allophone of /t/: there's no exclusive place reserved for it. Further, other phonetic data (for which, see Gimson 1994: 155–6) make it clear that the glottal stop can also: (i) be a realisation for other voiceless phonemes, notably the stops /p, k/ where these occur finally in an utterance, or (ii) occur as a boundary marker between syllables, or (iii) occur as a 'reinforcement' before syllables beginning with stressed vowels.

So while the glottal stop may be a *possible* – even likely – *realisation* of /t/ in many varieties of English, because the environments in which it occurs aren't predictable then it is not an allophone.

Compare the allophone [tʰ]. This has an *exclusive* place reserved for it: it's the allophone of /t/ that occurs initially in a (stressed) syllable.

The IPA symbol for the glottal stop is [ʔ].

4.4 Recap on consonants

Let's recap a little and remind ourselves of the work we've done on English consonants, and on the system – English phonology – of which they're a part. We have, among other things:

- Examined the notion of *contrastiveness*, and put it to work in devising *minimal pairs*
- Established a basic inventory of *consonant phonemes* for English
- Consolidated that inventory by looking at *voice, manner and place* features associated with English consonant phonemes

- Looked at the possible distribution of these consonant phonemes within the syllable
- Noted the existence of allophones, and in doing so reinforced the distinction we've been making throughout between *underlying structure* (phonology) and the *possible realisation of that structure* (phonetics)

It's tempting to proceed by moving rapidly on to cover vowels, but we shall not do so right away. Because a great deal of work in this chapter has focussed on the distribution of consonants within the *syllable*, and because we have only, to date, a sketchy notion of the structure of English syllables, it makes sense to look in more detail at syllable structure before we begin to analyse vowels and vowel systems. Syllable structure will be the topic of the next three chapters.

Exercises

Exercise 4a   Re-read the section on allophones (4.2). Now think about the phonemes /h/ and /ŋ/. One – /h/ – only ever occurs at the beginning of a syllable, the other – /ŋ/ – only ever occurs syllable-finally.

Both /h/ and /ŋ/ seem on the face of it to be phonemes – minimal pair tests strongly suggest as much – but given the distributional facts, are /h/ and /ŋ/ best analysed as phonemes? What else could they theoretically be analysed as? (Note: this problem will be revisited in chapter 11.)

Exercise 4b   This is an exercise concerning what we have symbolised so far as /r/. There's no need at this stage to make transcriptions, but study the following list of words, pronounce each one as neutrally and normally as possible, and note where, and to what extent, /r/ is present in your variety of English:

rip	*reap*	*ripe*
bring	*pray*	*try*
hard	*burp*	*blurt*
fear	*lure*	*fair*

I've given these examples (and you've already done an exercise – which you might like to revisit – focussing on /r/ in the previous chapter) because it's helpful for you to be able to judge whether your own accent is a *rhotic* accent, i.e. an accent of English that has /r/ in the coda of syllables. It may be that you have /r/ where that consonant occurs alone in the coda (*fear*), but not when /r/ is followed by another consonant (*blurt*). Try to judge the degree to which your accent has rhoticity.

Exercise 4c   (It might be helpful to reread 3.2–3.3 before completing the following.) What follows is a list of *phonetic* transcriptions of single words. Notice that these phonetic transcriptions are set within square brackets and use diacritics (i.e. those diacritics we've encountered in this chapter). For each transcription, notate what the underlying (= simple phonemic) transcription would be. I've completed the first example for you:

1. [pʰɪn] Simple phonemic /pɪn/ 'pin'
2. [fɪt̚]
3. [seʔ]
4. [ʔɪnɪŋz]
5. [pʰɪʔ ʧɪŋ]

Exercise 4d   In the last chapter we began an exercise that might help us to establish what the well-formed two-consonant clusters are that might begin English syllables. Below I repeat the list you encountered first in 4.1. Your task is simply to complete the list as fully as you can, noting as you do which two-consonant onsets are ill-formed or non-occurring (as in the right-hand column below). This is probably the trickiest exercise you will have completed so far in this book, so take your time with it. Completing it thoroughly will, however, help you not only to understand some of the distributional facts we've looked at so far, but also help you to anticipate the work we shall be doing on syllables.

Distribution of English consonants

Well-formed two-consonant onsets		Ill-formed (or non-occurring) two-consonant onsets	
/pl/	play	/lp/	Example: *<lpay>
/pr/	pray	/rp/	Example: *<rpay>
/br/	brown, bride	/rb/	Example: *<rbit>
/bl/	blue	/lb/	Example: *<lbue>
/fr/	free	/rf/	Example: *<rfee>
/fl/	flee	/lf/	Example: *<lfee>
/vr/	?vroom	/rv/	Example: *<rvoom>
(/vl/ non-occurring?)		/lv/	Example: *<lvoom>
/θr/	three	/rθ/	Example: *<rthee>
/θw/	thwart	/wθ/	Example: *<wthart>
(/θl/	non-occurring)	/lθ/	Example: *<lthee>
(/ð/ doesn't seem to occur with a following consonant in a well-formed onset)			

/tr/	*try*	/rt/	Example: *\<rty>
(/tl/	non-occurring)	/lt/	Example: *\<lty>
/dr/	*dry*	/rd/	Example: *\<rdy>
/sp/	*spin*	/ps/	Example: *\<psin>
/st/	*step*	/ts/	Example: *\<tsep>
/sk/	*skin*	/ks/	Example: *\<ksin>
/sf/	*sphere*	/fs/	Example: *\<fsin>
/sn/	*snow*	/ns/	Example: *\<nsow>
/sm/	*smooth*	/ms/	Example: *\<msooth>

Key terms introduced in this chapter

allophone
British English
classes
coda
complementary distribution
contrastive distribution
General American
nucleus
onset
rhotic
stressed syllables

Further reading

Gimson, A. C. 1994. *Gimson's pronunciation of English*. 5th edition, revised by
    Alan Cruttenden. London: Arnold. Opening of chapter 5.
McMahon, April. 2002. *An introduction to English phonology*. Edinburgh
    University Press. Chapter 4.

Syllables (1): introduction

In this chapter …

In this chapter we look more systematically at the structure of English syllables, about which up to now we've been simply using our linguistic intuitions. We see that syllables may interestingly be distinguished into two classes – lexical monosyllables, and non-lexical ones – and that these classes also have a bearing on the linguistic stress (or lack of it) of particular syllables. Presence or absence of stress also correlates to some extent with the presence of schwa in phonemic transcriptions. Schwa is almost invariably diagnostic of stresslessness. At the end of the chapter we refine our work on one aspect of the English stress system, and we'll see that there are generalisations to be made about *primary stress*, *secondary stress* and *unstress*. We introduce that work by thinking about the phonology, and to some extent the morphology, of English **compound words**.

5.1 Preliminaries, and a note on schwa

Because you've completed exercise 4d you're in a position to understand that the consonant system of English isn't distributed, and therefore doesn't work, merely randomly: the terms of the system – the consonant phonemes – are, in terms of their distribution, *constrained*. What does 'constrained' mean?

> Think back to exercise 4d. If a syllable begins with two consonants, and the first of those consonants is, for instance, /b/, then what can the second consonant be? Try to think of at least six words that begin with /b/ followed by another consonant. Each word should be one, and only one, syllable.

You might have constructed a list like the following (where each item is given in its standard alphabetic form):

blue
bran
bland
breed
blend
brunt ...

The relevant observation is that if a monosyllable begins with two consonants, and the first of those is /b/, then the second consonant *must be* /r/ or /l/. It *cannot* be /s/, or /f/, or /g/, or /p/. In fact, this observation holds 99 percent good for two- and three-syllable words beginning with two consonants, the first of which is /b/: *bracket, blender, broiling, blandishment* ... The only apparent exception is the word *bwana*, which is a loanword from Swahili. You'll probably *feel* the word *bwana* to be in some way anomalous, and infer that it's a loanword – precisely *because* the way in which the word begins (/b/ followed by /w/) is not normative in English.

What's at stake here is the relationship between /b/ and an immediately following consonant. The vowel that follows the second consonant doesn't seem to play any role in constraining what the second consonant of a syllable-initial group of two consonants might be. The cardinal relationship seems to be between /b/ and whatever consonant might follow it.

> It's not just /b/ that behaves in this way. Try the same exercise (4d) with (mono)syllables beginning /f/ + consonant, and /p/ + consonant.

Distributional constraints obtain within the English consonant system. Those constraints can be understood and analysed with reference to *syllable structure*. That is, the two (or more) consonants that may begin English syllables seem somehow to be in a special relationship with each other. From observing that relationship we can infer that these two (or more) consonants might form a **constituent** of the syllable. That's one of the reasons why we're going to look at syllable structure now. Looking at syllable structure helps to deepen our understanding of how the consonant system works.

This leaves the problem of the relatively impoverished inventory of vowels with which we're going to analyse syllables. Let's address that matter directly.

By some miracle of the textbook-writer's art, so far we've used only a small set of vowel phonemes to illustrate the examples. You may not have noticed this: in many word lists, and some exercises, I've set examples in italic (therefore implying the written form), or specifically set examples in angled brackets (e.g. <brunt>), which convention can only ever mean 'this is a written form, not a spoken one'. If I've transcribed vowels at all, I have done so using a very small range of vowels: /ɪ/ (short, as in /hɪd/, *hid*), /iː/ (long, as in /hiːd/, *heed*), /e/ (/hed/, *head*), and – on one occasion – /a/ (/had/, as in standard Northern English *had*).

In illustrating the *structure* of syllables we don't, in fact, need many extra vowels, since we can readily exemplify syllable *structure* by using a restricted vowel inventory. Further, even though we'll use a restricted inventory of vowels to illustrate syllable structure, the generalisations we can develop – even with a restricted range of vowel segments to play with – should hold good for *all the rest of the English vowel system*.

In what follows, then, I'll use examples with /ɪ/, with /iː/, and (occasionally) with /e/, trusting that you will probably have a very good intuitive idea of the contrasts in vowel involved, most importantly that between <hid> and <heed>, /hɪd/ and /hiːd/. I am, though, going to use one other vowel in order to illustrate the structure of (stressed) English syllables. That's the vowel very many English speakers have in words such as *hide*, *bide* or *night*. In my accent, such a vowel is symbolised as /aɪ/. In varieties of New York, New Zealand, or Bristol English, this vowel might be represented as /ɑɪ/. At this point in our work, it doesn't matter too much what the relevant symbol is (we'll revisit this vowel in chapters 8–10). What is critically important is that you can hear the following vowel contrasts within your own vowel system:

hid	heed	hide
/hɪd/	/hiːd/	/haɪd/

> To reassure yourself that these, or similar, vowel contrasts obtain in your own variety of English, construct at least three more examples (i.e. three groups of three words) where the same contrasts hold.

You might have constructed a list like this:

hid	heed	hide
/hɪd/	/hi:d/	/haɪd/
bit	beat	bite
/bɪt/	/bi:t/	/baɪt/
nit	neat	night
/nɪt/	/ni:t/	/naɪt/
fit	feet	fight
/fɪt/	/fi:t/	/faɪt/

It doesn't matter, at this stage, whether these are accurate transcriptions of underlying structure for your particular accent. What *is* important is that you perceive, irrespective of your accent, that there are vowel *contrasts* in your system of spoken English.

There's one other vowel that you'll come across in this chapter. As an introduction to this vowel, consider the following word list, read it aloud (preferably, more than once, and/or listening to someone else read it aloud), paying particular attention to the boldened syllables. (The boldening doesn't mean you should read these syllables with any special emphasis or extra loudness. Just read the list back as neutrally and normally as possible, paying attention to how the boldened syllables sound.)

appal	(compare *apple*)
appalling	
appealing	
affirm	(compare *affirmation*)
ado	(compare *addle*)
undo	(compare *unit*)
invert	(compare *invitation*)
balloon	(compare *ballot*)
despair	(compare *desperate*)
disgrace	(compare *dismal*)
ci**ty**	
hap**py**	
sit**ter**	
ne**ver**	

Take the top five examples. Each word begins with a syllable that doesn't bear stress, and typically, speakers and listeners perceive the stressless vowel in such a syllable as a 'murmur vowel'. Such a vowel sound has been described to me by students as 'a sort of hesitation noise', or 'an unemphatic "uh"'. More technically, this vowel is pronounced with no particular raising or retraction of the tongue, the tongue is more or less central in the oral cavity, and there is no particular lip-spreading (which we associate with vowels such as /iː/) or lip-rounding (which we associate with vowels such as the one we will eventually symbolise as /uː/ – /muːn/, *moon*).

This 'murmur vowel' occurs very frequently in English (see also the section of text below). It occurs so frequently, and is in many ways so remarkable, that this vowel is given a special name. That name is **schwa**. If we return to the top five examples in the above list, it's a safe bet that whatever your particular accent, you will pronounce the first syllables of the words in question with schwa.

Schwa is diagnostic of lack of stress. If, for example, we wanted to specify where the main word stress of the top five examples fell, we might say something like: 'On the second syllable of *appal* … and on the second syllable of *appalling* … and *appealing* … and *affirm* … and, yes, *ado*, too …' These second, stressed syllables are produced with vowels other than schwa. If we use a slash mark above the relevant vowels to graphically indicate (primary) 'stress', we might construct a list something like this:

appál   (compare *ápple*)
affírm   (compare *affirmátion*)
adó   (compare *áddle*)

The first syllable of the words in question, though, is *never* stressed. It may be *written* <a>, but it isn't pronounced like the <a> of *apple* or *addle*. It's pronounced with that fairly reliable diagnostic of stresslessness, schwa.

Schwa has a special symbol. It is /ə/.

Symbolising schwa. I've seen many longhand horrors masquerading as schwa over the years. Schwa is *not* best thought of as 'just an upside-down <e>'. The best way to construct a longhand representation of schwa is to imagine a clock face. Begin with your pen in the 9 o'clock position, then draw an ellipse through 12 o'clock, then 3 o'clock, then 6 o'clock, and then almost (but not quite) back to 9 o'clock again. Just before you reach your starting point at 9 o'clock, draw a horizontal bar rightwards across the shape you have just drawn. On PCs, the symbol for schwa may be found in Doulos SIL (www.sil.org)

It would be neat if we could say that stressless syllables in English were *always* pronounced with the vowel schwa. True, where schwa occurs you can be almost 100 percent certain that the syllable in which it occurs is stressless, but there's another vowel that also occurs in stressless syllables, and that is the vowel /ɪ/. Consider the following examples:

in**vert**
despair   (compare *desperate*)
disgrace   (compare *dismal*)
city
hap**py**

The boldened syllables are perceived to be stressless relative to the stressed syllables adjacent to them, and in fact, for some speakers the vowel of the first syllable of e.g. *despair* might be pronounced with schwa. But for the vast majority of English speakers, the relevant unstressed vowels have the underlying shape /ɪ/. (For speakers of Tyneside English, the vowel in the final syllables of e.g. *city* and *happy* is perceived as long, and somewhat like /iː/. Nevertheless, as we'll discuss in chapter 8, the underlying vowel phoneme can plausibly be analysed as /ɪ/.)

We might say, with accuracy, two things: (i) that the vowels schwa (/ə/) and /ɪ/ are sometimes in free variation in unstressed syllables, but (ii) where schwa does occur, it is reliably diagnostic of stresslessness.

5.2 Lexical and non-lexical monosyllables

We've begun to talk about stress. For most speakers, stress in English words is relatively easy to perceive: stressed syllables are perceived as 'more prominent', or louder, or longer, or 'more complex', or produced with more apparent effort, than the less stressed or unstressed syllables that might lie adjacent to them. And in fact, there are many phonetic cues to stress: vowel length, pitch change, fundamental frequency and loudness can all play a part in our perception of a given syllable as stressed. We're usually quite unaware of such phonetic factors. We simply have no trouble discerning syllables as stressed or unstressed. If you read back the following short lists, for example, you'll be able to discern immediately where the main word stress falls in each example:

Column 1	Column 2	Column 3
balloon	*orange*	*agenda*
cigar	*flower*	*important*
reply	*river*	*awaken*
bizarre	*cellar*	*repulsive*
affair	*rabbit*	*redundant*

67

In column 1, main stress falls on the *final* syllable of each word; in column 2, on the *initial* syllable of each word; and in column 3, stress falls on the *middle* syllable of each example. (Notice, particularly in column 3, that what we perceive as the stressed syllables are surrounded by unstressed syllables pronounced with either /ə/ or /ɪ/.)

There's a further way of thinking about stressed and unstressed syllables. In columns 1–3 above, we looked at what happens in words of two or more syllables. What happens, in terms of stress, in words containing one and only one syllable – that is, in *monosyllables*?

There are certain monosyllables in English where the words in question are full of semantic content – that is, the words are meaningful, and we can look those meanings up in a dictionary. The monosyllable *dog*, for instance, has the dictionary definition 'a domesticated flesh-eating animal ... ' And the word *house*? 'a building for human habitation ... ' And so on. Since they're full of semantic content, and are important parts of the *lexicon* of English speakers, we can call such words **lexical monosyllables.**

On the other hand, there's a class of words in English which are, certainly, monosyllables, but which have no semantic content ('no meaning' – except, as we'll see, *grammatical* meaning). Such monosyllables are items like *and*, *but*, *with* and *the*. Imagine yourself asking 'What does "the" mean?' Unlike a lexical monosyllable, *the* has no semantic content, though it does have a range of *grammatical functions* – as do words such as *and*, or *or*, or *from* ...

Consider the example formed by the little word *and*. This word is a *conjunction*: its grammatical function is to join together units of syntactic structure:

Merel was happy **and** Tom was overjoyed.	[*and* joins two sentences]
There are times when I crave fish **and** chips.	[*and* joins two nouns]
The writing of books is both pleasurable **and** painful.	[*and* joins two adjectives]

Monosyllables like *and*, *the*, *from* don't behave like lexical monosyllables, insofar as they have grammatical *functions*, rather than 'meanings'. Therefore we call such monosyllables **non-lexical monosyllables.** (Because such words have grammatical functions, some linguists call such items 'function words', but I'm going to stick with the term 'non-lexical', because the term contrasts so simply with 'lexical'.)

There's another important consideration in the classification of lexical and non-lexical (mono)syllables. Lexical words will *always carry stress on one or more of their syllables* (something we've already seen in the words of columns 1–3 above, all of which were *lexical* words). It follows, then, that *if a lexical word has one, and only one syllable, then that syllable will always be stressed*. We might claim that *lexical monosyllables are inherently stressed* – and since the vowel schwa is diagnostic of lack of stress, we can make the further claim that *lexical monosyllables will never be produced or perceived as having a pronunciation with schwa*. Therefore, lexical monosyllables like *cat*, *dog*, *house*, *chair*, *desk*, *match*, *mug* and many thousands of others are inherently stressed. They'll *never* have a pronunciation in schwa.

Non-lexical monosyllables, on the other hand, are often, if not typically, pronounced with schwa: *the*, for instance, is in many instances pronounced with schwa. The only exceptions are formed when the following word begins with a vowel (compare the pronunciation of *the* in the phrases *the dog* and *the egg*), or when we want to give the definite article *the* added emphasis ('I said pass me *the* book, not just *a* book'). Under emphasis, *the* acquires stress, and when it does, it may readily acquire a pronunciation with the vowel /iː/ (although there are other conceivable pronunciations in the example I've just used).

The generalisations about syllable structure that you'll find in this chapter are almost invariably generalisations *about the structure of lexical monosyllables*.

5.3 A further note on English stress

Much ink has been spilled on the extent to which the system of English stress ('stress phonology') is regular, that is, governed by rules or other principles. Since the topic is so very large I don't intend to offer you anything other than a short note here, one directed only to clarifying *what kinds of syllable* are stressed, and what kinds of syllable are typically unstressed. This limitation allows us to key the following note to the other material we've introduced in this chapter.

First, it's at least useful to think of lexical *monosyllables* as **always** bearing some sort of stress – i.e. as we've seen, the pronunciation of these words will **never** include schwa. Examples of such lexical monosyllables are *dog*, *house*, *shed*, *sky*, and so on. But there's also a linguistic situation in which lexical monosyllables may be *less stressed* than a lexical monosyllable that immediately precedes them.

> **Can you think of what that situation might be, and construct relevant examples?**

I have in mind **compound** words such as *doghouse*, *housemate*, *potting shed* and *skydive*. How and why are they *compounds*?

The best clue to the structure of these words lies in their *morphology*. Morphology, which can be thought of as the study of 'word-building', among other things, studies how new words can be *derived* from those words that already exist in a given language. This branch of morphology is called, transparently, ***derivational morphology.***

One of the ways in which speakers of English have always been able to derive new words is to join, or 'compound', two existing words together. (This property of English is shared without exception by all the other Germanic languages, and we can find many examples of compounding from written records that are at least 1400 years old.)

> **To see how compounding works, take the lexical monosyllable *house*, and insert another lexical monosyllable before it in order to make another word at least two syllables long. An example would be *DOG-house*, where the added word appears in capital letters. Try to construct at least five such examples. Don't worry about whether to spell such words with hyphens or not.**

Examples might be

tree house
greenhouse
madhouse ...

From our point of view the interesting thing is that both *tree* and *house* are themselves lexical monosyllables. Both are **nouns,** too: they *behave* as nouns in that they may be preceded by definite or indefinite articles (*a house, the tree*) and may be pluralised (*tree-s, house-s*). We can indicate their status as lexical monosyllables belonging to the class 'noun' by inserting each word into square brackets, and then labelling those brackets (with 'N' or 'Noun'), like this:

[tree]$_N$ [house]$_N$

When we compound the two words, though, we make another lexical item, another noun: the new word *tree house* can be preceded by articles ('the/a tree house') and be pluralised ('the tree houses'), just like any other noun. We might formalise the procedure of compounding like this: (a) we take the original words, and their brackets, and (b) we insert them, and their brackets, within a new, outer frame of brackets that encloses both words. Then we label this outer set of square brackets:

[[tree][house]]$_N$

The lovely thing about compounds is that they usually behave very regularly with respect to their stress patterning. For instance, because the words that make up compounds begin and end life as lexical items in their own right, they will *never* (or at least, very rarely, and then over a long period of time) acquire a pronunciation with schwa, i.e. they will never (or rarely) become stressless. And yet of the two words in our list of compounds above, one syllable or word will almost invariably be perceived as being 'more stressed' than its partner. If my hunches are right, you'll immediately perceive that in our list of '-house' words above, it's in every case the *first* word or syllable that is in some way 'more stressed' than its rightward partner. Compounds usually have a very distinctive 'falling' stress pattern.

What does a 'falling' stress pattern mean? The word 'falling' is a metaphor, used here simply to try to capture your possible intuitions. More technically, we could with accuracy claim that what we're producing and perceiving when we analyse English compounds is actually a *three-way stress distinction*:

1. Syllables that are most prominent within individual words bear **primary stress**
2. Syllables that are less prominent than those in 1, but which do not have pronunciations (in schwa, or /ɪ/, or possibly a syllabic consonant like /r/, /n/ or /m/) diagnostic of stresslessness, may be said to have **secondary stress**
3. Syllables having pronunciations diagnostic of stresslessness may be said to be **unstressed**

In compounds like *tree house* what you're hearing is *primary stress on the first word and secondary stress on the second*.

> **To make the three-way stress distinctions available in English analytically clear to you, think about the stress patterning of the three syllables of the compound word *skydiver*. Which word bears primary stress, which weak stress, and which syllable is unstressed?**

You should have found that *sky* bears primary stress, *dive* secondary stress, and the little suffix <-er> is stressless.

Notice that this pattern of stress within compounding ('primary–secondary–weak') also usually holds good in compounds whose internal words have more than one syllable each. An example here might be something like [application] and [committee] (both nouns). Compound the two words together – [[application][committee]], 'committee that considers job applications' – and you should find that the word *application* bears the primary stress of the compound word, while the word *committee* carries the secondary stress.

What has this got to do with phonology?

First there's a systematic point. One of the phonological hallmarks of lexical words, when these are pronounced in isolation, is that *one* of their syllables will *always* bear primary stress. There may well be other, secondary-stressed syllables within that same word, but one syllable, and one syllable only, will bear the primary stress of the whole word. From this it follows logically that where there's only one syllable present in a lexical word – *dog*, *house*, *shed* – than that syllable is *inherently stressed*. Such syllables can *never* be transcribed with schwa, or any other vowel (or consonant) diagnostic of stresslessness.

Second, compounds. Because compounds consist of two lexical words, they almost invariably have the 'primary–secondary' structure we've been discussing. *Secondary-stressed syllables are not unstressed syllables.*

Third, something very practical, to do with transcriptions. One of the errors many of my students make – and which I have made myself – is to transcribe *from* the page *to* the page. Few students ever appear to *pronounce* (even silently, as it were) the piece of discourse they are at that moment trying to transcribe. Accordingly, in judging transcriptions I find many mistakes where *unstressed* vowels are transcribed with vowel qualities *other than* schwa or /ɪ/, and conversely, mistakes where *stressed* syllables are transcribed *with* schwa. Therefore, it always pays to be alert not simply to what's written on the page, but to the *sounds of the discourse* that's being *indicated* on a page. Pronounce everything (even if you do the pronouncing silently) before you attempt to transcribe it. Pay particular attention to any compound words.

To help you practise, the first exercise you'll complete below requires you to make precisely those kinds of transcriptions where *listening*, and paying particular attention to *stress patterning*, is especially important.

Exercises

Exercise 5a   **Make simple phonemic transcriptions of the following words, as these are pronounced in your own accent of English. Pay particular attention to the pronunciation and structure of any *compound words* you are transcribing. Use schwa to transcribe the articles *the* and *a*. For other unstressed syllables, you may use either schwa, /ɪ/, or possibly /r/, as appropriate:**

    a.   the sin bin
    b.   it's a pitch
    c.   the sinner
    d.   the wedding singer
    e.   a pin-sticker

Exercise 5b   In the exercises – here and elsewhere – you'll find that certain words recur. That's partly because we're still working with a very limited range of vowels (the /ɪ/ of *hid*, the /iː/ of *heed*, and the /aɪ/ of *hide*) but also because the same words can be used to illustrate many topics of relevance to the work we've done in chapters 2–4. First, then, study the following phrases (there are ten of them) and *make a simple phonemic transcription of each.* Remember that with these simple transcriptions you are illustrating the *underlying system* of speech sounds that is operative in your own variety of English.

You may use either schwa or /ɪ/, as appropriate, for the transcription of unstressed vowels.

There may be some few speakers reading this for whom the vowel of e.g. <fine> isn't /aɪ/ . If so, don't worry – just leave that part of the transcription blank and come back to it after you've read chapter 7.

   a.   He's in Leeds.
   b.   She's nice.
   c.   Leeds is a fine city.
   d.   A pin is tiny.
   e.   It's a bit of a grind.
   f.   Finish it.
   g.   It isn't itching.
   h.   She denied it.
   i.   Bitterness is fine.
   j.   He's pimping my ride.

Key terms introduced in this chapter
compound
constituent
lexical monosyllables
morphology
non-lexical monosyllables
noun
primary stress
secondary stress

Further reading
Gimson, A. C. 1994. *Gimson's pronunciation of English*. 5th edition, revised by
   Alan Cruttenden. London: Arnold. Chapter 10. Sections 10.1–10.3.5 are a
   succinct descriptive survey of distinctive patterns of English stress, while section
   10.3.5 is devoted specifically to compounds.

CHAPTER 6

Syllables (2): constituents

In this chapter …

In this chapter we look in more detail at how English syllables are structured. We take some terms and concepts we introduced earlier – those of syllabic onset, nucleus and coda – and use them to describe the internal structure of syllables. In doing so, we see how nucleus and coda are themselves gathered into a higher-level internal constituent of the syllable, called the rhyme.

We observe that onsets and rhymes are the *immediate constituents* of the *syllable*. The immediate constituents of the *rhyme* are the nucleus and the coda.

Once we've established the existence of these internal constituents we also see that there are principles at work – principles possibly based on 'sonority', which we reanalyse as 'openness' – which govern how segments can appear in well-formed syllables (and within internal constituents of those syllables).

We also look at apparently onsetless syllables and suggest that in English, onsets may be *obligatory*, and that therefore it makes sense to explore the concept of a 'zero phoneme' which might fill an erstwhile empty onset position, as in words such as *eye* or *egg*.

We close this chapter by briefly reconsidering the notions of the optionality and obligatoriness of internal syllable constituents, and aligning those notions with a typology that might obtain in the world's languages.

6.1 The constituents of English syllables

In chapter 4 we claimed that we could think about syllables as containing constituents such as *onset* (the consonant or consonants that might begin the syllable), *nucleus* (the vowel at the heart of the syllable), and *coda* (the consonant or consonants that might end the syllable). We developed this terminology because we needed to find a simple way to refer to 'the consonant or consonants that begin or end a syllable', and the terminology 'onset–nucleus–coda' offers just that straightforwardness. But we haven't yet begun to *justify* this terminology. Let's do that.

On the face of it, we could analyse syllables just as a concatenated string of segments. If we use the symbol C to stand for one consonant phoneme and V to stand for one vowel phoneme, a syllable such as *hid*, /hɪd/, would be analysed as CVC.

> Using C to stand for one consonant phoneme and V to stand for one vowel phoneme, try the same procedure on the following syllables: *hint*, *print*, *pitch*, *ship*. (Hint: you'll need to make a simple phonemic transcription of these syllables first.)

Written form	Transcription	C and V array
<hint>	/hɪnt/	CVCC
<print>	/prɪnt/	CCVCC
<pitch>	/pɪʧ/	CVC (/ʧ/ is *one* consonant phoneme)
<ship>	/ʃɪp/	CVC (/ʃ/ is *one* consonant phoneme)

> Look at the Cs and Vs that are aligned with the word *print*: CCVCC. There's nothing inherently wrong with such a representation. We've truly aligned one consonant phoneme with one C, and the vowel phoneme /ɪ/ with one V. But there's something that seems to be missing from such a representation. What is it?

What's missing is the material we introduced in the last chapter and which you started to analyse in some of the questions and exercises you found there. That is, if there are two consonants that begin a syllable, and the first of these is /b/ or (as in the above example, *print*) /p/, then the second consonant can only ever be /r/, /j/ or /l/: *print*, *pew* and e.g. *plinth* are well formed; **pwint*, **pmint*, **pbit* are not.

> Once again, you need to distinguish carefully between the common alphabetic forms of English, and phonemic transcriptions. For example, the words <psychology> or <pneumatic> seem to begin with 'p' followed by 's' and 'n' respectively. In English, though, syllable-initial <ps> is phonemically /s/, and syllable-initial <pn> phonemically /n/. Similarly, the word <physics> doesn't begin with */ph/ but /f/ (/fɪzɪks/). It's a good idea *always* to make simple phonemic transcriptions of the examples we're discussing.

So there seems to be a special relationship between syllable-initial /p/ and whatever consonant might follow it in a two-consonant syllable opening. The problem is that a notation that handles syllable structure as something that is merely a string of Cs and Vs doesn't address this relationship. One C is followed by another C, without implying anything about the relationship between the two Cs.

We can extend these observations to the consonants that can close English syllables. Consider the syllable *print* again. In terms of its C and V array, it's a CCVCC syllable, ending with two C segments. But what the CV notation fails to engage with is the fact that if the first of two closing consonants is /n/, then the second, and final, consonant can only be one of a limited set – it could be /t/ (*print*); it could be /s/ (*prince*, /prɪns/); possibly, too, it could be /z/ (*pins*, /pɪnz/) or /ʃ/ (*pinch*, /pɪnʃ/). But the consonant that follows /n/ in a two-consonant syllable closure can *never* be /m/ (**pinm*) or /f/ (**pinf*) or /r/ (**pinr*). Just as in the two-consonant clusters that can open well-formed syllables, there are *restrictions* on what kind of two-consonant clusters can close well-formed syllables in English.

There appear, then, to be constraints on syllable openings and constraints on syllable closures. The existence of these easily verifiable constraints suggests strongly that a well-formed English syllable isn't just an array of segments, of Cs and Vs. Rather, a well-formed syllable has *internal constituency*, including the onset, the nucleus and the coda.

Let's try to diagrammatise this. In the following, I'm going to use the Greek lower-case sigma symbol, <σ>, to stand for 'syllable'. What we're saying is that a diagram like the one found in (1) below is accurate as far as it goes, but limited in its implications, in that it says nothing about internal constituency:

(1)   **C and V array**

Syllable (σ)

C   C   V   C   C
/p   r   ɪ   n   t/

On the other hand, a diagram such as 6.(2) is both more intuitively and more observationally adequate:

(2)   Onset, nucleus and coda

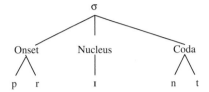

Diagram (2) claims that there are *three constituents* within the syllable. It's within these constituents that constraints appear to hold. Accordingly, one of our jobs will be to ask questions such as 'What makes a well-formed onset?' and 'What constraints hold in English codas?'

We're not done with the internal constituency of the syllable yet. One thing we could do, for instance, is reconsider the nucleus and coda. One commonplace way of thinking about these constituents is to claim that together they form a constituent of the syllable called the **rhyme**, like this:

(3)   Nucleus and coda as a rhyme

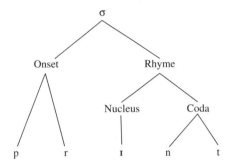

(3) claims that the *immediate constituents* of the syllable, i.e. those constituents branching directly off the 'σ' label, are the onset and the rhyme. The existence of the rhyme constituent is implied not only by the practice of generations of English poets (the 'rhyme' is exactly that chunk of the word used to chime with other words which have different onsets but identical rhymes, thus e.g. *h<itch>* rhymes with *p<itch>*), but also by another, properly phonological factor.

> **Can you work out what is the phonological factor that suggests nucleus and coda together form a rhyme constituent?**

Look again at diagram (3): the onset is filled with consonantal material (i.e. segments we could unambiguously label C); the nucleus looks like it's filled with vocalic material (i.e. a segment – or, in other examples, segments – we'd unambiguously label V); and the coda is filled with material we'd label C. That seems straightforward (although life isn't quite as straightforward as it might look, so keep reading). What might not be apparent is that within the onset, /r/ is actually somewhat more 'vowel-like' than /p/. /r/ can, for instance, function as a syllable in its own right in some English accents, notably varieties of American English, where a word like e.g. *bitter* has two syllables, the second of which is comprised of /r/ – GA /bɪtr/. On the other hand, /p/ is among the most 'consonant-like' of the consonants, insofar as it is a voiceless stop. From this, one might begin to infer that well-formed onsets consisting of two segments have their 'most consonantal' material at the leftmost periphery. The 'less consonantal' or 'more vowel-like' material in a two-segment onset will typically be found *between* the leftmost edge and the nucleus (e.g. the /l/ that can follow /p/ in words such as *play, plinth, plight,* or the /r/ that can follow /b/ in words like *bray, brawl, bright*).

Within the coda, the 'most consonantal' material seems to be found at the right periphery of the syllable, while the 'less consonantal' or 'more vowel-like' material of a two-segment coda seems to occur not at the rightmost periphery, but between that periphery and the vowel within the nucleus.

Put this together, and what you get is a generalisation: *the most consonantal, least vowel-like segments are found at the margins of the syllable, while the most vowel-like segments are found in the nucleus.*

If that is so, then it's uniquely in the *rhyme* that we get a rightwards gradient from 'most vowel-like' (the (leftmost segment in the) nucleus), to 'most consonant-like' (the segment that lies at the right margin). Conversely, it is within the *onset* that we get a gradient movement from 'most consonant-like' (the segment that lies at the left margin) to 'more vowel-like'. We can add this intuition, and its generalisation, to the diagram (3), here modified as (4):

(4)   **The margins and the centre of a well-formed syllable**

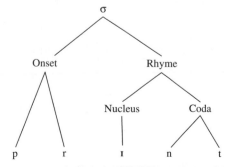

<<<<most consonant-like<<<<CENTRE>>>>most consonant-like>>>>
<<<<least vowel-like<<<<<<<CENTRE>>>>least vowel-like>>>

We can observe something else. In the example *print*, we've correctly spotted that /p/ and /t/ are 'most consonant-like' (they're both voiceless stops), and both lie, as expected, at the right/left margins. Further, it seems likely that /r/ is closely bound to /p/ within the onset. What is *not* so certain, and thus far seems only likely, is that the /n/ of *print* belongs in the coda.

> If the /n/ of e.g. *print* doesn't belong in the coda of the syllable, where else might it belong?

It would be tidy if we could say 'onsets are filled by consonants, nuclei are filled by vowels, and codas are filled by consonants'. But there's no structurally compelling reason why the /n/ of e.g. *print* can't belong in the nucleus, like this:

(5) **What kinds of segment can be in the nucleus?**

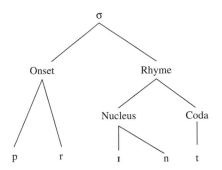

In (5) /n/ forms the second, or rightmost, of the two segments that lie in the nucleus. There's no reason why that shouldn't be allowed to happen. Nowhere have we said categorically that 'nuclei must be filled with segments that are unambiguously V'. What we *have* said is that the nucleus of a well-formed syllable must be filled with a segment or segments that are 'more vowel-like' than the segments that might lie in that syllable's margins. Despite being a consonant, /n/ is in fact more 'vowel-like' than the /t/ to its right. For one thing, /n/ – like /r/ or /l/ – can itself function like a syllable peak, e.g. in words such as *happen* or *button*. That said, /n/, as a C, is less vowel-like than the true vowel segment /ɪ/, which lies to its immediate left within the nucleus.

It's clumsy to have to write 'more/less vowel-like' or 'more/less consonant-like'. What I'm suggesting is that the segments of English phonology seem to have particular properties that can be mapped onto syllable structure. For example, the property 'oral stop' (/p, b, t, d, k, g/) seems to be aligned with 'the kind of consonant that can begin a two-segment onset', while the property 'vowel' seems readily to be aligned with 'the kind of segment that can begin a two-segment nucleus'.

In fact, there seems to be a unifying, and therefore simplifying, fact at work in the sound structure of English that helps us make better sense of notions like 'more/least consonant-like'. Many linguists have claimed that the kinds of properties of segments we hinted at in diagram (4) can be understood by thinking of the inherent **sonority** of a segment. That is, there may well be a *scale* at work in English sound structure, whereby the least sonorous (= 'least vowel-like') segments – segments such as oral stops – lie at one end of the scale, and true vowels (= 'least consonant-like') at the other. We can diagrammatise this, using the symbols < to mean 'less sonorous than' and > to mean 'more sonorous than':

(6)   **A first look at sonority**

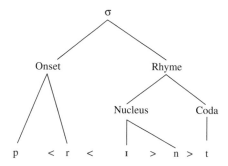

The easiest way to interpret such a diagram is to begin in the centre, with the vowel segment /ɪ/. This is more 'sonorous' (= 'more vowel-like', or 'less consonant-like') than the segment /n/ to its immediate right, which is in turn more sonorous (= 'more vowel-like') than the segment /t/ that lies at the right margin of the syllable. Starting again from /ɪ/, but this time working leftwards, /ɪ/ is more sonorous (= 'more vowel-like') than /r/, and /r/ is more sonorous than /p/.

The further claim would be that *all* well-formed syllables in English are structured like this: if such syllables have two segments in their onset, then the first is less sonorous than the second; if such syllables have two segments in their codas, then the second is less sonorous than the first. That is, 'sonority' – a concept we've yet to define in anything other than an intuitive sense – might provide a more elegant way of thinking about issues such as 'what kind of segment is "less consonant-like" than, say, /m/', as well as exposing with slightly more rigour the properties of English segments as these are aligned with behaviour within syllables.

Before moving on I need very briefly to look again at notions of C and V.

Recall that we've used C to stand for 'one consonant segment' and V to stand for 'one vowel segment', noting that a syllable like *print* would pan out as CCVCC. Then we said that analysing a syllable merely as a concatenated string of Cs and Vs wasn't a perspicuous way of analysing structure. Nevertheless, the claim that a syllable is filled with one or more *segments* is still valid, and we might want to suggest incorporating such a claim into a syllable diagram as follows, where the symbol X stands for a single segment, irrespective of whether this is a C or a V segment:

(7)   **The tiers of syllable structure**

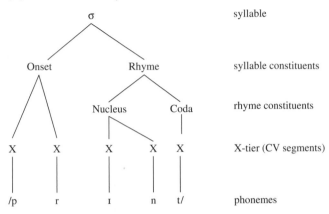

All we seem to have done is introduce a new level (a *tier*) of syllable structure between the constituents of the syllable and the phonemic segments that are the exponents of those constituents. Nevertheless, this diagram shows how richly layered English syllables might be, and in fact the X-tier of structure will turn out to play an interesting role in the analysis later. For the present, do no more than notice *the hierarchy of constituents* involved in syllable analysis. We'll return to them.

6.2 Sonority, classes and openness

We've hinted that *sonority* might be the key to understanding notions such as 'more vowel-like' and 'more consonant-like'. We might claim that the more intrinsic sonority a segment has, the more vowel-like it is (and therefore the most likely to lie towards the centre of the syllable), and conversely, that the least sonorous sounds will be the 'most consonant-like' (and therefore the most likely to lie at the syllable's margins). But what is 'sonority'?

The term refers to energy relative to effort, or more informally to the 'carrying power' of a sound. A sonorous sound is one with high output relative to the articulatory effort required to produce it, and sounds can therefore be ranked according to their degree of sonority. The vowel in *hawk* is more sonorous than the vowel in *hook*, which in turn is more sonorous than a consonant such as *l* or *r*. We can say in general that the points of greatest sonority in an utterance will be interpreted as syllable peaks. But the concept is … not entirely satisfactory. (Clark and Yallop 1990: 97)

A similar definition is given in McMahon (2002: 107): the acoustic properties of sonorant segments, she writes, 'gives them greater carrying power'. McMahon, Clark and Yallop, and several others, suggest that sonority is a *scalar* property, i.e. that there is a gradient set of values at work in English segmental phonology in which segments with low sonority are found at one end of the scale, those with high sonority at the other. Further, several writers note that a general principle at work in the creation and perception of well-formed syllables is a principle of **sonority sequencing**, where the sonority peak of a well-formed syllable lies in the (first position of the) nucleus, and where sonority decreases the further you move towards the syllable's margins. If you re-examine a syllable such as *print* (diagram (6) above), then what's been called the *Sonority Sequencing Generalisation* does seem to be at work: /ɪ/ is most sonorous – it lies in the first position of the nucleus – and it's surrounded by segments whose sonority decreases; /p/ – a voiceless stop, and therefore, one might imagine, of low 'carrying power', or sonority – lies at the leftmost margin, and /t/ – another voiceless stop – at the right margin.

Given all this, we might want to claim the following:

(1) the more vowel-like a segment is, the more sonorous it is – and therefore the more likely *not* to lie in the margins of a syllable;
(2) the less sonorous a segment is, the more consonant-like it is, and therefore the less likely to lie in the nucleus of the syllable.

We could go further, constructing a sonority scale in which the least sonorous sounds (e.g. segments such as voiceless stops) would be low-ranked, and the most sonorous sounds (e.g. vowels) high-ranked. Several such attempts have been made in the literature, but none of these scales seems to work particularly well *on its own* as an explanation of the underlying structure of syllables.

First, they seem *arbitrary*: linguists will them to be tidy and true, but often, the messy nature of the data only partly supports (and sometimes might not at all support) such analytical tidiness.

Second, sonority scales sometimes make *wrong predictions*: if, for example, we think of the consonants /f/ and /s/, both of which are voiceless fricatives, then we might expect that both segments have the same sonority value. If we do give /f/ and /s/ the same sonority value, then we're implying that these segments should behave the same way with respect to their role in syllable structure. But they don't: /s/ can readily be followed by /n/ or /m/ in syllable onsets (<snick>, <smith>), but can /f/ be followed by /n/ (*/fnɪk/) or /m/ (*/fmɪθ/)? Clearly not. If we retain sonority, together with its accompanying scale, in our descriptions of syllable structure, then we're obliged to supplement the explanations offered by such a scale with a list of separately stated restrictions on which segments can co-occur with others. For example, in order to handle the problems created by the behaviour of /s/ and /f/ in onsets, we'd have to state: 'Well, /s/ can be followed by /n/ or /m/, and that's OK, because it's predicted by sonority sequencing, but ... er ... On the other hand, /f/ simply can't be followed by /n/ or /m/, even if this is predicted by sonority sequencing, so let's list onset clusters like /fn/ and /fm/ as *exceptions* to the rule ...'

Third, sonority scales run into trouble when it comes to handling the behaviour of the segment /s/ within English syllable structure. The problem created by /s/ isn't just a matter of its apparently anomalous behaviour compared with other voiceless fricatives, it's also a matter of *how many consonant segments can begin well-formed English syllables.*

> **Can you think of a range of examples where well-formed lexical monosyllables have *three* consonants in their onsets, and/or *three* consonants in their codas?**

You might have come up with examples such as <school> or <sphere>, but if so, you'd be wrong: <school> begins with the segments /sk/, and <sphere> begins with /sf/. (Both are loanwords, too, which might mean that their phonotactics have been borrowed from the loaning language, cf. the discussion of the loanword *bwana* earlier.) If you found examples like *scrimp*, *stripe*, *scream*, *spray*, *splint* you'd be correct: onsets in these syllables appear to begin with /s/ followed by a voiceless stop, which in turn is followed by an approximant (/r/ or /l/). If you constructed words that appear to end with three consonants, you might have come up with examples such as *splints*, *scrimps*, *prints*, and again you'd be right. But notice: all these examples in one way or another contain /s/, which occurs either as the first consonant in the onset, or the last one in the coda. This behaviour is very difficult to predict if we tie our analysis of syllable structure too closely to the concept of sonority, and whatever scale comes with it.

There's a fourth problem with sonority. It's defined as being related to the 'carrying power' of segments, and that seems sensible: we perceive vowels as syllabic peaks even in a noisy environment. However, we also perceive syllable structure (including those peaks formed by whatever lies in the nucleus of a syllable) when syllables are *whispered*, and have no carrying power at all.

For these reasons I'm not going to develop the analysis of sonority any further. Even if we were to put this notion to work, we'd still have to state some restrictions on which segment can co-occur with what, and do so quite separately from whatever might be predicted by a sonority scale. Instead, I'm going to use some of the material we looked at in chapter 2, namely those features of **place, manner,** and **voice.**

> **At this point, please revisit the list of consonants ('inventory and diagnostic') found in section 3 of chapter 3.**

We could reorder this list so that consonants produced with some stoppage of the airstream in the oral cavity are ranked below consonants produced with frication, and below consonants produced as nasal stops. That is, if we are to construct a form of ranking appropriate to the behaviour of consonant segments within English syllables, we could do worse than to correlate the ranking with the 'openness' of a segment.

- *Oral stops* involve total, if momentary, closure of the oral cavity.
- *Fricatives* involve the kind of partial openness whose phonetic correlate is friction.
- *Nasal stops* involve closure of the oral cavity, but openness of the nasal cavity.
- *Approximants* involve no closure, but rather, modification of the oral tract in ways that may be phonetically hard to distinguish from vowels – and after all, many approximants can also function as syllabic peaks, just like vowels.

What we've been calling 'most consonant-like' (= 'least sonorous') can be correlated with the *degree of closure* present in the vocal tract; and what we've been calling 'most vowel-like' can be correlated with the *degree of openness* present in the vocal tract. With that in mind, let's try reordering our list of consonants:

Consonant classes and openness			
Consonant	**Voice**	**Manner**	**Place**
/p/	–	plosive	bilabial
/b/	+	plosive	bilabial
/t/	–	plosive	alveolar
/d/	+	plosive	alveolar
/k/	–	plosive	velar
/g/	+	plosive	velar
(The class of plosives)			
/ʧ/	–	affricate	palato-alveolar
/ʤ/	+	affricate	palato-alveolar
(The class of affricates)			
/f/	–	fricative	labio-dental
/v/	+	fricative	labio-dental
/θ/	–	fricative	dental
/ð/	+	fricative	dental

/s/	–	fricative	alveolar
/z/	+	fricative	alveolar
/ʃ/	–	fricative	palatal
/ʒ/	+	fricative	palatal
/h/	–	fricative	glottal
/ʍ/	–	fricative	labio-velar
(The class of fricatives)			
/n/	+	nasal (stop)	alveolar
/m/	+	nasal (stop)	bilabial
/ŋ/	+	nasal (stop)	velar
(The class of nasal stops)			
/l/	+	lateral (approximant)	alveolar
/r/	+	approximant	post-alveolar
/j/	+	approximant	palatal
/w/	+	approximant	labio-velar
(The class of approximants)			

What's suggested by such a list is that sounds are produced and perceived not so much in terms of a sonority scale, but in groups – classes – whose membership is defined by the acoustic properties, whether of manner or place, held in common by those segments belonging to the group. With these classes in mind, let's now return to examining what constitutes a well-formed onset in English syllables.

First, onsets may consist of one segment – or of none. You can readily construct a list of lexical monosyllables that appear to have no consonant whatsoever in the onset (*egg*, *isle*, *id*, *eye*...). How do we handle such onsetless syllables in terms of syllable structure? Do we claim that the onset simply isn't present?

(8a)   **Onsetless syllables**

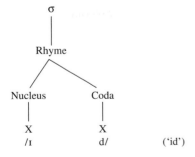

Or, more radically, could we claim that the underlying representation of apparently onsetless syllables is structured as follows, where 'ø' represents a segment that at this underlying level has no place or manner features associated with it?

(8b) Onsetless syllables

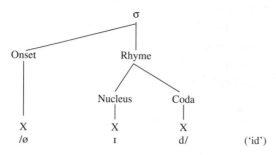

If we adopt (8b), then we're suggesting that there is a segment /ø/ that operates precisely like a phoneme. We're also implying that *onsets are obligatory* – even if they turn out to be filled with /ø/. These are radical claims, but we can test them. If, for instance, the segment /ø/ is a 'zero phoneme' then it should *contrast with* other phonemes that occur in the same position, i.e. the words containing this null phoneme should be susceptible to exactly the same minimal-pair tests that we used in chapter 2. If we can establish, via such tests, that /ø/ does indeed function as a phoneme, then it will look as if onsets have to be obligatory constituents of syllables in English – because there will be no syllables, even ones ostensibly beginning with a vowel, that will *not* contain onsets. So can we use minimal-pair tests on /ø/? We can:

/øɪd/	*id*
/hɪd/	*hid*
/bɪd/	*bid*

There are many other examples: *egg* and *leg*; *eye* and *buy*; *eat* and *meat*. These suggest that /ø/ *could* with appropriacy be added to the inventory of English consonants. If so, it would be added as a null term, and would *in itself* have no phonetic content (i.e. it could never be voiced or voiceless, nor a stop, a fricative, or anything other than the phoneme /ø/). On the other hand, if we *do* allow /ø/ into the phoneme inventory, we could claim that like other phonemes, it underlies one or more *allophones* (just as /p/, for instance, underlies [pʰ]). One idea might be that the phoneme /ø/ underlies an allophone that is the *glottal stop*, [ʔ]. This isn't as odd as it might seem. Many phoneticians have noticed that the glottal stop often occurs before a stressed vowel: 'any initial accented vowel may be reinforced by a preceding glottal stop when particular emphasis is placed on the word, whatever the preceding sound …' (Gimson 1994: 155). Therefore, we *might* analyse a lexical monosyllable like *id* as follows:

Spelling	<id>
Underlying phonemic representation	/øɪd/
Surface phonetic representation	[ʔɪd]

Representations like this are controversial (and may turn out to be simply wrong). *If* the zero phoneme *is* part of the underlying inventory of English segments, then clearly it has no place, voice or manner features associated with it. In terms of distribution it seems to contrast with other phonemes only in absolute syllable-initial position (*egg* and *leg*, *id* and *bid*, and so on). It seems not to contrast with any other consonant phonemes in syllable-final position, largely because there are no lexical monosyllables like **ge* (cf. *get*) or **bi* (cf. *bit*, *bid*, *biff*, *big*). Of course, one might argue that *if* the zero phoneme is present in the underlying inventory, then perhaps there *should be* lexical mono-syllables attested such as **ge* and **bi*. But arbitrarily, the distribution of the zero phoneme (or more cautiously, 'what might turn out to be the zero phoneme') could be restricted just to the 'empty onset' position. There are other consonant phonemes whose distribution is restricted (/ʒ/, /ʌ/, /j/), and there's no theoretical reason why the zero phoneme's distribution cannot also be restricted.

On the plus side, the zero phoneme – if we include it in the underlying inventory – actually helps us to make a range of generalisations about the structure of well-formed English lexical monosyllables (although note again that such generalisations hold true *except* where /s/ is involved).

A well-formed lexical monosyllable in English:

- has an obligatorily filled onset
- obligatorily has a *minimum* of two Xs somewhere within its rhyme constituent – either two Xs in the nucleus (*eye*, /aɪ/), or one in the nucleus, one in the coda (*bit*, /bɪt/)
- has an obligatory contour whereby the 'most consonantal' (= least open) segments appear in the periphery of syllables, the 'most vocalic' (= most open) in the nucleus
- has up to two Xs in the onset, up to two Xs in the nucleus, and up to two Xs in the coda

Given these constraints, then a *minimal* lexical monosyllable in English is a syllable such as *id*, *eye*, *egg*, *hid* or *bit*. A *maximal* lexical monosyllable is an item such as *grind*, /graɪnd/. All items, in order to be well formed, are subject to the constraint on openness.

Having said this about the zero phoneme, let me emphasise again that including such an item in the list of English phonemes would be very con-troversial, largely because including such an item would generate more problems than its existence would solve! We'll be exploring some of those problems later, in chapter 11, and in what follows I *won't be making use of zero phonemes in any transcriptions we undertake in the text, or which I ask you to complete in the exercises.* (In that connection it's worth noting that the zero phoneme is *not* a standard IPA consonant symbol, and *never* appears in transcriptions of English based on the IPA.)

6.3 **A note on syllables and typology**

The work we've done in 6.2, and the thinking that sustains it, allows us to fit English into a **typology** of the world's languages. That is, constituents such as onset, nucleus and coda are apparently *universal*. That's not to say that all languages have onsets, nuclei and codas disposed in just the same way as English. It *is* to say that these syllable constituents are present underlyingly in the terms of the typology, but may be employed differently by different languages. If, for example, we use the term O to stand for onset, N to stand for nucleus, and C to stand for coda, then it's apparent that languages *love onsets*: there are many, many languages attested whose preferred, even obligatory syllable structure is to begin syllables with an onset: O. And *all* languages have syllabic nuclei: N. Thus, one very widely attested pattern for underlying syllable structure is ON (so-called 'CV languages'). Such languages don't have syllable structures that permit codas – perhaps a better way of expressing that would be ON̶C̶, where the strikethrough means 'debarred'. There are *no languages* whose syllables consist simply of O̶N̶C̶ (such languages would have no non-syllabic consonants!) or – more surprisingly – of O̶NC (obligatorily onsetless syllables). On the other hand, English is like many other languages in that (if we're right in the thinking we've developed in this chapter) it has *obligatory onsets*, *obligatory nuclei*, and *optional codas*. If we stand our symbol C (for coda) inside parentheses, we can allow that symbol to stand for 'optional'. Therefore, we might claim that English patterns like other ON(C) languages. If, on the other hand, we regard English as patterning with those languages which have *optional onsets*, then our abbreviation would run (O)N(C). We'll touch on this matter again in 11.6.

Exercises

Exercise 6a   Draw appropriate syllable trees for the following monosyllables (which are here given in their standard alphabetic forms):

   a.   itch
   b.   pitch
   c.   imp
   d.   pimp
   e.   pip

Exercise 6b   This exercise anticipates work we're going to do in the next chapter. You are not expected to 'get this exercise right', but to think about how you might get it right. That is, the exercise is meant to be difficult!

Below you'll find two words, both of which have two syllables (i.e. the words are *bisyllabic*). Both words are stressed on their initial syllables – something which may turn out to be important later. I have transcribed both of them for you. Study the word *pimping* first, and try to decide which of the two syllables the second /p/ belongs to – to the end of the first syllable? Or the beginning of the second? Most people have fairly clear intuitions about this.

Now study the word *pipping*. Again there are two (and only two) /p/ phonemes in the word, one beginning the entire word, and the other in the middle. (Note that the word could never be transcribed as */pɪppɪŋ/. It has to be / pɪpɪŋ/.) Your second task in this exercise is to try to determine which syllable the medial /p/ might belong to, *and why*. This is tricky, and most people have much shakier intuitions here.

pimping   /pɪmpɪŋ/
pipping   /pɪpɪŋ/

Exercise 6c   Construct appropriate syllable trees for the words *hymn* and *imp*. You should find that in the first word, /m/ belongs unambiguously to the coda of the syllable. In *imp*, though, the /m/ belongs to the nucleus (and this would be quite according to the principles we've discussed above, section 6.2). Do you find this analysis useful, and does it match your hunches about 'where /m/ belongs'? Or is there another, equally explanatory way of handling the alignment of segments to the nucleus and coda in such words?

Key terms introduced in this chapter
rhyme
sonority
sonority sequencing
typology
zero phoneme

Further reading
Linguists conducted a great deal of work on syllable structure in the 1970s and 1980s, and the partial analysis developed in this chapter looks back to some of that. For instance, onsets, nuclei and codas are beautifully explored in:

Selkirk, Elisabeth. 1982. 'The syllable'. In H. van der Hulst and N. Smith eds. *The structure of phonological representations* (part II). Dordrecht: Foris Publications, 337–83.

Another version of this paper may be found in John A. Goldsmith ed. 1999. *Phonological theory: the essential readings*. Oxford: Blackwell, 328–50. Goldsmith's volume also collects other important papers relating to syllables and syllable structure, among them 'Syllables' by Erik Fudge (first published in *Journal of Linguistics* [JL] in 1969 [*JL* 5: 253–87]).

The work on zero onsets which we've incorporated into this chapter was first developed by Heinz Giegerich in the 1980s. Three relevant publications are:

Giegerich, Heinz. 1980. 'On stress-timing in English phonology'. *Lingua* 51: 187–221.
Giegerich, Heinz. 1983. 'On English sentence stress and the nature of metrical structure'. *JL* 19: 1–28.
Giegerich, Heinz. 1985. *Metrical phonology and phonological structure: German and English*. Cambridge University Press.

Interestingly, the account of the English syllable you will find in Giegerich's *English phonology: an introduction* (Cambridge University Press, 1992 – see especially chapter 7) is rather different from the account found in that scholar's earlier work, and does *not* include zero constituents. (Instead, the onset itself is made an optional constituent, rather than being obligatorily filled.) The fact that Giegerich's views on the syllable have apparently changed – as indeed have Selkirk's – can be taken as a good indication of just how controversial a topic syllable structure still is.

CHAPTER 7

Syllables (3): structure

In this chapter …

In this chapter we develop our work on English syllables so as to say more about the structure of their internal constituents (the onset, nucleus and coda). Particularly important will be our work on the internal structure of the *nucleus*, since this will allow us to give a much more precise definition to our hunches about those phonological entities we've called long and short vowels (a short vowel is aligned with one and only one X-slot, while a long vowel is, like a diphthong, aligned with precisely two X-slots). We conclude the chapter by looking at the notions of *light* and *heavy* syllable, noting their complex relationship with stress as this is manifested within English words, and we also note issues that concern syllabification.

7.1 **More on the structure of the onset**

If we look first at onsets comprised of a single X, what kind of segment can that single X be? It can in fact be *any consonant segment (including, possibly, /ø/)*, **with the exception of** ...

What are the exceptions? They are /ʒ/ – which doesn't seem to occur as readily as a single-consonant onset as, say, /d/ or /m/ or indeed its voiceless equivalent, /ʃ/ – and /ŋ/. There's no way of predicting their absence from onsets in English (though they can occur as single-X onsets in other languages), and I here adopt the brutal tactic of making a *list of exceptions*. So let's place our generalisation about what can occur in single-X onsets on the left-hand side of the page, adding arbitrary exceptions on the right:

Generalisations about single-X onsets

Prediction	*Exceptions*
Any C can function as a single-X onset	/ʒ/ and /ŋ/

If we consider onsets spanning two X-slots, then openness (as we've defined it in the previous chapters) comes into play, so that the less open segments occur at the left margin, the more open segments as the second of the two Xs, reading these from left to right. You should here revisit the list of consonants you found in the list in section 3.3. Recall that we constructed classes of consonants, based on place and manner features. What I'm going to do here is label these classes numerically, where class 1 = the class of plosives, class 2 = the class of affricates, and so on:

Class 1	plosives
Class 2	affricates
Class 3	fricatives
Class 4	nasal stops
Class 5	approximants

> Recall that we're embarking on an analysis of what sequencing principles govern the behaviour of two-X onsets. With that in mind, try to work out why I have just constructed a class list for English consonant segments. Hint: you might like to revisit the list of two-segment onsets you've already constructed.

A class 5 segment – an approximant – can apparently *never* be followed by another class 5 segment within the same onset. There are simply no onsets in English of the form */wj/ or */wr/ (note: <wr>, as in *wring*, is phonemically /r/ in present-day Englishes). Nor can a class 5 segment, where this is the first segment in a two-X onset, be followed by a segment belonging to any lower class (*/wn/, */lm/, */rs/ etc). A good prediction, then, is that where a class 5 segment appears in the *first* X of an onset, then that will be the *only* X in the onset.

Class 4 segments – nasals – can be followed neither by another class 4 segment (*/mn/ etc), nor by a segment belonging to any other lower class (*/np/, */nz/ etc) A strong prediction is that where a class 4 segment appears in the *first* X of an onset, then this will be the *only* X in the onset.

With class 3 segments – fricatives – our analysis becomes more complex. Certain fricatives, like /f/ or /s/, can apparently be followed by segments belonging to class 4 (/snɪp/) or class 5 (/swɪm/). Notably, the segment that seems to lend itself particularly readily to such profligate behaviour is /s/: the fricative /f/ can *never* be followed by /m/ or /n/ (*/fnɪp/). If /f/ does occur as the first segment in a two-X onset, then it must be followed by another segment from class 5 (/flɪp/, /friː/, *free*). Further, where /f/ occurs in such a position, the following segment must be /l/ or /r/. It can *never* be /w/ (*/fwɪp/).

It's worth dwelling on the non-occurrence of onset clusters such as */fw/, because their absence in English **phonotactics** (literally 'phonos' = sound + 'tactic' = touching, thus 'sound-touchings') is *systematic*. In two-X onsets, that is, it seems that many clusters don't occur *if the two segments in question share the same place of articulation*. On these grounds, /fl/ is OK (/f/ is labio-dental, /l/ is alveolar), as is /fr/ (/f/ is labio-dental, /r/ is post-alveolar). Additionally, /fj/ would be OK, too (<few>, <fuse>), since /j/ is palatal. What *isn't* OK is for a labio-dental such as /f/ to be followed by another consonant whose place of articulation includes the feature of labiality (/w/ is *labio*-velar).

This said, we've said nothing so far to preclude the existence of possible onset clusters such as /fn/. These are non-attested in English, and it's hard to see why they might be: after all, /sn/ is fine, but */fn/ apparently isn't.

We've also said nothing so far to debar other theoretically possible two-X onsets: given what we've discussed, */zn/ would be predicted to occur, as would /vr/ (a cluster that seems to exist only in the onomatopoeic word <*vroom*>).

At least part of the problem with the phonotactics of fricatives concerns the nature and representation of the segment /s/. As a long and inconclusive analytical literature attests, /s/ is a real problem for theories of English syllable structure. So extensive are the problems posed by this segment that I'm going to defer a fuller discussion of them until chapter 11 (see particularly 11.3), where I'll extend our analysis of English syllables and examine further problems related to the analysis as we've developed it in this book.

Even though this section has been brief, what we've suggested is the following:

(i)   The consonant segments that may fill the onset belong to *classes*, where membership of a class is determined by the acoustic properties held in common by the items that make up the same class.

Thus, for example, we might claim that there is a *class of voiceless stops* in English, since these have both voicelessness and momentary cessation of the egressive airstream ('stoppedness') in common. In view of the foregoing, what we're now saying is that each member of this class of sounds (and that means /p, t, k/) is predicted to behave in precisely the same way in terms of its position in the onset and the potential that each member of that class has to appear with other consonants in the onset. Some examples:

- /p/ can occur on its own in the onset   <pat>   /pat/
- /p/ can occur before an approximant (class 5)   <pray>   /preɪ/
(but not where both /p/ and a following approximant share the same place of articulation, e.g. *<pwit> */pwɪt/, where /p/ and /w/ have *labiality* in common)
- /p/ can occur after /s/ in syllabic onsets   <spat>   /spat/

Further, since /p/ belongs to the same class as /t/ and /k/, the predictions we've just made for /p/ should also hold good for the other members of the class. And this is what happens: /t/ and /k/ can occur on their own in onsets (/tɪp/, /kɪt/), or before an approximant (where this last doesn't share the same place of articulation), as in /trɪp/, /twaɪs/ 'twice', or after /s/ (/stɪl/ 'still', /skin/).

(ii) Ideally, adjacent consonant segments in a well-formed onset belong to non-identical classes, where the second of the two consonants belongs to a class at least one higher than the first.

Examples of the preference for two consonants in the onset to belong to non-identical classes would be /pleɪ/ 'play', where /p/ and /l/ belong respectively to classes 1 and 5; or /brat/ 'brat', where /b/ belongs to class 1 and /r/ to class 5; or /fri:/ 'free', where /f/ belongs to class 3 (the class of fricatives) and /r/ to class 5. Note: this seems to be precisely a 'preference', and it's easy to construct examples where two adjacent consonants in an onset belong to adjacent classes, e.g. /snɪp/ 'snip', where /s/ belongs to the class of fricatives (class 3) and /n/ to the class of nasal stops (class 4). However, this last example involves the very problematic segment /s/, which behaves somewhat irregularly with respect to its phonotactic behaviour.

A further thing we should notice is that an onset seems to be the more well-formed, the more the second of two adjacent consonants is 'vowel-like'. For instance, many well-formed two-consonant onsets have the segments /l/ (/slɪp/), /w/ (/swɪg/), /m/ (/smɪθ/ 'smith') etc in their second slot. These last segments are 'vowel-like' to the extent that they are all voiced, or – like all vowels – are pronounced with no stoppage (or even any particular occlusion) of the airstream, or (and this holds for /l/ and /m/) can even – again like vowels – function as syllabic peaks (nuclei) in their own right.

(iii)   Adjacent consonants in a two-segment onset may not share the same place of articulation.

We've already seen this principle in action. Of course, the alert reader will have noticed that if consonants are put into classes, then the principles we've just discussed under (i – ii) will to some extent mean that adjacent consonants in the onset won't necessarily share the same place of articulation. Nevertheless, we still need this principle, because there are possible, but still ill-formed, examples where adjacent consonants belong to maximally different classes but nevertheless share the same place of articulation. One instance is a hypothetical example we've just looked at, */pwɪt/. This is ill formed even though /p/ (stop) and /w/ (approximant) are classes apart. And it's ruled out precisely because these two consonants are both in some way *labial*.

These seem to be general, and relatively robust, principles.

7.2 More on the structure of the coda

Just like onsets, codas may contain single consonant segments. There is, however, a more extended list of exceptions as to which consonants *can't* form single-X codas. Can you think what these exceptions are?

Generalisations about single-X codas

Prediction	*Exceptions*
Any C can function as a single-X coda	/j, w, ʍ, h/

While two-X onsets contain consonants belonging almost *obligatorily* to non-identical classes (with the second consonant belonging to a class at least one, and preferably two or more, higher than the first), two-X codas pattern so that consonants should *preferably* belong to non-identical classes, with the first consonant belonging to a class at least one higher than the first:

<grind>	coda= /n+d/	class 4 + class 1
<fiend>	coda= /n+d/	class 4 + class 1
<yield>	coda= /l+d/	class 5 + class 1

> You may be tempted to include clusters like <mp> (<imp>) and <lm> (<film>) as possible two-X coda strings. Is there any good reason to analyse these and similar examples as containing just one-X codas?

95

In examples like /fɪlm/ or /ɪmp/, the work we looked at in chapters 5 and 6 suggests that in these and similar examples, the coda of the relevant syllables contains just one X – the final consonant of the entire word. Recall earlier examples like *print* and *hint*. There we analysed the /n/ as occupying the second available slot of the nucleus. There's no reason to suppose that /fɪlm/ or /ɪmp/ should be analysed differently: the /l/ and the /m/, respectively, would belong to the second available slot of the nucleus, leaving /m/ and /p/ to be single-X codas.

There's another way in which codas differ from onsets. Remember that in onsets, two adjacent consonants weren't allowed to share the same place of articulation, thus barring possible onsets like */bm/, */dn/ or */fw/. In codas this restriction doesn't seem to obtain in quite the same way (although the *preference* for class structuring remains). There are many examples of two-X codas where the two consonants share the same place of articulation: /graɪnd/ 'grind', where /n/ and /d/ are both alveolar, or /paɪnt/ 'pint', where /n/ and /t/ are again both alveolar, are representative.

Codas also differ in how possible two- and three-X strings might be analysed. In onsets, three-X strings do of course occur, but their first term is always /s/, and that /s/ is always part of the **root** of the word (i.e. the most basic, non-inflected form of a given lexical word, such as [tɪp] 'tip', compared with its inflected form [tɪp]+s 'tips'). Therefore, and with respect to onsets, we find many examples such as <string> (/strɪŋ/), <sprint> (/sprɪnt/) and <script> (/skrɪpt/), where the initial /s/ is definitely part of the root of the word, since it would be totally implausible to divide the word into morphological units such as *s+[print], *s+[tring] and so on.

In codas, /s/ (/z/) again forms part of the problem, but in the following examples, notice how the word-final /s/ (/z/) isn't part of the word's root, but is actually an inflectional ending (i.e. a piece of grammatical structure tacked onto the root in order to indicate some extra grammatical information):

Codas and inflectional endings

Written	Transcribed	Coda	Inflection
<film+s>	/fɪlmz/	/m(+z)/	/z/
<imp+s>	/ɪmps/ (or /øɪmps/)	/p(+s)/	/s/
<hint+s>	/hɪnts/	/t(+s)/	/s/
<grind+s>	/graɪndz/	/nd(+z)/	/z/
<field+s>	/fiːldz/	/ld(+z)/	/z/

Our job is to account for the phonological structure of word **roots**, rather than engage with an analysis of the principles of English inflectional morphology (these would require a different book). Therefore we might want to make the claim that in terms of basic syllable composition, *codas consist maximally of two X-slots.*

Although this has been a relatively short section, you'll find further work relating to the structure of the coda in the exercises that conclude this chapter.

7.3 More on the structure of the nucleus

Here I'm going to confine our discussion to the nuclear structure of those three vocalic segments mentioned in chapter 5, and which have been the segments we've been using in some of the transcriptions we've completed:

<hid>   <heed>   <hide>
/hɪd/   /hi:d/   /haɪd/

I'm also going to add one other example, the syllable <hint>, /hɪnt/.

In the syllable *hid* things seem straightforward. The segment /ɪ/ belongs in the nucleus, the segment /d/ in the coda:

(1)

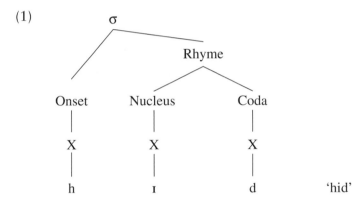

'hid'

Intuitively, we'd call the /ɪ/ of *hid* a short vowel. Notice that the nucleus contains just one X-slot. In fact, in turns out that nuclei containing one and only one X almost invariably display vowels we would think of as short: further examples are *ban, bed, bun, bad; cat, cup, keg, cog;* and so on.

Those vowels which, by contrast, we'd want to call long have a subtly different nuclear structure.

> If the vowel /i:/ (*heed*, /hi:d/) is distinct from the vowel /ɪ/, how could
> you express that difference in terms of syllable structure? Essentially,
> if there is a difference (and there is), then you need to construct a
> syllable tree different to the one immediately above. But how would you
> do that?

The answer appears to be that we can express what we intuitively think of as vowel length by aligning the relevant long vowels with *two* X-slots, as follows:

(2)

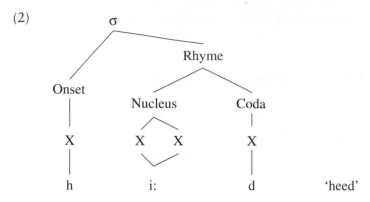

'heed'

And then there are vowels such as the shape we've so far represented as /aɪ/ (/haɪd/). Now, the nucleus containing a vowel such as /i:/ spans two X-slots, each of which has identical content (though see also chapter 9). In the case of vowel shapes such as /aɪ/ we can suggest that although the nucleus contains two X-slots, these are filled with *two segments whose phonetic characters are non-identical*. Compare the tree above with the following:

(3)

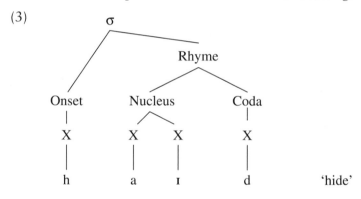

'hide'

Vowel shapes like /ɪ/ or /i:/ we may call, using traditional terminology, **monophthongs**. Vowels such as /aɪ/ are called **diphthongs**.

> I've seen many incorrect spellings of the words <monophthong> and <diphthong> over the years. These words aren't spelled *<monophtong>, <diptohng>, *<diptong> or – the commonest misspelling – *<dipthong>. Thinking about etymology might help you to spell the words correctly. The root of each word is in fact a Greek term that can be transliterated as *phthongos*, 'voice' or 'sound'.
> A *di-phthong* is therefore a 'two-voiced' or 'two-sounded' vowel phoneme; a *mono-phthong* is a 'one-voiced' or 'one-sounded' phoneme.

Lastly in this section, I want to look briefly at the syllable structure of the word <hint>, /hɪnt/. We've already looked at some issues concerning the syllable structure of a similar word, *print*, and there suggested that the /n/

could equally well belong to the nucleus as to the coda. We'd claim the same for the structure of /hɪnt/:

(4)

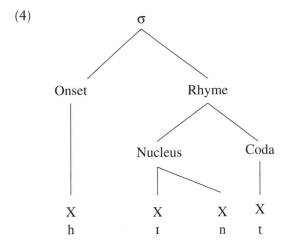

It seems that a well-structured nucleus must have the following properties *when that syllable is stressed* (on the nucleus in unstressed syllables, see below):

(i)   the leftmost position must be occupied by a segment that is unambiguously a vowel ('least consonant-like'). In one-X monophthongs this condition is self-explanatory, and in diphthongs, too, the first element is invariably vocalic (e.g. /haɪd/). We need this provision, though, since there appear to be nuclei whose second segment may be a consonant: a good example here is the word 'print' /prɪnt/, with /pr/ in the onset, /ɪn/ occupying the nucleus, and /t/ in the coda;

(ii) the second, rightmost X-slot of the nucleus may be filled with a copy of the leftmost segment (in which case we have a monophthong). An example here would be a monophthong (and a monosyllable) such as 'heed' (/hi:d/ – see the diagram above);

(iii) the rightmost X-slot of the nucleus may be filled with a vocalic segment that is non-identical to the leftmost segment in the same nucleus (in which case we have a diphthong). A good example here is /haɪd/ 'hide'.

These summaries leave problems. One special problem for syllable structure is posed by the role played by /n/, /m/ and – in some varieties of English – by /r/. Notice that these segments seem to be able to stand as the nuclei of syllables in their own right, in words such as *button, chasm* and (in GA and other varieties) *bitter*.

We'll be doing some more work on the problematic segment /r/ in chapter 11, but here it's worthwhile saying something about /n/ and /m/ in the context of their appearance in codas and/or as syllables in their own right.

Data first. The *written* (normal alphabetic) form of words such as *button* and *bottom* implies that the second syllables of these words consist of a vowel followed by /n/ and /m/ respectively. In careful pronunciations of these two words there does seem to be a vowel present – often the 'murmur vowel' schwa, which occurs typically in unstressed syllables. In such careful pronunciations we might well want to transcribe the relevant words as something like /bʌtən/, /kæzəm/. (Note here that you'll learn much more about the transcriptions of vowels, and about the 'murmur vowel' schwa, in the following chapters, see particularly 8.2.) Yet at a normal speech tempo what seems to happen is that /n/ and /m/ somehow acquire *the property of being syllables in their own right.* More explicitly, we might wish to transcribe the words as /bʌtn/, /kæzm/, but there's no way we'd want to claim that such words had become *monosyllables.* /n/ and /m/, in these respective cases, do not appear to belong to the coda of a monosyllable, but to an entirely separate syllable. Many linguists therefore suggest that in certain contexts segments such as /n/ and /m/ are 'syllabic nasals'. Our immediate problem is how we might represent this, since in all the work we've done so far we've implied, and strongly, that if there's only one X-slot in the nucleus then this *must* be filled by a segment that is unambiguously vocalic.

One crucial piece of explanation that bears on the representation we can give syllabic nasals is that nasals can only ever be syllabic when they occur in *unstressed syllables*, as indicated by the following list of examples:

Word	Careful pronunciation	'Normal' pronunciation
chasm	[kæzəm]	[kæzm]
button	[bʌtən]	[bʌtn]
captain	[kæptən]	[kæptn]
bottle	[bɒtəl]	[bɒtl]
butter	[bʌtər]	[bʌtr]

For each example (and many like them), it's apparent that syllabic nasals, together with /l/ and /r/, only ever occur in *unstressed* syllables. Significantly, the generalisations we've so far worked through with respect to syllable structure are based on those structures that occur in *stressed* syllables. With respect to the nucleus, however, it appears that the generalisation we've made above must be weakened – or perhaps better, separately stated – when unstressed syllables and their structure are to be analysed. Here goes:

Generalisations about the structures of syllabic nuclei:

(i) **Stressed syllables**
  - Nucleus may contain up to two X-slots
  - If leftmost X-slot is filled, the segment must be unambiguously a vowel
(ii) **Unstressed syllables** (and see also Giegerich 1992: 166)
  - Nucleus must contain only one X-slot
  - Nuclear X-slot of an unstressed syllable may be filled by the non-vocalic segments /n, m, l/, and in rhotic accents, by /r/.

That means that for syllabic nasals *in unstressed syllables* we might construct

representations such as the following:

(5)

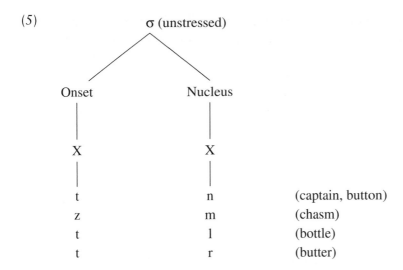

t	n	(captain, button)
z	m	(chasm)
t	l	(bottle)
t	r	(butter)

7.4. Syllabification; light and heavy syllables

Words in every language may be classified according to whether they're *monosyllabic* (contain one and only one syllable), *bisyllabic* (contain precisely two syllables), *trisyllabic* (contain precisely three syllables), or contain even more syllables (in which case we'd refer to *polysyllabic* words). 'Polysyllabic' simply means 'containing more than one syllable', so includes the class of bi- and tri-syllables. In what follows I'll give examples of such words, and – although some of the vowel symbols will at this stage be unfamiliar to you – I'll also make a simple phonemic transcription of each (and here it's particularly important to note the single /p/ in *happy* and the single /m/ in *hammer*):

(6)

Monosyllabic words	Polysyllabic words		
	Bi-syllabic	**Tri-syllabic**	**More than 3 syllables**
pit	pity	departing	depilatory
/pɪt/	/pɪtɪ/	/dɪpɑːtɪŋ/ BrE	/dɪpɪlət(ə)rɪ/
hat	happy	happening	unhappily
/hat/	/hæpɪ/	/hapənɪŋ/	/ʌnhapɪlɪ/
ham	hammer	hammering	deification
/ham/	/hamə/ BrE	/hamərɪŋ/	/diːjɪfɪkeɪʃn/
ground	gudgeon	fabulous	glorification
/graʊnd/	/gʌdʒn/	/fabjələs/	/glɔːrɪfɪkeɪʃn/

101

Syllabification is a matter that concerns *polysyllabic* words, and in particular concerns the syllables to which the consonants within the polysyllable belong. To illustrate the problem, consider the following examples, given here in normal orthography:

ham   hamper   hammer

In *ham*, clearly the /m/ belongs to the coda of the one syllable of the word. In the bisyllabic word *hamper*, though, we have to think through the question 'To which syllables do the /m/ and the /p/ belong?' Notice that this question was something you considered for the first time while completing exercise 6b. (You might like to revisit that exercise before reading further.)

> **Use your intuitions – or the work you've already done on exercise 6b – to decide where you would insert the syllable division in a word such as *hamper*. You should use the symbol '.' to indicate the syllable division.**

We could syllabify the word *hamper* as follows: (a) ha.mper; (b) ham.per; (c) hamp.er. I've asked many classes of students to use their intuitions about the syllabification of this word, and the result has almost invariably been an overwhelming preference for the syllabification shown in (b): *hamper* comprises two syllables, the first of which is *ham-*, the second of which is *-per*. Notice that this preference puts /p/ into the onset of the second syllable.

There are reasons behind these instincts and preferences. First, ask yourself why a syllabification such as (a) seems so disfavoured. The answer is that such a syllabification places 'mp' into the onset of the second syllable, and this is impossible: /mp/, while it's at first glance acceptable as a coda, *isn't a well-formed onset* of an English syllable. Second, ask yourself why (c) is (usually) disfavoured. After all, 'hamp' is a perfectly well-formed syllable (it just happens not to occur, although cf. e.g. *hemp*, *damp*). Such a syllable (where /m/ belongs in the nucleus and /p/ in the coda) is also predicted to be well formed given the work we did earlier, in chapter 6, on monosyllables such as *print*, *hint* and *imp*. However, there seems to be a principle at work in the syllabification of English words that says the following: 'If you can make a well-formed onset, then you must'. With *hamper*, such a principle would favour the syllabification *ham.per* (where we've made a good onset from /p/) over *hamp.er* (where we've failed to make the onset that we *could* have made from /p/). This principle is so important for English syllabification that it's given a special name: the *Principle of Maximal Onsets* (PMO). (You'll also encounter the same principle elsewhere in the relevant literature under the guise of the 'Law of Initials' or 'Initial-Maximal Syllabification'. We'll be looking again at this important principle in chapter 11.) What the PMO says is: 'If you can make a well-formed onset, do it.' More formally (and concisely): *onsets are maximised.*

> Below you'll find a list of examples – given here in their normal alphabetic forms – which require syllabification. Using the PMO as a guide, syllabify each example. I've done the first examples for you.

Syllabification

ample (am.ple)	empire (em.pire)	emperor (em.pe.ror)
handy	haunted	unthinking
laughing	laughter	laughingly
listing	listless	lustreless
complete	shimmer	simpering

There's a further problem we need to discuss, concerning the syllabification of words such as *shimmer* or *hammer*. If you completed the last question, you probably came across the problem as you tried to syllabify the words in the last row. The PMO instructs you to 'maximise onsets', but if you do that with the word *shimmer* (/ʃɪmə/ or /ʃɪmr/ according to your variety of English) then you're left with the syllabification /ʃɪ.mə/. Many students find such a syllabification counter-intuitive. In fact, when I set this exercise in class many students want to syllabify the word as *shim.mer* – but of course that's impossible. (Why?)

The problem concerns stress. Notice that the first syllables of *shimmer* and *hammer* are stressed (i.e. they will never have a pronunciation in schwa and are always perceived as prominent relative to the final syllable of the words). In all varieties of present-day English (insofar as these varieties have been studied) there seems to be a strong preference among speakers for *stressed syllables in bisyllabic words to contain codas **when the first syllable of those words contains only one X in the nucleus***. For example, we've already noted that if they contain a short vowel then lexical monosyllables *invariably* have codas (e.g. syllables such as *id*, *itch*, *hitch*, *thin*, *hint* and so forth). What we're considering now is merely a logical extension of that principle.

Syllables containing filled codas are called *heavy syllables*. Syllables containing no codas (e.g. the first – and unstressed – syllables of *appal*, *aghast*, or the final syllables of *button*, *chasm* etc) are called *light syllables*. Therefore it seems to be the preference for *heavy syllables to be stressed*.

> If we return to our example *shimmer* then the observation is that the first syllable is stressed, and therefore the implication is that it has a coda (/m/). On the other hand, the PMO states that the problematic segment, /m/, must be unambiguously an onset. What's the solution?

One idea is that in this and similar examples the inter-vocalic consonant belongs to *both syllables simultaneously*. The technical term for this is *ambisyllabic*: the /m/ of *shimmer* is a prime candidate for ambisyllabicity. How might we represent this in the kind of syllable tree we've been using throughout?

We can propose a structure like the following:

(7)

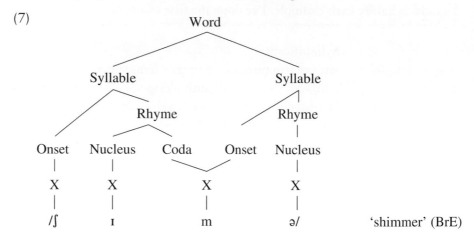

'shimmer' (BrE)

Here the coda of the first syllable is filled *and* the PMO is satisfied since the onset of the second syllable is filled.

Ambisyllabicity is controversial. Then again, the written system of present-day English suggests that many speakers and writers do perceive consonants occurring in the same environment as the /m/ of *shimmer* as ambisyllabic, since so many of these consonants are written with two graphemes, despite being single phonemic segments:

Written evidence for ambisyllabicity
shimmer
litter
glitter
hammer
hummer
simmer
better
slumming
winning…

Unfortunately, the written evidence isn't conclusive, since there are many exceptions. There are some words which are written with single consonants even though those consonants may be ambisyllabic: *coming* or *clever* are good examples. Nevertheless, the written evidence is at least suggestive, and here I shall treat ambisyllabicity as a real phenomenon of present-day English, rather than something that linguists have dreamed up out of hope or despair.

In the following chapter we're going to extend our analysis of vowels, both monophthongs and diphthongs. (That will, among other things, enable us to make extended phonemic transcriptions.) Before racing ahead to chapter 8, though, you're strongly advised to complete the exercises below.

Exercises

Exercise 7a   Reread 7.4 on ambisyllabification and the PMO. Using '.' to indicate syllable divisions, syllabify the following words (here given in their standard alphabetic forms – you don't have to make phonemic transcriptions, though it would be a good idea to do so). I have done the first example for you.
a. pimping syllabified as pim.ping
b. itching
c. city
d. happily
e. finishing

Exercise 7b   In 7.4 you studied generalisations about light and heavy syllables, and how syllables containing codas are stressed. Look at the following list of words (these are again given in their standard alphabetic forms, and you may decide to make a phonemic transcription of them, if you've not already done so, in order to help you with this exercise). Decide whether the underlined syllable in each word is light or heavy. Then decide whether syllables with codas are *always* stressed, and whether light syllables are *always* unstressed. (Note: our generalisation about stress says that 'syllables with codas are always stressed'. It *doesn't* say that light syllables are always unstressed.)
imp
hymn
impish
hippy
litter
city
grinding
he

Exercise 7c   This exercise begins to analyse what kind of segments may occupy the last position of a maximally filled coda (i.e. a coda filled by two consonants). Look carefully at the list of syllables below. Reassure yourself that the final segment of each word can (indeed, must) occupy the second slot of a maximally filled coda. Now try to work out whether the consonant segments that may occupy the last slot of the coda have anything in common. (Note: you'll find it very useful to make a simple transcription of each word if you haven't already done so in a previous exercise.)

I'm setting this exercise now because it anticipates work we'll be doing in subsequent chapters, particularly chapter 11. Here's the list:

imps
scrimped
grind
rinsed
sixth
seethed
wisps
means

Key terms introduced in this chapter
ambisyllabicity
diphthong
heavy syllable
light syllable
monophthong
phonotactics
Principle of Maximal Onsets (PMO)
root

Further reading

Some of the material developed in this chapter relies heavily on one source, which is the clearest and most explanatory statement known to me of the internal structure of the syllabic nucleus. That source is:

Giegerich, Heinz. 1992. *English phonology: an introduction.* Cambridge University Press. See especially chapter 6. (You might also like to look at chapter 7, which concerns syllables and stress.)

CHAPTER 8

Vowels (1): short vowels

In this chapter …

In this chapter we focus largely on the system of short vowels as this is manifest in different varieties of English. Building on the work we've already done in chapter 7, we'll review the linked notions that short vowels are associated with one X-slot within the syllabic nucleus, whereas long vowels are associated with two X-slots. Then we proceed to draw a distinction between vowel quantity (length) and vowel quality (*where* and *how* a vowel is produced). In the remainder of the chapter we develop our analysis of vowel quality, and see that the crucial diagnostic for the description of vowels is the relative height and position of the tongue. This relative height and position can be matched against a stylised diagram of the oral cavity. Such a diagram is known as a *vowel trapezium*. Distinctive positions within that trapezium are associated with numbered reference points, which in turn are associated with the *primary Cardinal Vowels*. We shall see that nearly all varieties of English seem to have *six* distinctive short vowels, plus a seventh (central) vowel which characteristically occurs in unstressed syllables, and which we encountered earlier – *schwa*.

8.1 Establishing an inventory of short vowels

You'll recall from the last chapter that short vowels are represented in syllable structure by the alignment of the relevant vowel segment with just *one* X-slot within the syllabic nucleus. The vowels that for many English speakers occur in words such as *pit*, *pat* and *pot* would, then, have identical representations in terms of syllable structure (though of course the *quality* of the vowel aligned with the X in the syllabic nucleus would be different in each case):

(1)

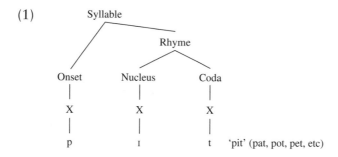

                                         'pit' (pat, pot, pet, etc)

Note that we have just made an important distinction between vowel **quantity** (whether a vowel is short or long) and vowel **quality** (where and how the vowel is produced in the oral cavity).

In this section of text our job is to look at vowel quality, and thereby begin to establish a plausible inventory of *short vowels*, i.e. those vowels aligned with just one X-slot in syllabic nuclei. This isn't an easy task, because there's some systematic variation in English accents of which we will need to take account, even in this introductory chapter. (You will find more about variety within the English vowel system in chapter 10.)

> To help you begin this task, consider the following substitution frame, and insert a selection of short vowels into it in such a way that well-formed English lexical monosyllables result:

Substitution frame 1

/p__t/

You'll recognise the test: it's designed to help us establish minimal pairs. Thus *pit* and *pot* form a minimal pair, and both contrast with *pet*, *pat* and (for many, though not all, speakers) with *put* and *putt* (the last being a golfing term). Notice that no English speaker is ever going to insert schwa (to which you were introduced in chapter 5.1) into the above frame, since the result would be a non-occurring lexical (mono)syllable. This particular substitution frame, then, can't establish the existence or distribution of schwa for us. But for many speakers, such a frame would be quite sufficient to confirm the fact that for them there are (at least) *six* contrastive short vowels.

You may wonder why throughout the last chapter so many of our examples used the short vowel /ɪ/. There was method in this madness. In the following fragment of a table, for instance, you'll see that *every* speaker of English, in *every* variety (at least as these had been recorded in 1982), had the vowel phoneme /ɪ/ – here recorded as occurring underlyingly in the word *pit* or *kit* – as part of their inventory:

The vowel systems of varieties of English (collected from Wells 1982).

(2)   The *pit* vowel

	RP	London	Norwich	Bristol	Birmingham	Leeds	Scottish	Irish	GenAm	NYC	Deep South[1]	Australia	New Zealand
KIT	ɪ	ɪ	ɪ	ɪ	ɪ	ɪ	ɪ	ɪ	ɪ	ɪ	ɪ	ɪ	ɨ ~ ə

Note: Vowel symbols separated by commas are vowels which exist side by side in given varieties, whereas vowel symbols separated by '~' are in free variation, i.e. there is no phonemic contrast between those vowels in that variety.

(RP stands for 'Received Pronunciation' – a once prestige British English accent – and NYC for New York City English. Don't worry about the symbol you'll find under the box for New Zealand English (NZE). At this point it's sufficient to notice that NZE apparently has a systematically different phoneme than /ɪ/ in this environment.)

Since /ɪ/ had (and has) such a widespread distribution, and would occur in the vowel systems of so many readers of this text, I thought it was a good idea to use this vowel for so many of our examples in previous chapters.

The vowel /e/ (*pet*) is also fairly widespread, though in the following table – again, it's a fragment – notice how some accents don't have the vowel symbolised /e/, but one symbolised /ɛ/, for monosyllables such as *dress* or *pet*. Indeed, I have /ɛ/ (in *pet*, *dress*, *net* and so on) in my own accent, which is Standard Northern British English. In the table below, you'll find the distribution of /e/ and /ɛ/ as this occurs in the same varieties of accents that were tabled above:

The following charts, like the one above, have been collated from the data presented in Wells (1982). The accents represented in these charts have no special or privileged status, and nothing is implied by the left/ right ordering of the accents displayed – there's no reason why RP, for instance, is 'better than' Leeds English. These accents just happen to be among the ones studied in Wells (1982). In chapter 10 I shall revisit some of these accents, and begin to compare the data collected in Wells (1982) with those collected and presented in Schneider, Burridge *et al.* (2004),

> which last is arguably among the finest research resources available to a student of English phonology in the early part of the twenty-first century.

(3) The *pet* vowel

	RP	London	Norwich	Bristol	Birmingham	Leeds	Scottish	Irish	GenAm	NYC	Deep South	Australia	New Zealand
KIT	ɪ	ɪ	ɪ	ɪ	ɪ	ɪ	ɪ	ɪ	ɪ	ɪ	ɪ	ɪ	ɨ ~ ə
DRESS	e	e	ɛ	ɛ	ɛ	ɛ	ɛ	ɛ	ɛ	ɛ	ɛ	e	e ~ ɪ

Our task, then, is really twofold. First, we need to establish an inventory of short vowels. Second, we need some terminology in order to analyse phonemic distinctions – for instance, right now we have no way of analysing the distinction between a vowel represented by /e/ and one represented by /ɛ/. We know (or we trust) that the distinction exists, but we know nothing about *where* the relevant vowels are produced, or about *how* they differ, or about *why* they contrast in the way they do.

Let's review the short vowels that for many readers would be netted by the minimal pairs established by the substitution frame /p__t/. They are as follows:

Alphabetic	Possible phonemic transcription
pit	/pɪt/
pet	/pet/, /pɛt/ …
pat	?
pot	?
put	?
putt	?

We now need to *describe the differences* between /ɪ/ and /e/, or between /e/ and all the other short vowels with which it contrasts. To undertake that description, we need to turn again to articulatory detail, and in particular, we need to study *how* and *where* vowels are produced in the oral cavity. Once we've done that, we'll be able to transcribe the short vowels that until now have been mere puzzles.

> First, repeat a simple exercise. Holding your lips open, and keeping them rounded to begin with (just make, and hold, an 'OH' shape with your lips) gently flick your right cheek with the middle finger of your right hand. You'll hear a resonant, somewhat hollow, sound. Now, and while you're continuing gently to flick the outside of your cheek, alter the shape of your lips – purse them, then spread them, and then go back to the lip position you started from. Repeat the same exercise, this time paying particular attention to the *height* and *position* of your tongue within the oral cavity. You'll find that if the tongue is perceptibly raised, a different

sound is produced by your gentle flicking than when the tongue is perceptibly lowered and/or retracted. As you move your lips and tongue like this, you are actually altering the shape of the *oral cavity*, which in the present context can be thought of simply as a hollow space containing air. If you strike the outside of that hollow space, you'll get a different resonance depending on the overall shape and dimensions of the space.

When we were describing consonants, we analysed and classified in terms of the active articulators – the lips, teeth, alveolar ridge and so on. In the production of consonants, the airstream was often radically modified by the touching, or near-touching, of some of these active articulators – think, for instance, of the production of *stops* (where the oral cavity is briefly sealed) or *fricatives* (where the near touching of e.g. tongue tip and alveolar ridge causes the frication you perceive when /s/ is produced). But when we're describing vowels, *what seems to matter crucially is*:

(a)   *the height and position of the tongue* and
(b)   *the position of the lips*.

After all, when we articulate and perceive vowels it's impossible to say: 'When I produce this vowel my tongue is touching the alveolar ridge, and when I produce this other vowel the quality of sound seems to be labio-dental ...' Rather, what is crucial for the classification of vowels is the relative *height* and *position* of the tongue.

Try another exercise. For this one, spread your lips into what is almost a smile (notice that you *are* spreading your lips), and then produce the vowel /iː/ that you would associate with a word such as *neat* or *keep*. Hold the pronunciation of the vowel on a long outbreath, and try to think about the position of your tongue. You'll probably feel the sides of your tongue touching your upper teeth, but where are the blade and tip of your tongue as you utter this vowel? (Hint: you can cheat. Try inserting the tip of your little finger between your teeth as you continue to utter /iː/.)

Now try another exercise, this one concerning the vowel you'd associate with words such as *cat* or *hand*. Just pronounce those two words, but notice as you do what happens to your lips, and to the position of your tongue. On *cat* and *hand*, the lips aren't spread to quite the same extent as they were for *keep*, and furthermore the tongue is *lower*. You can actually feel the tongue rising and lowering if you insert your little finger between your teeth as you pronounce *keep* and then *cat*.

If we're to start classifying vowels, then, the *position and movement of the tongue* are critical for our purposes. Therefore, we need to develop a keen

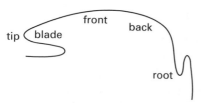

Figure 8.1 The general shape of the tongue

self-consciousness about the shape, flexibility and dimensions of the tongue. It may help you to study a diagram of the tongue, as this is seen from the speaker's left-hand side. Please pay particular attention to the terms used to label the different parts of the tongue, especially the terms *blade* and *tip*.

In the production of some vowels, for instance, the *blade* of the tongue is *raised* towards the front of the hard palate, while the *tip* of the tongue is lowered (this would be the vowel /ɪ/ or /iː/ for many speakers). In other vowels, the *body* and *blade* of the tongue alike are *lowered* and *retracted* – the vowel heard in words like *carp* would, for many speakers and hearers, be of this lowered, retracted type.

There are two further things to notice. In all varieties of English, vowels are in principle non-nasal, i.e. they are produced with the velum (the soft palate) raised, thus sealing off the nasal cavity. It's true that in certain environments, such as that provided by a vowel followed by a nasal consonant (e.g. words such as *ban, pin, numb*), that vowels do *become* nasalised, but this is a feature of production, and is contextually determined. (Since it's contextually deter-mined it is a feature of *production*, and therefore has a phonetic, allophonic character.) Interestingly, in other languages there are indeed vowels that could be confidently analysed as *underlyingly* nasal, but these don't occur in English. In all varieties of English, vowel phonemes are resolutely *oral*.

The other thing to notice is this: we can assume that in all varieties of English, vowels are *voiced*. I can't immediately think of any vowel – any vocalic segment that contrasts with any other such segment – that is voice-less. (Can you?) Again, in other languages it's possible to conceive of vowels that are *underlyingly* voiceless, but these don't seem to occur in English.[2]

Below you'll find a diagram that looks like a trapezoidal shape into which symbols have been inserted, and to which numbers have been attached. Try to work out, if you can, what such a shape might symbolise.

The trapezium – often known as a *vowel trapezium* (and also by other, less technical, names of which 'the washing machine' is my own favourite) – is a highly stylised representation of the oral cavity as this might be seen by someone standing to the speaker's left. If I superimpose the vowel trapezium on a diagram of the mouth, you'll see immediately how the trapezoidal shape stylises that space in the oral cavity within which the tongue moves to generate distinct vowel phonemes:

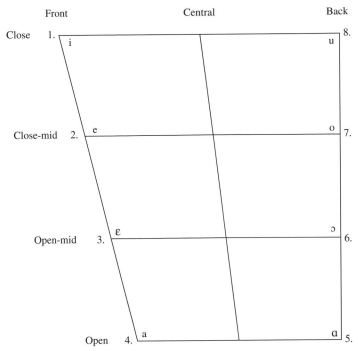

Figure 8.2 A vowel trapezium, showing the eight Cardinal Vowels. Note that the Cardinal Vowels are here set as reference points, and nothing is implied about whether such reference points are pronounced as long or short

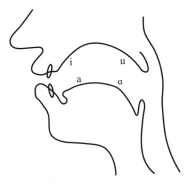

Figure 8.3 The oral cavity and four Cardinal Vowel points

The vowel trapezium gives us a way in which to start thinking about the vowel-shaping movement of the tongue in the oral cavity. The pioneers of phonetics, for instance, thought of the vowel trapezium as containing *stylised reference points*. In the diagram above, these points are numbered 1 through to 8. Reference points 1 through 4 represent vowel shapes produced by the *fronting* of the tongue ('front vowels'), while points 5 through 8 represent vowel shapes produced by the *retraction* of the tongue ('back vowels').

You'll also see from the above diagram that sections of the oral cavity are subclassified: the term 'close' means that the jaws are in a relatively close position, and the tongue blade is *raised towards* the front part of the hard palate, and furthermore, is raised as far as it can go without actually touching the hard palate and thereby producing a consonant. (A term which is also often used for vowels produced with maximal tongue-raising is 'high', thus vowels such as /ɪ/ and /ʊ/ are referred to as 'high vowels'.) The term 'close-mid' (or 'half-close' in some reference texts) means that the tongue is raised, but not as raised as it is when it's in the most close position. The term 'open-mid' ('half-open' in some reference texts) means that the jaws are relatively *open*, and the tongue is relatively *lowered*, while 'open' means that the tongue is in the most lowered position. (Again, note that a term also often used for vowels produced with maximal tongue-lowering is 'low', thus vowels such as /ɑ/ and /ʌ/ are referred to as 'low vowels'.)

There's nothing magical or even inevitable about such numbers and labels. Indeed, both the numbers and labels are *abstractions* designed simply to help us talk with accuracy about how vowels are produced. Equally, it's important to notice that these numerical reference points are not, themselves, vowels. It doesn't automatically follow that 'number 1 = /ɪ/'. What *does* follow is that the position associated with number 1 on the vowel trapezium indicates the kind of vowel that is produced with the tongue 'as far forward and raised as it can go without occluding the airflow in such a way as to produce a consonant' (a similar definition may be found in Roach 1991: 13).

These reference points are so useful to analysts that for a century and more they have been known by a special generic name. The vowels associated with positions 1 through to 8 are known as the **primary Cardinal Vowels**. The word 'primary' implies that there may be *secondary* Cardinal Vowels, and indeed there are – you'll be looking at a diagram of them in the next chapter.

With these notes in mind, I'd like you to concentrate on positions 1 through 4, i.e. those slots that function as reference points for the description of *front* vowels.

Describing /ɪ/ as a 'high front short vowel' isn't too difficult. The tongue is indeed fronted, the blade of the tongue is raised towards the hard palate (but doesn't touch it), and the tip of the tongue is lowered. (You can in fact feel that tip-lowering if you produce, then hold, the vowel found in the word *kit*, and then insert the tip of your little finger into the gap between your upper and lower teeth.) What is more difficult is hearing the difference between the vowels different speakers may have in *pet*. For some speakers, that vowel is half-close (/e/); for others, that vowel is mid-low (/ɛ/).

To help you identify the difference between /e/ and /ɛ/, try a small exercise. On a held outbreath, try pronouncing a lengthened version of the 'i' vowel (we have already seen this vowel symbolised as /iː/,

> and it occurs in many varieties of English in words such as *need, heed* and so on). It helps if you imagine you are *singing* this vowel. As you pronounce a long-held version of /i:/, lower your bottom jaw. This will automatically have the effect of lowering the *body,* and to some extent the *front* and *tip,* of the tongue. As the tongue body lowers, you should notice that the quality of the vowel you are producing alters: it will move through an /e(:)/ shape, then through an /ɛ(:)/ shape.

There's another interesting observation to make about the short vowels /e/ and /ɛ/. It's not theoretically inconceivable that some speakers might have the short vowels /ɪ/, /e/ *and* /ɛ/ in their vowel inventories, since the vowels offer phonemic contrast. But this doesn't seem to happen in present-day Englishes: speakers of *all* varieties of present-day English seem to have a three-, not a four-way contrast in the system of short front vowels. There's a high (close) front short vowel (/ɪ/); then there's either a half-close (/e/) or half-open (/ɛ/) short front vowel; and there's another short front vowel, too – the vowel which occurs in words such as *pat.*

Let's describe the short vowel which can occur in words such as *pat, mat.* For *all* speakers, this vowel occurs in a low (open) position. You can actually feel the tongue-lowering involved if you pronounce the word *pat*, and at the same time insert a finger into the front of your mouth, as you do so feeling that the tip of your tongue lies just behind your lower teeth.

There's a difference, however, in how this low front vowel is implemented. Some speakers have a slightly *raised* vowel in this position (i.e. the body of the tongue is slightly raised, though not so raised so as to confuse this vowel with /ɛ/), while others have a slightly *retracted* vowel. (I have this phoneme in my own variety of English.) You can see (and hear) the difference if you study the following table of varieties:

(4)   The *pat* vowel

	RP	London	Norwich	Bristol	Birmingham	Leeds	Scottish	Irish	GenAm	NYC	Deep South	Australia	New Zealand
KIT/ PIT	ɪ	ɪ	ɪ	ɪ	ɪ	ɪ	ɪ	ɪ	ɪ	ɪ	ɪ	ɪ	ɨ ~ ə
DRESS/ PET	e	e	ɛ	ɛ	ɛ	ɛ	ɛ	ɛ	ɛ	ɛ	ɛ	e	e ~ ɪ
TRAP/ PAT	æ	æ	æ	æ	a	a	a	æ	æ	æ,æɜ, æ,æɪ ɛɜ	æ	ɛ ~ æ

The contrast that I've tried to get at in the foregoing paragraph is that between /æ/ (which speakers of some British English, GA and

Antipodean Englishes have) and /a/ (which other speakers of Midlands, or Northern British English have). From the table you'll also notice that speakers of some varieties of American English – NYC, the Deep South – have pronunciations which are *diphthongal*. (Diphthongs will be discussed in the next chapter, so if you're concerned about symbols such as /æe/ or /æɪ/ – don't be. The table above is simply to help you understand the range of possible variation, rather than compel you to transcribe all of it.)

> I stress again that a diphthongal pronunciation of the *pat*, *trap* vowel (NYC, Deep South) isn't *wrong*. It's not 'ugly', not 'sub-standard'. From a phonological point of view all that matters is that speakers *contrast* the vowels which occur in words such as *pit*, *pet* and *pat*. A speaker from New York City, for example, whatever his or her underlying vowel phoneme in *pat*, makes a lovely contrast between that vowel and the vowels occurring in *pit* and *pet*. To that extent, his or her English is highly *effective*: it makes exactly those contrasts necessary to allow vowel phonemes to be, and to remain, distinct from each other.

To make the distinction between /a/ and /æ/ clear, study the following fragment of a trapezium. The fragment shows short monophthongal vowels that may occur in the low (open) front position. (If you can access recordings of RP from the period 1950–70 you can also hear speakers of that once prestige British accent, RP – some politicians, newsreaders, some sports commentators – using pronunciations of the *pat* vowel in /æ/. For such speakers, *the cat sat on the mat* sounds something like 'the ket set on the met' – although of course that's merely a crude graphic stylisation, and such speakers had, and some still have, a perfect phonemic contrast between /æ/ and /e/.)

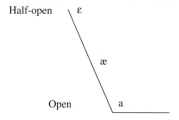

We're now going to study the short back vowels, i.e. those monophthongal vowels, pronounced short, which occur aligned with positions 5 through 8 of the vowel trapezium. As with the front vowels, we're going to start with back vowels produced with relative tongue-raising, and will therefore begin our analysis with a vowel associated with position 8 of the trapezium.

> Before we proceed, repeat the exercise you performed above, only this time begin with a long-held (better, a *sung*) version of the vowel that for many speakers occurs in the word *moon*. Eventually we'll symbolise this vowel as /u:/ – a high back vowel – but for the moment you can think of the first part of this exercise simply as the production of a long-drawn-out "ooh" sound. Notice that your lips are *rounded*, not *spread*, as you produce this sound. Now (and while still singing!) lower your bottom jaw. This will automatically have the effect of lowering the body (and to a lesser extent, the blade and tip) of your tongue. What vowel sounds do you produce in the process?

The first short back vowel we're going to study is the vowel which for many speakers occurs in the word *put*. Pronounce this word carefully, and several times. Now pronounce the word *foot*, where you should find exactly the same vowel phoneme. You may well find that as you pronounce *put* or *foot*, your lips are somewhat *rounded*. That's important. While lip-*spreading* is something that's more often associated with front vowels, lip-*rounding* is something that's more often associated with back ones. Moreover, in producing the vowel of *put*, your tongue is both *retracted* and *raised*. That's much more difficult actually to feel (by inserting a finger into your mouth) than is the case with any of the front vowels – largely because the blade and tip of the tongue *are* retracted. Nevertheless, and particularly if you pronounce *put*, then *pot*, you should notice that in the former, the blade and tip of the tongue are slightly more raised than in the latter.

The phonemic symbol we use for the *put* vowel isn't simply */u/. It's tempting to use the familiar graphic <u> in this way, but unfortunately, if we did so use that familiar symbol in this context we'd risk confusion with the vowel so many speakers have in a word such as *moon*. This vowel – the *moon* vowel – we'll eventually symbolise as /u:/, so it seems both wise and necessary to use a separate, disambiguated symbol for the *put* vowel. That symbol is /ʊ/. If you're writing in longhand, practise writing the symbol, and make sure it's distinct from <u> (or later, from /u:/). It may help you, too, if you think of this symbol, and the vowel it represents, using some special name: if you're going to be entirely accurate, you could think of this vowel as 'short high back – and relatively round – vowel'. If you're going to be informal, you could do worse than to call this vowel what many of my students call it (referring to the shape of the phonemic symbol): 'the chamber pot'.

The varietal distribution of the *put/foot* vowel – a short high (close) back vowel – can be expressed in the following table:

(5)   The *put/foot* vowel

	RP	London	Norwich	Bristol	Birmingham	Leeds	Scottish	Irish	GenAm	NYC	Deep South	Australia	New Zealand
KIT/PIT	ɪ	ɪ	ɪ	ɪ	ɪ	ɪ	ɪ	ɪ	ɪ	ɪ	ɪ	ɪ	ɨ ~ ə
DRESS/PET	e	e	ɛ	ɛ	ɛ	ɛ	ɛ	ɛ	ɛ	ɛ	ɛ	e	e ~ ɪ
TRAP/PAT	æ	æ	æ	æ	a	a	a	æ	æ	æ, æɘ, ɛɘ	æ, æɪ	æ	ɛ ~ æ
FOOT/PUT	ʊ	ʊ	ʊ	ʊ	ʊ	ʊ	ʊ	ʊ	ʊ	ʊ	ʊ	ʊ	ʊ

What interests me about the table above is how, for many speakers, the high front and high back positions seem to be subject to so little variation. That is, such a position seems among other things to function as a kind of oral/aural reference point. The short vowel that occurs in that position (positions 1 and 8) can *never* be confused with any other short, lower vowel.

Let's move on to the other short back vowels. One such is the vowel that for many (though by no means all) speakers occurs in words such as *putt* or *strut*. If you do have a phonemic contrast between *put* and *putt*, notice that when you pronounce the latter vowel the tongue is lowered from the /ʊ/ position, and the lips lose their rounding. If you now (and to anticipate a little) pronounce the word *part*, and compare both *put* and *putt*, you'll feel that in *putt* the tongue isn't quite as lowered as in *part*. Therefore with *putt* we are in some varieties of English dealing with a mid vowel, though whether this is half-open, half-close, or something else entirely, is a question we haven't yet answered.

To answer that last implied question – is the *strut* vowel half-close or half-open? – then we must appeal to some very precise description. It would be misleading to say, for instance, that there was a neat *symmetry* between short front vowels and short back ones, wherein the front system had a close vowel (/ɪ/), a mid vowel (either half-close /e/ or half-open /ɛ/), and a low/open vowel (/a/ or /æ/) and the back system equally had a close vowel (/ʊ/), a mid vowel (the *strut* vowel) and a low/open one. That wouldn't be accurate, unfortunately – not for present-day Englishes, anyway.

Instead we have to enquire again about *where* the back vowel which occurs in *strut* words actually occurs. To help us, let's make a further contrast, involving the vowel which occurs in many varieties in words such as *pot* or *lot*.

> Try pronouncing *pot*, then *put*; *put*, then *pot*. Now pronounce the three words *put*, *putt* and *pot*. (You may find you have no contrast between *put* and *putt*, but if not, do please keep reading, and see in particular the final paragraph of this section of text.) Remain very conscious of the movement of your tongue as you switch from one to the other vowel.

> You should find that when you pronounce *putt*, the tongue is lower than when you pronounce *put*, and at the same time, lip-rounding won't be at all marked (and may well be absent). When you pronounce *pot*, the tongue may well be even lower than when you pronounced *putt*, and at the same time, you should notice some lip-rounding.

Gimson describes the *putt/strut* vowel as being 'articulated with a considerable separation of the jaws and with the lips neutrally open; the centre of the tongue (or a part slightly in advance of the centre) is raised just above the fully open position, no contact being made between the tongue and the upper molars' (1994: 104).

He describes the *pot/lot* vowel as follows: '[t]his short vowel is articulated with wide open jaws and slight, open lip-rounding; the back of the tongue is in the fully open position' (1994: 108).

Notice the contrast. The *putt* vowel has 'the centre of the tongue … *raised*', whereas the *pot* vowel has 'the back of the tongue … in the *fully open* position' [my italics: McC].

There's also a further contrast we can observe. In *pot/lot*, the tongue is more or less fully retracted, whereas in *putt/strut*, the centre of the tongue is not only raised, but raised towards the *centre* of the oral cavity.

What does all this mean, in the terms we're trying to develop in this chapter? It means that the short vowel found in *pot* words is associated with position 5 of the trapezium, i.e. it's a short open back vowel. The vowel found, for some speakers, in *putt* words is, if anything, nearest to position 6 (i.e. it's a half-open but unrounded vowel), but at the same time it's centralised (the tongue isn't fully retracted).

The symbol for *putt* vowels can't be */u/, for reasons we've already discussed. Instead, we use the symbol /ʌ/. For *pot* vowels we may use the symbol /ɒ/, or /ɑ/ for the markedly lowered and retracted pronunciation found in some dialects (see the table below).

We might chart the pronunciation of the *putt/strut* and *lot/pot* vowels in terms of English varieties as in the following table:

(6)   The *put/putt/pot* vowels

	RP	London	Norwich	Bristol	Birmingham	Leeds	Scottish	Irish	GenAm	NYC	Deep South	Australia	New Zealand
KIT/PIT	ɪ	ɪ	ɪ	ɪ	ɪ	ɪ	ɪ	ɪ	ɪ	ɪ	ɪ	ɪ	ɨ ~ ə
DRESS/PET	e	e	ɛ	ɛ	ɛ	ɛ	ɛ	ɛ	ɛ	ɛ	ɛ	ɛ	e ~ ɪ
TRAP/PAT	æ	æ	æ	æ	a	a	a	æ	æ	æ, æə, ɛə	æ, æɪ	æ	ɛ ~ æ
FOOT/PUT	ʊ	ʊ	ʊ	ʊ	ʊ	ʊ	ʊ	ʊ	ʊ	ʊ	ʊ	ʊ	ʊ
LOT/POT	ɒ	ɒ	ɒ	ɑ	ɒ	ɒ	ɔ	ɒ	ɑ	ɑ, ɑə	ɑ	ɒ	ɒ
STRUT/PUTT	ʌ	ʌ	ʌ	ʌ	ʊ ~ ʌ	ʊ	ʌ	ʌ	ʌ	ʌ	ʌ	ʌ	ʌ

Notice that some speakers (of e.g. Northern British English – look in the 'Leeds' column) do not have a vowel contrast in words such as *put* and *putt*. This doesn't mean, of course, that their inventory of vowels is somehow 'worse' than that of other speakers. In fact, the pronunciation of words such as *cut, sun, love* in /ʊ/ is in historical terms very significant, since until the seventeenth century *all* these words, in all varieties, had a pronunciation in /ʊ/. Some varieties of English – but not Northern British English – were then subject to phonological changes which affected the quality of some short vowels – including, of course, /ʊ/. The original vowel was subject to unrounding and lowering (except where it was followed by a palatal or alveolar fricative, which helps to account for the fact that RP *bush* /bʊʃ/ retains its historical pronunciation) and then to centralisation (in this case, becoming less 'back'), becoming /ʌ/ by the nineteenth century. This didn't happen in the north of England, which retained the original pronunciation of the words in question. (This interesting issue is discussed further in chapter 10, see especially 10.4.)

We have so far discussed *six* short vowels – three front vowels and three that might be plausibly distinguished as varieties of back vowels. There is, however, a seventh short vowel. It is so important that it deserves a section to itself.

8.2 Schwa, and other vowels in unstressed syllables

We've already seen (chapter 5.1) that schwa characteristically occurs in unstressed syllables. In such syllables, schwa may be in relatively free variation with /ɪ/. Consider, for instance, the word *captain*. In my variety of spoken English, the phonemic transcription would usually be /kaptən/, but a speaker of RP might well have a pronunciation that reflected underlying /kæptɪn/ (/ɪ/ in such unstressed syllables is in fact a hallmark of old-fashioned RP).

But although we've noted the fact of schwa's distribution in unstressed syllables, and said something about its variation with /ɪ/, we haven't yet said *where* the vowel is produced.

> **Pronounce the following words aloud, paying particular attention to the height and position of the tongue when you pronounce the underscored syllable in each word (you may not have schwa in every instance, but if not, make a note of what short vowel or other sound occurs): *appear; undo; comma; sherbet.***

With the possible exception of the vowel occurring in the first syllable of *undo* (where some speakers will have /ʌ/, particularly in very slow, careful speech), my guess is that almost all speakers will have schwa as the vowel of the relevant syllables. And what is the height and position of the tongue when schwa is produced? Many students find this difficult to state with precision, and that's not surprising. The tongue is neither markedly raised nor lowered, nor is it markedly fronted or retracted. Furthermore, when schwa is produced, the lips have no degree of spreading (which one would associate with front vowels) or rounding (which would be associated with back ones). Precisely. Schwa is a vowel produced in the *middle* of the oral cavity – a *central* vowel. Gimson's description may be of interest: ' … a central vowel with neutral lip position … ' (1994: 117).

Although schwa contrasts with other short vowels (as it must, in order to be a vowel phoneme!), it is unlike other short vowels in that it has no potential contrast with a vowel in an adjacent higher/lower slot of the vowel trapezium. It isn't, for instance, 'lower than /e/' in the same way that /e/ is lower than /ɪ/, nor 'higher than /a/' in the same way that /e/ is higher than /a/. It is simply … central. Yet because there are no immediate *central* contrasts available, schwa itself may be produced in subtly different ways according to the context in which it is produced. Gimson, for example, notes the following variations (1994: 117–18):

The vowel system of varieties of English
(7)   Schwa

Context and example	Underlying	Phonetic (= tongue position)
(1) non-final – *fatigue*	/ə/	central
(2) adjacent to velars – *long ago*	/ə/	slight raising and retraction
(3) final – *father, comma, China*	/ə/	slight lowering

Matters are also complicated by the fact that for many speakers of *rhotic* varieties of English (i.e. those varieties that have /r/ in syllable-final position in words such as *father, organ*), words such as *father, butter, never* may have syllabic /r/ in their final syllables, or, in other varieties and in careful speech, may have schwa+/r/. (You'll find more on **rhoticity** in chapter 10.6.)

These data mean that although we're quite correct in calling schwa an underlying short central vowel, schwa itself is actually quite difficult to characterise in phonetic terms since it 'shifts about' within the central region of the oral cavity according to the environment in which it appears. Unfortunately, too, schwa is subject to speaker-specific variation: I don't *always* have schwa in *captain* (sometimes, and not in any contextually determined way, I have /ɪ/) … and I'm more likely to have /ɪ/ in *captain* than in e.g. *mountain*, because I instinctively prefer to avoid any hint of homophony between *mountain* and *mounting*.

Put all this together, and it means that we can't immediately look at all the contextually determined phonetic varieties of underlying schwa and without further ado call them allophones. The wanderings and idiosyncracies of schwa are, at least at this stage of our work, simply too unpredictable for that.

In the table below you'll find a somewhat simplified distribution list for schwa as this may (or may not) occur in the word *letter* (note the presence of 'r' there) and *comma* (note the absence of 'r' there). The list is again adapted from Wells (1982):

(8)   Schwa in final position: *letter* and *comma*

	RP	London	Norwich	Bristol	Birmingham	Leeds	Scottish	Irish	GenAm	NYC	Deep South	Australia	New Zealand
KIT/PIT	ɪ	ɪ	ɪ	ɪ	ɪ	ɪ	ɪ	ɪ	ɪ	ɪ	ɪ	ɪ	ɨ ~ ə
DRESS/PET	e	e	ɛ	ɛ	ɛ	ɛ	ɛ	ɛ	ɛ	ɛ	ɛ	e	e ~ ɪ
TRAP/PAT	æ	æ	æ	æ	a	a	a	æ	æ	æ, æɔ, ɛɜ	æ, æɪ	æ	ɛ ~ æ
FOOT/PUT	ʊ	ʊ	ʊ	ʊ	ʊ	ʊ	ʊ	ʊ	ʊ	ʊ	ʊ	ʊ	ʊ
LOT/POT	ɒ	ɒ	ɒ	ɑ	ɒ	ɒ	ɔ	ɒ	ɑ	ɑ, ɑə	ɑ	ɒ	ɒ
STRUT/PUTT	ʌ	ʌ	ʌ	ʌ	ʊ ~ ʌ	ʊ	ʌ	ʌ	ʌ	ʌ	ʌ	ʌ	ʌ
*lett*ER		ə	ə	ər	ə	ə	ər	ər	ə(r)	ər	ər	ə	ə
*comm*A		ə	ə	ə	ə	ʌ	ə	ə	ə	ə	ə	ə	ə

> Please note one error many students make when attempting to transcribe schwa. Because everyone reads back to themselves, silently or aloud, the stretch of English they're transcribing (and may continue to laboriously pronounce every syllable, even as this is being transcribed) then transcription errors may creep in. This is particularly the case with unstressed syllables whose vowels are candidates for transcriptions in underlying schwa. Because such syllables are read back very slowly, and because each syllable of the transcription is pronounced emphatically, a syllable containing a vowel such as the schwa of e.g. *appear* may surface in an ultra careful read-back not as schwa but as a vowel whose pronunciation is something like /ʌ/. But transcribing the first syllable of *appear* with /ʌ/ would simply be wrong. Because /ʌ/ appears in stressed syllables, we'd be implying that the first syllable of *appear* is stressed, which would be incorrect. To avoid this problem, the best thing is to adopt a crude rule of thumb by which **the symbol /ʌ/ is reserved exclusively for representing vowels in stressed syllables.**

There's one other issue we need to discuss while we're analysing the phonology of short vowels, and that is an issue relating to /ɪ/ where this occurs syllable-finally in words such as *happy*. Many speakers (including me) have underlying /ɪ/ *and* surface [ɪ] in vowels occurring in that context – but many do not. Some speakers of rather old-fashioned RP, for instance, have underlying /ɪ/ but surface [e] (even [ɛ]) in such a context, whereas speakers of Tyneside English have a markedly tensed (and lengthened) surface [iː] in the same context. Still other speakers have a close front surface variety that is a shortened version of the long vowel [iː].

Consider a word such as *busy*. Using the symbols we've introduced so far, one plausible phonemic transcription would be /bɪzɪ/. There'd be no dispute about the transcription of the initial, stressed syllable. The problem would come with the final, unstressed syllable. Many speakers would look at a transcription such as /bɪzɪ/ and express some misgivings ('But that's not how I pronounce the final vowel … and even as a transcription of an underlying vowel that final /ɪ/ seems a bit … dodgy.') These same speakers often report using a longer (tensed) variety of underlying /ɪ/, a variety with more overt lip-spreading, while others report using a more centralised, slightly lower vowel sound.

There is a solution available to us, but (yet again) it's a fairly controversial one. So far in this book, and quite in accord with classical phonological theory, we've been assuming that there are underlying entities such as long vowels and short vowels. Indeed, vowels so far have been discussed and analysed as being either 'long' (associated with two Xs in the nucleus of a syllable) or 'short' (associated with one X). We've not seen or heard any vowel yet that is 'both long *and* short'.

What I'm going to do here is follow in the spirit if not the letter of Roach (1991). I'm going to maintain the use of the symbol /iː/ for the underlying long vowel, and /ɪ/ for the underlying short vowel, *but* I'm going to assume that there is a surface representation of underlying /ɪ/ which in syllable-final position can be symbolised as [i] (the same symbol as that used for /iː/, but without the length marks). In using this symbol, and in hinting that this surface vowel is 'neither long nor short', I'm aware that I'm storing up problems for us (not least, problems relating to how to match such a vowel with X-slots in a syllabic nucleus). However, if we regard the *underlying* vowel – the phoneme – as unambiguously short, then this also allows us for the moment to analyse variation in the pronunciation of (the final syllable of) *busy* as primarily a matter belonging to phonetics.

Some possible variations in the pronunciation of *busy* you'll find in (9). Below that, you'll find a familiar distribution chart (adapted from Wells 1982), where *all* the short vowels we've discussed so far appear. Note there are *six* such vowels associated with Cardinal Vowel positions – and, of course, there is the central vowel, schwa.

The vowel system of varieties of English
(9)   /ɪ/ in final, unstressed syllables

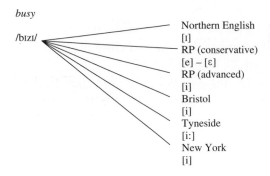

busy

/bɪzɪ/

Northern English
[ɪ]
RP (conservative)
[e] – [ɛ]
RP (advanced)
[i]
Bristol
[i]
Tyneside
[iː]
New York
[i]

(10)   *happy* and *busy*

	RP	London	Norwich	Bristol	Birmingham	Leeds	Scottish	Irish	GenAm	NYC	Deep South	Australia	New Zealand
KIT/PIT	ɪ	ɪ	ɪ	ɪ	ɪ	ɪ	ɪ	ɪ	ɪ	ɪ	ɪ	ɪ	ɨ ~ ə
DRESS/ PET	e	e	ɛ	ɛ	ɛ	ɛ	ɛ	ɛ	ɛ	ɛ	ɛ	e	e ~ ɪ
TRAP/ PAT	æ	æ	æ	æ	a	a	a	æ	æ	æ, æɜ, ɛɜ	æ, æɪ	æ	ɛ~æ
FOOT/ PUT	ʊ	ʊ	ʊ	ʊ	ʊ	ʊ	ʊ	ʊ	ʊ	ʊ	ʊ	ʊ	ʊ
LOT/POT	ɒ	ɒ	ɒ	ɑ	ɒ	ɒ	ɔ	ɒ	ɑ	ɑ, ɑə	ɑ	ɒ	ɒ
STRUT/ PUTT	ʌ	ʌ	ʌ	ʌ	ʊ ~ ʌ	ʊ	ʌ	ʌ	ʌ	ʌ	ʌ	ʌ	ʌ
*lett*ER		ə	ə	ər	ə	ə	ər	ər	ər	ə(r)	ər	ə	ə
*comm*A	ə	ə	ə	ə	ə	ə	ʌ	ə	ə	ə	ə	ə	ə
*happ*Y	ɛ	ii	[i]	i	[i]	ɪ	e, ɪ, i	iː	ɪ	i	i	iː	iː

That concludes, for the moment, our work on the short vowel system, although we must bear the last problem – the problem posed by a possible three-way surface contrast of length and tenseness – in mind. We shall revisit it.

It's time now to look at those vowels associated with two X-slots within the syllabic nucleus – the long vowels and diphthongs. They are the topic of the following chapter.

Exercises

Exercise 8a   **Look at the following list of words. In most varieties of English these words will all contain some kind of short vowel, a description and symbolisation of which are to be found in this chapter. Try to make a *phonemic transcription***

of *all* of these words, paying particular attention to the transcription of the vowels. Here's the list:

rough	cut	midge	met
rock	bread	cough	hymn
head	friend	leant	cap

Exercise 8b Study the following list of vowel symbols. For each symbol, write out the full descriptive classification for the vowel represented by the symbol. You will need to say whether a vowel is *close, half-close, half-open, open,* then state whether it's *front, back* or *central.* I have completed the first part of the exercise for you.

/ɪ/ close front

/ʌ/

/ʊ/

/a/

/ɛ/

/ɒ/

/ə/

Exercise 8c Draw a vowel trapezium. On it, insert the following short vowels, symbolised and positioned correctly: (a) a close front vowel; (b) a close back vowel; (c) a half-open front vowel; (d) a half-close front vowel; (e) an open back vowel; (f) a half-open back vowel.

Exercise 8d Indicate which Cardinal Vowel position is associated with the following vowels (i.e. your answers will be something like 'associated with Cardinal Vowel 5' etc):

/ɪ/

/ʌ/

/ɒ/

/e/

Exercise 8e Make two *phonemic transcriptions* of the following three pieces of connected English. (All the vowels which should feature in your transcription are vowels we have discussed in this chapter, i.e. they are all short vowels.) Your first transcription should reflect the structure of *your own* spoken variety of English; your second should capture the structure of a *different* variety of spoken English, perhaps that of a colleague, friend or co-worker. Note what differences there are in the two transcriptions – do those differences show up primarily in consonants or in vowels?

i. 'It was a lovely cat,' Pam said, a little sadly. 'Pity it's dead.'
ii. The bull rushed to the fence.
iii. Upon inspection, the goods were (/wə/) damaged.

Key terms introduced in this chapter
Cardinal Vowels
vowel quality
vowel quantity

Notes
1. 'Deep South' – a term you'll find both here and in other tables – is a simplification. For further detail, see Wells (1982, III: 527–53).
2. That's not to say that there may not be vowel segments in English that are underlyingly devoid of articulatory content – so-called underspecified vowels. After all, we came across good (though still controversial) reasons for including a zero consonant in our inventory of consonants, and it's entirely possible that English phonology encompasses underspecified vowels as well as zero consonants. Even given that possibility, though, it seems most analytically straightforward if we proceed by claiming that *in principle, all English vowels are voiced*. I shall not write further about underspecification in this book.

Further reading
Gimson, A. C. 1994. *Gimson's pronunciation of English*. 5th edition, revised by Alan Cruttenden. London: Arnold. Particularly chapter 8, pp. 97 ff.
Roach, Peter. 1991. *English phonetics and phonology*. 2nd edition. Cambridge University Press. Chapter 2, particularly sections 2.2–2.3.
Wells, J. C. 1982. *Accents of English*. vol. III. Cambridge University Press. Chapter 6, particularly sections 6.5–6.11.

CHAPTER 9

Vowels (2): long vowels and diphthongs

In this chapter …

In this chapter we look at the distribution of long vowels in English. We note that the set of these vowels can reliably be associated with those Cardinal reference points on a vowel trapezium that we first looked at in chapter 8. Therefore we can speak fairly confidently about the existence of 'high front/back vowels', 'low front/back' and so forth.

The long vowel systems of English, however – unlike the consonant systems and even the short vowel systems – seem to be subject to a great deal of variation. We start to look at some of that variation in 9.3, 'A tour of long vowels', and in section 9.4–9.5 examine further features of variation, particularly that concerning the existence of rhotic and non-rhotic accents. That discussion leads to a very brief consideration of triphthongs in 9.6. The methodological and principled difficulties we encounter in 9.4–9.6, however, mean that we must reconsider the nature of 'variation', together with the idea of underlying representation. Those will be the topics explored respectively in chapters 10 (which looks at 'variation' in more detail) and 11 (where we'll revisit the idea of underlying structure).

9.1 **Describing long vowels and diphthongs**

You'll remember from chapter 7 that while short vowels are associated with just *one* X-slot within the syllabic nucleus, long vowels and diphthongs are associated with *two* X-slots within the nucleus. In our test examples, the minimal pair *heed* (/hi:d/) and *hide* (/haɪd/), where the first contains a long vowel, and the second a diphthong, the respective structures looked like this:

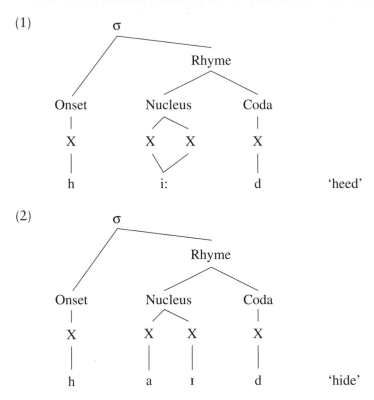

(1) ... 'heed'

(2) ... 'hide'

In both cases, the syllabic nucleus is maximally filled (i.e. up to the two X-slots permitted as well formed). In (1), the case of the 'pure' long vowel /i:/, the two X-slots are associated with a vowel that is assumed (at this stage) to have component parts with an identical quality. In (2), the respective X-slots are associated with vowel segments that have non-identical qualities.

There are in fact some descriptive difficulties hidden within such a simple characterisation. For example, many analysts seem to assume that a long vowel such as /i:/ is in some way 'pure' ('the pure long vowel /i:/' would be a phrase straight out of many of the standard handbooks), and in truth diagram (1) does imply this acoustic purity, namely that in e.g. *heed* there is *one* and only one 'pure' vowel phoneme. For diphthongs, diagram (2) implies that a diphthong has two non-identical *and quite separate* internal components, which are themselves vowel segments – in our example, the low front vowel /a/ and the high front vowel /ɪ/.

Roach (1991: 20) uses the phrase 'pure vowel' to contrast with the term 'diphthong', but interestingly, in his chapter 13, tellingly titled 'Problems in phonemic analysis', he notes that there may be other ways of thinking about the so-called 'pure' long vowels. For instance, a phonemic inventory of vowels *might* consist just of basic, short vowel phonemes (vowels such as /a, ɪ, e/ etc.). If that were indeed the case, Roach notes, 'it would then be possible to make up long vowels by using vowels twice' (1991: 114). One example he gives is of the long vowel /iː/, which, if analysed as 'twice short', might plausibly be transcribed /ɪɪ/. In terms of how this might be represented in terms of syllable structure, look back to diagram (1), and then compare (3), the diagram immediately below:

(3)

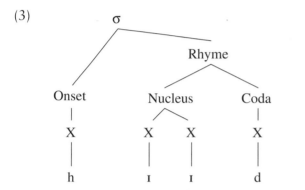

'heed'

If we were to admit such an analysis then long vowels and diphthongs would have directly comparable internal structures: long vowels align with two nuclear X-slots, each of which would be filled with a segment of an identical quality, while diphthongs would align with two nuclear X-slots, each of which would be filled by segments with non-identical qualities.

We could be yet more radical. Here's an interesting quote, again from Roach (1991: 114):

Another way of doing this kind of analysis is to treat long vowels and diphthongs as composed of a vowel plus a consonant; this may seem a less obvious way of proceeding, but it was for many years the choice of most American phonologists. The idea is that long vowels and diphthongs are composed of a basic vowel phoneme followed by one of **j, w, h** (in the case of RP).

If we were to follow this idea, then of course the idea that there were such things as 'pure' long vowels would vanish. A long vowel such as the /iː/ of *heed* would in this view be transcribed as /ɪj/, and a diphthong such as the /aɪ/ of *hide* would be transcribed /aj/. If we were to adopt this idea, then there would be an even more direct analogy between long vowels and diphthongs: not only would each consist of two X-slots in the syllabic nucleus, but those X-slots would be filled by non-identical phonetic material.

For the moment I am – perhaps disappointingly, to the radically minded reader – going to stick to the traditional view and graphic symbolism of long

129

vowels and diphthongs, i.e. the view that long vowels are to be symbolised as e.g. /iː/ (where the two dots function as a diacritic marker indicating length) and have the syllabic representation as seen in (1). I adhere to the old-fashioned view simply because it's easier to teach, and to learn, transcriptions such as /iː/ and /aɪ/ than it is to teach and learn transcriptions such as /ɪɪ/ or /aj/. (If this seems boringly practical and overcautious, I urge the same radically minded reader to pay particular attention to chapter 10, where I revisit the idea that 'pure' long vowels may not in fact be at all pure.) Before we proceed with what will at this stage be a fairly conservative analysis of long vowels and diphthongs, however, I'd like you to pose the following two questions to yourself.

> **Do your intuitions about the long vowels in your own phonemic inventory suggest that these vowels are 'pure'?**

> **What theoretical advantages might there be if long vowels were to be analysed as consisting of two non-identical short phonemes? (Clue: think back to syllable structure, and to the notion of a strength hierarchy correlated with the phonetic openness of segments.)**

There's one further point to note before we establish an inventory of long vowels. It concerns diphthongs. We've so far thought about diphthongs as consisting of two non-identical vowels, each of which, separately and discretely, fills one X-slot. But in fact, speakers and auditors don't perceive diphthongs as consisting of *two* separate elements that have somehow been acoustically stuck together. They simply hear the diphthong as unitary, as *one* contrastive vowel phoneme. This perception comes about because diphthongs are uttered with a *gliding* motion of the tongue. When pronouncing any diphthong – take our familiar example /aɪ/ – no speaker pronounces /a/, then stops (however briefly), then pronounces /ɪ/. (If that were the case, then we might expect also to perceive some transitional phenomena as the speaker's articulatory musculature shifted from one segment to the other. But we do *not* perceive any such transitional phenomena in the case of e.g. /aɪ/, or any other diphthong. We simply hear *one* contrastive vowel.)

With those notes and caveats in mind, let's proceed.

9.2 Establishing an inventory of long vowels

We can proceed to establish an inventory of long vowels using exactly the same descriptive methodology we used to establish an inventory of short vowels in the last chapter – namely, we can use *substitution frames* to help us decide what the contrastive long vowel (or diphthong) phonemes are, for any given variety of English; we can use the *vowel trapezium* to display *where* such vowels are produced in the oral cavity, and how they contrast with other vowels; and we can use the *primary Cardinal Vowel* reference points to help us classify vowels along the continua 'high–mid–low' (i.e. close–mid–open) and 'front–central–back'.

It bears repeating here that what so many textbooks and handbooks dub the 'Cardinal Vowels' are not, in and of themselves, vowels. The *Cardinal Vowels* can best be thought of as *contrastive reference points*. As the *Principles* of the IPA put it, 'Most letters [i.e. those graphic shapes symbolising phonemes: McC] ... not only represent particular sounds but also have to do duty for other shades of sound near to these. Hence the need for establishing systems of "cardinal" sounds ... A convenient system of cardinal vowels consists of a series of eight basic vowels of known formation and acoustic qualities, which serve as a standard of measurement, and by reference to which other vowels can be described.' (1949: 4)

It is entirely possible, even desirable, therefore, to use descriptions such as 'the vowel closest to Cardinal point 1, pronounced short' (this would be the phoneme /ɪ/), and 'the vowel aligned with Cardinal point 1, pronounced long' (this would be the phoneme /iː/).

To begin, consider the following substitution frame, and consider what long vowels or diphthongs could be inserted into it. Try to start, if you can, with a *high front* vowel. Then try to insert a *high back* vowel into the frame. To complete the task, of course you should not use any of the short vowel phonemes whose existence we established in chapter 8.

Substitution frame 1
/b__t/

A good vowel to start with is the vowel represented by either <ee> (*beet*) or, in some varieties of present-day English, <ea> (*beat*). Unless you're a native speaker of an Antipodean variety of English, it's highly likely that the vowel you have in *beet* or *beat* is a long variety of a vowel aligned with Cardinal position 1. Such a vowel is produced with very perceptible tongue-raising and fronting. If you produce and then hold such a vowel, and insert your little finger between your teeth, you will feel that the blade of the tongue is raised and fronted, while the tip is lowered. At the same time, the lips are perceptibly spread (a secondary diagnostic of the production of (high) front vowels).

This vowel we can represent as our familiar /iː/.

Next, a high back vowel. This might have been harder for you to analyse, since many beginning students find front vowels easier to perceive and describe than those vowels produced with tongue-retraction. To help you, recall the secondary diagnostic we used to identify short back vowels: lip-rounding. If, for example, you produce the vowel /i:/, then retract the tongue (while still keeping its blade high), and at the same time rounding your lips, you'll eventually produce …?

That's right. You'll produce the vowel that many speakers have in a word such as *boot*. This is the vowel associated with Cardinal position 8, here pronounced long. The (blade and tip of the) tongue is retracted, the lips are relatively rounded.

This vowel we can symbolise as /u:/.

> Now try to construct two lists, the first containing examples of monosyllables containing /i:/, the second a list of monosyllables containing /u:/. Try to find at least six examples (a total of twelve: six front, six back), and if you can, make each pair of examples a *minimal pair* (such as *beat* and *boot*). Note: if your variety of English doesn't have these long vowels (e.g. in words such as *peat* or *moon*), don't worry. The main purpose of the exercise is simply to reassure you that many (in fact, almost all) varieties of English *do* have these vowels, and even if your variety doesn't have them, it's a sure bet that you'll be exposed daily to a variety which does. A secondary purpose of the exercise is to provide us with two reference points – the highest possible long vowels, front and back – by which we can establish the existence of contrastively lower long vowels.

Your lists might have looked something like this:

Long high front vowels	Long high back vowels
Cardinal 1	Cardinal 8
beet	boot
mean	moon
meat	moot
mead	mood
feed	food
fleet	flute

> A helpful two-part exercise at this stage, and one that will help us to establish the existence of *almost all* the other long vowels in Cardinal positions 1 through 8, is to do the following:
>
> i.   Produce and hold a long /i:/ vowel (you might want to sing it). Now, still holding that vowel, i.e. trying to keep the tongue height

constant, slowly start to lower your bottom jaw. Note how the quality of /i:/ begins to change as the jaw lowers. Why might that be so?

ii.   Produce and hold a long /u:/ vowel (you might want to sing it). Still holding that vowel, i.e. trying to keep the tongue height constant, slowly start to lower your bottom jaw. Note how the quality of /u:/ begins to change as the jaw lowers. Why might that be so?

In both cases you began the exercise using the highest possible long vowel phonemes, front and back respectively. In each case, if you lower your bottom jaw this will have the inevitable consequence that the blade of the tongue will be *lowered* too. As the tongue lowers, what you hear are some of the long vowel shapes that function as Cardinal reference points 2 to 4 (the remainder of the set of long front vowels) and 7 to 5 (the set of long back vowels, described from higher to lowest).

Taking the front set as an example, what you will have heard as you completed the last exercise are a mid-high long front vowel (some speakers may recognise this as something like 'a long version of French e-acute'), a mid-low long front vowel ('a long version of French e-grave'), and a low long front vowel. Taking the back set, we begin in Cardinal position 8, with /u:/, and the tongue then moves through position 7 (the long vowel some – though by no means all – varieties of English have in *boat*), then through position 6 (the long vowel some varieties have in e.g. *bought*), and then – in the lowest, most retracted position – the long back vowel many speakers have in words such as *part*, *heart* or perhaps *bath* (although speakers of Northern British English do not have a long, low back vowel in that environment).

The point of this last exercise is to help establish exactly those Cardinal reference points we've been discussing. What the exercise establishes is precisely that set of reference points which you'll find symbolised on a vowel trapezium in the figures below. (Again, don't worry if your variety doesn't contain *all* of these hypothetically possible long vowels. It is in fact highly unlikely that your variety contains all of them. Mine certainly doesn't: I have Cardinal 1, Cardinal 8, Cardinal 6 and Cardinal 5 as reference points in my own inventory. We'll discuss the gaps and apparent inconsistencies later in this chapter, and again in chapter 10.)

The first diagram you'll see below is repeated from chapter 8, and shows the Cardinal reference points. The second diagram indicates how the set of hypothetically possible long vowels are matched with the Cardinal reference points, and shows how such long vowels may be symbolised (note the presence of the length diacritic ':' in each case):

Figure 9.1 Cardinal reference points

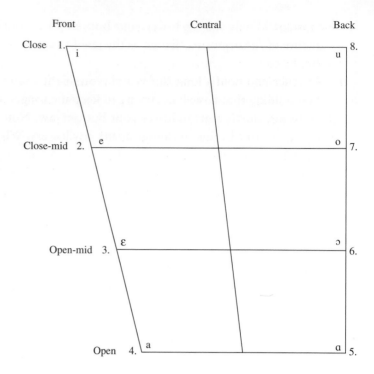

Figure 9.2 The possible set of long vowels in Cardinal positions 1 through 8

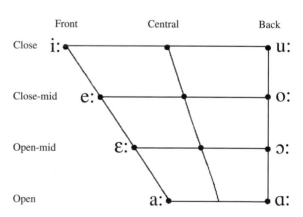

There's one other long vowel we need to add. We can establish its existence if we use the following substitution frame:

Substitution frame 2
/b__d/

We could possibly – and plausibly – insert /iː/ (*bead*), possibly /ɔː/ (*bored*), possibly /ɑː/ (*bard*). (I'm using the word 'possibly' because while there are many varieties with long vowels in such words, there are also some varieties of English which don't have long vowels in words such as *bored* and *bard*. Instead, in these words such varieties have a *short* vowel, followed by the consonant /r/. I'll discuss such varieties below.) But we could also, and equally plausibly, ask: 'What about, for example, *bird*?' In many varieties, a monosyllable such as *bird* (or *word*, *term*, *hurt* and so forth) contains a long vowel which is neither markedly front, nor back; the tongue is neither perceptibly raised, nor retracted; the lips are neither markedly rounded, nor are they spread.

We can think of the vowel many varieties have in e.g. *bird* as a long *central* vowel. In some ways this vowel can be thought of as the long equivalent of schwa (although it doesn't 'derive from' schwa – it's merely produced in what is roughly the same part of the oral cavity, with roughly the same tongue height and position).

This long central vowel is symbolised /ɜ:/.

> Some of the vowel symbols we're now using are unfamiliar and need practising. This is important. Many students, for instance, sometimes transcribe e.g. /ɜ:/ as /ɛ:/, or /ɔ:/ as /or/. The best way to practise is to keep making substitution frames, and keep transcribing, having your transcriptions checked by a colleague as you work.

You'll have spotted in the foregoing paragraphs that I've been particularly cagey about what varieties of English may, or may not, have a particular long vowel as part of their inventory of long vowels. This caginess stems from the fact that there's a great deal more variation between varieties of English in their long-vowel systems than in their short-vowel systems. For example, most varieties have a neat three-term short-front-vowel system (/ɪ/, then /e/ or /ɛ/, then /æ/ or /a/), but there are few varieties that have a similarly neat three-term long-front-vowel system. Indeed, in my own inventory there is only *one* front vowel that might be described as unambiguously long (and, I suppose, 'pure') – and that is /iː/. That's not to suggest that I don't have other vocalic shapes which begin their articulatory lives at the front of the oral cavity, as it were – but these shapes may best be described as *diphthongs*, which we'll discuss further, and in some detail, below.

To help us think about variety in English long-vowel systems, we can appeal once again to the description of Wells (1982). In what follows I'm going to attempt a quick phonological tour of long vowels, noting where they occur in some varieties of English (and equally, noting where they don't occur). I'm going to begin with the distribution of /iː/, then move to the distribution of /uː/, and thereafter through the remaining possible long back vowels, working from higher to lowest, and then will move into a discussion of the front vowels, working from lowest to higher.

This isn't going to be a tidy tour. Given the very different nature of the English accents covered, you'll notice that while some varieties have long vowels in e.g. words such as *start*, others have short vowels (or even diphthongs) in the same environment. Nevertheless, it's worthwhile attempting the tour, since at the very least it will give some idea of the beautifully complex nature of English accents, and will provide us with further things to discuss.

9.3 A tour of long vowels

Let's begin, then, with the distribution of the high front vowel /i:/. Notice that many varieties have this vowel, or something very like it:

(4)   The vowel systems of varieties of English (adapted from Wells 1982): /i:/

	RP	London	Norwich	Bristol	Birmingham	Leeds	Scottish	Irish	GenAm
FLEECE	i:	ii	i:	i	i:	i:	i:	i:	i:

This table lacks much of the detail Wells adduces because I have simplified it very radically, merely for the purposes of clarity. However, even from this simplified table you'll see that many varieties of British English have /i:/, the exceptions being London (which has an incipient diphthong in words such as *fleece*, *beet* etc) and Bristol (which has a shortened variant of /i:/).

If we turn now to /u:/ (the vowel found in many varieties in words such as *moon* and *goose*) the distribution table looks like the following (and again, this is simplified):

(5)   The vowel systems of varieties of English (adapted from Wells 1982): /u:/

	RP	London	Norwich	Bristol	Birmingham	Leeds	Scottish	Irish	GenAm
GOOSE	u:	ʉ:	ʉ:	u	u:	u:	u	u:	u

Again, it looks as if /u:/ enjoys a wide distribution, the exceptions being London and Norwich. The symbol /ʉ:/ is Wells's own, and 'covers a considerable range of actual phonetic realizations' (1982, II: 307), including what is almost a diphthongal realisation of the *goose/boot* vowel in Cockney. In Scottish, too, what is elsewhere pronounced /u:/ is pronounced shorter – and, as Wells notes (1982, II: 401–2), may in many varieties of Scottish English be indistinguishable from the short vowel /ʊ/. Nevertheless, the /u:/ phoneme is relatively widespread, and even if a particular variety of English does not have that actual phoneme, it will indeed have a variant vowel phoneme in that position, one that will be aptly contrastive with other potential vowels in that variety.

Let's discuss something trickier. This is the back vowel phoneme that may (or in some varieties, may not) occur in a word such as *boat*. For speakers of many varieties of English the vowel that occurs in *boat, coat, hope* is not a 'pure' long vowel, but is a diphthong (indeed, it is a diphthong in my own variety). Yet for many other speakers of English these words contain a long vowel, one associated with Cardinal reference point 7 (a mid-high back vowel). In the following table, again adapted from Wells (1982), look carefully at the vowel recorded under 'Leeds, Scottish, Irish', noting also that whatever the vowel that occurs in the other columns it could in no case be described as a 'pure' vowel:

(6)   **The vowel systems of varieties of English (adapted from Wells 1982): /oː/**

	RP	London	Norwich	Bristol	Birmingham	Leeds	Scottish	Irish
GOAT	əʊ	ʌʊ	ʌʊ, uː, (ʊ)	ɔʊ	ʌʊ	oː	o	oː

Persisting for the moment with long back vowels, let's try to characterise the vowel associated with Cardinal position 6 – the mid-low slot. This vowel, which for many speakers would be the vowel heard in words such as *bored, core, thought* and *hall*, has a fairly wide distribution, as the following table shows:

(7)   **The vowel systems of varieties of English (adapted from Wells 1982): /ɔː/**

	RP	London	Norwich	Bristol	Birmingham	Leeds	Scottish	Irish	GenAm	NYC	Deep South	Australia	New Zealand
THOUGHT	ɔː	ɔː, ɔə	ɔː	ɔ	ɔː	ɔː	ɔ	ɔː	ɔ	ɔə	ɔ	ɔː	ɔː

Moving on to the lowest, most retracted long vowel, that associated with Cardinal position 5 – this is the vowel that for many speakers would occur in words such as *heart, calm* and *start* – we find again that the low back vowel phoneme is widely distributed, while for some speakers the vowel that occurs in these words isn't a low back vowel, but a low front one (/aː/), while for yet other speakers, those having *rhotic* accents (i.e. accents that have post-vocalic /r/ as part of their phonology), words such as *heart* and *start* are characteristically pronounced with short low front /a/+/r/:

(8)   **The vowel systems of varieties of English (adapted from Wells 1982): /ɑː/**

	RP	London	Norwich	Bristol	Birmingham	Leeds	Scottish	Irish	GenAm	NYC	Deep South	Australia	New Zealand
START	ɑː	ɑː	ɑː	ar	ɑː	aː	ar	aːr	ɑ(r)	ɑə(r), ɑr	ɑɾ~ɑː	aː	aː

Turning now to the set of long front vowels, those associated with Cardinal positions 4 through to 1, we've already seen that *some* speakers (e.g. those in Leeds or Australia) do have a long vowel in position 4 in words such as *start*:

137

(9)   The vowel systems of varieties of English
(adapted from Wells 1982): /aː/

	Leeds	Australia
START	aː	aː

But as (8) shows, many speakers of other accents have /ɑ:/ in this position, and in fact /a:/ isn't a part of their phonological inventories (it isn't part of my own, despite the fact that I was born less than twenty miles away from Leeds).

Then there are the two vowels in the system of possible long front vowels we haven't yet discussed, those in Cardinal positions 3 (mid-low, /ɛ:/) and 2 (mid-high, /e:/).

As far as Cardinal 3 goes, some speakers of non-rhotic accents have /ɛ:/ in words such as *square* and *fair*:

(10)   The vowel systems of varieties of English (adapted from Wells 1982): /ɛ:/

	RP	London	Norwich	Bristol	Birmingham	Leeds	Scottish	Irish	GenAm	NYC
SQUARE	ɛə	eə	ɛ:	ɛir	ɛ:	ɛ:	er	e:r	ɛ(r)	ɛə(r)

However, according to Wells (1982) *no* speaker of *any* variety of contemporary English has /e:/ as an unambiguous part of their underlying long-vowel phonology. That's surprising, given the fact that the back equivalent of /e:/ – that is /o:/ – *does* occur in some varieties. Further, /e:/ appears to occur in e.g. varieties of English Spoken in Leeds and parts of Ireland, although there it perhaps reflects a monophthongisation of the diphthong /eɪ/. Nevertheless, the absence of /e:/ in many varieties of contemporary Englishes appears merely to be an accidental gap, as it were. (Further, its absence in contemporary varieties of English doesn't mean that such a mid-high long vowel couldn't and didn't occur in historically prior varieties, as we'll see in the following chapter.)

That concludes, for the moment, our quick tour of long vowels in some varieties of present-day English. It's unlikely that your own variety of English has been entirely unrepresented, but don't worry if you haven't found an exact representation of your particular long-vowel phonology in this section of text. Your English, like mine, may well be full of gaps, inconsistencies and weirdnesses. For what it's worth, here are some features of my own long-vowel phonology that reflect some of the inconsistencies I mean:

Subject: 50-year-old white male, born Bradford, Yorkshire (1958)
Long-front-vowel phonology:
/iː/   *heed* etc
/e:/   doesn't occur

/ɛ:/ doesn't occur (in words such as *square*, subject has /ɛə/)

/a:/ doesn't occur

Long-back-vowel phonology:

/u:/ *moon* etc

/o:/ doesn't occur (in words such as *goat*, subject has /əʊ/)

/ɔ:/ *bought, taught, court* etc

/ɑ:/ *start, calm* etc

Long-mid-vowel phonology

/ɜ:/ *bird, heard, word* etc

On the face of it, an analyst might expect my own long-vowel phonology to be exactly the same as that of a speaker born in Leeds, a city a mere handful of miles down the road. But it's not the same: in words such as *square* I don't usually have a long vowel (/ɛ:/), but a diphthong (moreover, the same diphthong found in prestige varieties such as RP in the same environment, /ɛə/) – although I have the 'pure' long vowel in rapid speech. In words such as *start* I don't have /a:/, but the vowel /ɑ:/ (again, the same vowel found in the same environment in prestige varieties such as RP). And in words such as *boat* I have a diphthong (/əʊ/) – once more, a phoneme from a prestige variety – whereas a Leeds speaker would have monophthongal /o:/. On the other hand, the same analyst would instantly identify my vowel phonology (considered in toto) as belonging to someone from the north of England: in words such as *pet* and *head* I have /ɛ/ rather than prestige /e/, in words like *none* and *nothing* I have /ɒ/ rather than prestige /ʌ/. So my own vowel phonology is a strange but commonplace mix: it has some prestige features – these possibly reflect my schooling, and/or my exposure to other varieties of English, even my exposure to other languages – but it nevertheless has enough features of 'Northern British English' to be confidently classified as that, rather than as, say, a variety of South-western British English, or the English of Australia or New York City. My guess is that if you analyse the vowel system of your own speech you'll find similar features.

That last sentence contains an implicit invitation which this exercise makes explicit. Analyse your own long vowel phonology. First state your ethnicity, then your gender, then the year in which you were born. Second, and in those terms I've just sketched for my own long-vowel phonology, detail your own, paying particular attention to any apparent inconsistencies or gaps in that system. What does such an exercise tell you about your own phonology and its assumed prestige (or lack of it)? Why do the inconsistencies arise? Where do they come from?

As a supplementary exercise it's useful to compare your findings with those of at least two colleagues, one born in the same year as you and

> raised in the same geographical area, and one born earlier or later and raised elsewhere.
>
> If you find that many of your long vowels aren't in fact 'pure' long vowels at all, read the next two sections of text and then revisit this exercise.

9.4 Diphthongs, non-centring

As 9.2 suggests, diphthongs can be thought of as vocalic *glides* in which the tongue begins in one position and then glides (without any transitional phenomena occurring) to another position. An example would be our familiar diphthong /aɪ/ (*hide*, *find* etc), where the tongue begins in a low, relatively front position and glides upwards, ending in a high front position on /ɪ/.

It's traditional (and useful) to classify diphthongs into (i) a group of vocalic shapes whose tongue movement ends in a *non-central* position in the oral cavity, and (ii) a group of vocalic shapes whose tongue movement ends in a *central* position in the oral cavity. The first group are called, transparently, **non-centring diphthongs**, while the second group are called **centring diphthongs**.

Given the many positions theoretically available within the oral cavity, it's surprising (and interesting) that non-centring diphthongs usually glide to one of only two end points: they glide to the high front position associated with /ɪ/, or the high back position associated with /ʊ/. An example of a front-gliding, non-centring diphthong would be /aɪ/; an example of a back-gliding, non-centring diphthong would be /aʊ/, in many varieties occurring in words such as *house*, *now* and *loud*.

It would be entirely possible in this section of text to continue what we were doing in the last section, namely, comparing a tabular display of non-centring diphthong phonemes as these were attested as occurring in varieties of English in 1982. I'm not going to do that, largely because it's the *principles* I'd like to make clear in this section of text, rather than focussing on how non-centring diphthongs are represented in different varieties.

To begin the discussion, take the entire set of front vowels as we've discussed it so far. The entire set includes all the possible long front vowels, and all the possible short ones. You'll find there is a total of eight possibilities (four long, four short).

> It's a fact that theoretically possible diphthongs such as */eːɪ/ or */aːɪ/ *never* occur in *any* variety of contemporary English. Can you work out why not? (Clue: think syllable structure.)

The observation we need in order to answer the question is that long vowels already take up the maximum two X-slots available in the nucleus of the syllable, and there's no provision for somehow finding an extra slot for putative 'diphthongs'. Therefore, for *all* diphthongs, what seems to happen is that the diphthong is (and may if you wish be defined as) *a transitionless glide between two short vocalic segments*.

That narrows the possibilities in a principled way.

Consider those narrowed possibilities in terms of the front-vowel set. If the subset of non-centring diphthongs, i.e. those gliding to /ɪ/, is in question, what might these diphthongs be *in principle*? Since /ɪ/ can't be copied to itself (there are no 'diphthongs' of the form */ɪɪ/, though see 9.1 on the possibility of there being a monophthong of that kind), then the theoretical possibilities would cover mid-high /e/ (/eɪ/), mid-low /ɛ/ (/ɛɪ/) and low /a/ (/aɪ/).

The theoretically possible /eɪ/ and /ɛɪ/ would in fact be very difficult to hear as contrastive, and it's not altogether surprising that *no* variety of contemporary English has *both* diphthongs, though many have the non-centring diphthong /eɪ/, whereas others have /ɛɪ/. However, the contrast between /eɪ/ and /aɪ/ *is* easy to perceive, and it's no surprise that many varieties also have /aɪ/. Equally, many varieties have a non-centring diphthong that begins articulatory life in a relatively back position, on /ɔ/, and glides to /ɪ/. The following table – again, adapted and simplified from Wells (1982) – makes these distinctions clear. The table uses the test words *face, voice* and *price*:

(11) **Non-centring diphthongs of some varieties of English (1: front-gliding)**

	RP	London	Norwich	Bristol	Birmingham	Leeds	Scottish	Irish	GenAm
FACE	eɪ	ʌɪ	æi	ɛi	ʌɪ	eː ~ ɛɪ	e	eː	eɪ
PRICE	aɪ	ɑɪ	ʌi	ɑɪ	ɒɪ	aɪ	ae	aɪ	aɪ
VOICE	ɔɪ	ɔɪ	oi	ɔɪ	ɒɪ ~ oɪ	ɔɪ	ɒɪ	ɔɪ	ɔɪ

Notice that although London speakers tend to have /ʌɪ/ in *face* (a non-centring diphthong whose first segment is relatively low and back), and Norwich speakers have the same diphthong in *price* words, no variety – obviously enough – has the same diphthong in both *face* and *price* words. (In such a variety, the words *dace* – a kind of fish – and *dice* would be homophones … but no variety like that has apparently ever existed, precisely because one central principle of phonological distribution is to ensure that phonemes – particularly vowel phonemes – keep their distance from one another.)

We can use the same principles as we've just employed above to analyse the back-gliding, non-centring diphthongs, i.e. those ending up on /ʊ/. Non-centring diphthongs of the back-gliding type are found in many varieties, in words such as *house/mouth* and *goat*:

(12)   **Non-centring diphthongs of some varieties of English (2: back-gliding)**

	RP	London	Norwich	Bristol	Birmingham	Leeds	Scottish	Irish	GenAm
GOAT	əʊ	ʌʊ	ʌʊ, uː,	ɔʊ	ʌʊ	oː	o	oː	o
MOUTH	aʊ	æʊ	æʉ	aʊ	æʊ	aʊ	ʌʊ	aʊ	aʊ

That nets us (at least) five non-centring diphthongs, distributed contrastively. The list below shows those non-centring diphthongs I have in my own variety:

(13)   **Non-centring diphthongs, front- and back-gliding**
A specimen distribution from Northern British English (50-year-old white male from Bradford):

/aɪ/	*price, child, fight*
/eɪ/	*fade, rate, stay*
/ɔɪ/	*boy, voice, toil*
/aʊ/	*house, now, found*
/əʊ/	*boat, load, though*

9.5 Diphthongs, centring

The second group of diphthongs whose existence we noted above is the group of *centring* diphthongs, those whose glides end up in mid-central position, at /ə/. There are a number of theoretically possible candidates, but in fact some varieties of English don't have *any* centring diphthongs (see below). This is particularly the case with varieties that have post-vocalic /r/ – a matter that will be touched on in the next section of this chapter, and further explored in chapters 10 and 11. The prestige, but now old-fashioned, variety of British English known as RP, though, has *three* centring diphthongs:

/ɪə/	*beard, Ian*
/eə/ (or /ɛə/)	*air, square*
/ʊə/	*poor, cure, tour*

The pattern of distribution is particularly messy. Some present-generation speakers of modified RP have /ɪə/ in *beard* but the long vowel /ɔ:/ in *cure*, while some speakers of Leeds English may have /ɪə/ in *near, beard* but /ɛ:/ in *air, square*.

If you look at the words associated with these diphthongs you'll notice that all of them – with the exception of the proper name *Ian* – contain <r>. That might give us a clue as to why the presence and distribution of centring diphthongs seems so messy across the varieties of English. For example, study the following table, which details a relevant subpart of the phonology of Irish English, GA and NYC vowels. Notice that Irish English is a variety that has no centring diphthongs at all – but interestingly, it does certainly have words containing long vowels (in the syllabic nucleus) followed by /r/ (in the coda). GA has *short* vowels in words such as *near*, *square*, but that short vowel is followed by /r/ in prestige varieties of that accent. And NYC English has a whole range of centring diphthongs, which may (= prestige) or may not (= non-prestige) be followed by post-vocalic /r/.

(14) 'Centring diphthongs' in some non-RP varieties of English (table adapted from Wells 1982)

Irish	GenAm	NYC
iːr	ɪ(r)	ɪə(r)
eːr	ɛ(r)	ə(r)
aːr	ɑ(r)	ɑə(r), ɑ(r)
ɔːr	ɔ(r)	ɔə(r)
oːr	ɔ(r)	ɔə(r)
uːr	ʊ(r)	ʊə(r)

As we've noted before, varieties of English which have /r/ after a vowel – *post-vocalic /r/* – are called *rhotic accents*. Such accents include Irish Englishes, varieties of SW British English, many prestige types of American Englishes, and Scottish English. For all these accents, /r/ is distributed not only in syllabic onsets, but also in syllabic codas. On the other hand, there are many other varieties of English, including RP, Northern English varieties and Antipodean Englishes, where /r/ does not *appear* to be allowed to occur in syllabic codas after vowels. Such accents would be described as *non-rhotic*.

There's an interesting set of problems associated with the simple distinction between rhotic and non-rhotic accents, and they are essentially problems of a phonological nature, concerning *underlying representation*. Although we're going to look at these problems in more detail in the following chapter, and in chapter 11, I'd like to begin to think about the problems now by asking some leading questions:

For speakers of *non-rhotic* accents, a seemingly plausible transcription of the monosyllable *fear* would be /fɪə/, with a non-centring diphthong. However, consider the following words and phrases and insert the relevant phonemic transcriptions in the fourth column, noting particularly carefully what may (or may not) happen with /r/ in each case:

Word	Transcription	Phrase	Transcription
fear	/fɪə/	*fear is*	…

143

near	/nɪə/	*near enough*	...
air	/eə/	*air is*	...

> For speakers of *non-rhotic* accents, what arguments might you find for suggesting that the *underlying* structure of e.g. *fear* could very well be /fɪər/, that for *near* /nɪər/, and that for *air* /eər/?

9.6 A note on triphthongs

The questions we've just posed also bear on another, highly complex kind of vowel that appears to be part of the phonology of many non-rhotic accents. Roach (1991: 23), for example, notes the existence of *triphthongs* in some varieties, notably RP. 'A triphthong', he writes, 'is a glide from one vowel to another and then to a third, all produced rapidly and without interruption' (1991: 23). Triphthongs of this kind *always* appear to end in schwa, and can be thought of as 'diphthongs gliding to schwa'. The examples Roach adduces are the following:

(15) **Triphthongs**

/eɪ+ə/	Example: *player*
/aɪ+ə/	Example: *fire, liar*
/ɔɪ+ə/	Example: *loyal, royal*
/əʊ+ə/	Example: *lower, mower*
/aʊ+ə/	Example: *hour, power*

Triphthongs are difficult to analyse, largely because their presence in any speaker's phonology can be difficult to recognise, is the subject of much apparently random variation, and is also subject to changes in speech tempo. For example, in slow, emphatic speech a word such as *loyal* might very well be pronounced with a glide (/j/) between the two syllables, while in rapid speech a syllable such as *hour* might well be pronounced with a diphthong (or even a 'pure' long vowel).

Nevertheless, the existence of triphthongs is interesting when considered in the light of those questions we posed at the end of the last section of text. Notice, for instance, that all the examples above, with the exception of *loyal, royal*, have <r> in their final (or only) syllables. Let's therefore end this note, and indeed this chapter, on a final question:

> What evidence could you find to support the view that the underlying representation of e.g. *fire* in a *non-rhotic* accent could better be analysed as /faɪr/ than /faɪə/?

Exercises

Exercise 9a This exercise is designed to help you recognise and transcribe diphthongs. Many students have particular difficulty with recognising and transcribing the diphthong /əʊ/, which in some varieties occurs in words such as *lone*, *boat* etc. The difficulty seems to be that having learned that the symbol for schwa is very often associated with unstressed vowels, there seems to be a reluctance to use the same symbol as the starting point for a diphthongal glide that may be found centrally in a stressed syllable.

The exercise is simple. Make a phonemic transcription of the following words as they occur in your own phonology. (Note: even if some of these words don't contain diphthongs in your variety, some will, and you should transcribe all of them anyway.)

boat	bite	bait	owl	airless
lonely	biting	baling	housing	hours
hopeless	boating	boiling	airing	royalty

Exercise 9b During the course of your progress through this book you've studied consonants and their distribution, syllable structure, and just completed two chapters' worth of work on vowels. It's time, therefore, to attempt some lengthier pieces of transcription. The following passage, which you should try to transcribe phonemically (in a transcription which captures the phonology of your own variety of English), is the beginning of a famous test passage given in four varieties of transcription in the pamphlet *The principles of the International Phonetic Association*:

The north wind and the sun were disputing which was the stronger, when a traveller came along wrapped in a warm cloak. They agreed that the one who first succeeded in making the traveller take his cloak off should be considered stronger than the other.

Make a note of any problems you encounter as you construct your phonemic transcription.

Exercise 9c Here is a continuation of the passage found in exercise 9b. I have transcribed the beginning of the next sentence of the passage in my own English. Your task is twofold: (i) read the transcription and rewrite it in 'normal' English; (ii) state what features of the transcription would allow you to identify the speaker as using a variety of Northern British English:

/ðɛn ðə nɔ:θ wɪnd blu: əz hɑ:d əz hi: kʊd bət ðə mɔ: hi: blu: ðə mɔ: kləʊslɪ dɪd ðə travlə fəʊld hɪz kləʊk əraʊnd hɪm/

Exercise 9d   We noted that some analysts propose that there are triphthongs in some varieties of English. One of Roach's examples is the word *liar*, for which he proposes the transcription /laɪə/ (for speakers of non-rhotic accents). The question I'd like to pose is twofold: (i) is *liar* a monosyllable? and (ii) if it is a monosyllable, what would its syllabic representation be?

Exercise 9e   In my own variety of English I have the following 'pure' long vowels: /iː/, /uː/, /ɔː/, /ɑː/ and /ɜː/. Sporadically, too (and particularly in rapid speech), I have /ɛː/ (in words such as *air*).

Try to establish the inventory of your own system of long vowels. (You will know exactly how to do this if you follow the diagnostic procedures we've used throughout this book.) It may look very similar to the one I've just outlined (which would be a commonplace inventory of long vowels for many speakers of British English) – but it might also be interestingly different.

Exercise 9f   This exercise is designed to reveal not so much the long vowel phonemes of your own variety of English, but a *range* of possible long vowels as these *might* occur in the phonology of other varieties of English, and indeed of other languages.

(i)   Pronounce and hold the vowel /iː/. Keeping your tongue height constant, begin to round your lips. What quality of vowel is produced?
(ii)   Do the same as in (i), but this time begin with the vowel /eː/.
(iii)   Do the same as in (i), but this time begin with the vowel /ɛː/.

Exercise 9g   The (no doubt slightly strangled-sounding) vowels you started to produce in the last exercise *can* function as English phonemes and, more certainly, they can and do function as part of the phonology of other languages. The lip-rounded version of /iː/, for instance, can be symbolised as /yː/ (and is part of the phonology of present-day Dutch, French, and other languages). The lip-rounded version of /eː/ can be symbolised as /øː/ (and is part of the phonology of French). And so on. In fact, whole pairs and sets of vowels can be produced by either *beginning to round* (*or retract*) front vowels, or *beginning to unround* (*or front*) back ones. In addition, high vowels might lower, low vowels might raise. In fact, part of the history of English phonology can be told by observing and reconstructing similar movements: originally back vowels start to front, high vowels begin to diphthongise, unrounded vowels acquire rounding, and so on. We'll be looking at a tiny part of that history in chapter 11, but for the moment, study the vowel trapezium in the IPA chart in the appendix (p. 212). You're not expected to learn all the vowel symbols in it, but the diagram itself will give you a further idea of the *range of possible variation* there is. In the diagram you will of course find the familiar Cardinal reference points, and you'll also find the symbols for the vowels you produced when you rounded (and retracted) /iː/, /eː/ and /ɛː/.

Key terms introduced in this chapter
centring diphthong
non-centring diphthong
triphthong

Further reading
Roach, Peter. 1991. *English phonetics and phonology*. 2nd edition. Cambridge University Press. Chapter 3.

CHAPTER 10

Vowels (3): variation

In this chapter …

In the last chapter, and as part of some formal work we completed on the representation and transcription of long vowels, we began to notice some details of the present-day variation that exists in the system of English long vowels. In this chapter we're going to say more about variation, and put 'variation' into a conceptual framework that will allow us to distinguish present-day variation (which we'll call *synchronic variation*) from those variations that seem clearly to be the products of historical change (*diachronic variation*). Although this isn't a book about diachronic phonology, we'll see that *any* account of synchronic phonology would do well to be aware of the history that underlies the system. (Further, many students simply are curious about, and like to know, how and perhaps even why their own phonology took shape in the way it did.) In terms of diachronic phonology we can't do everything in a book of this kind, of course, but we can analyse key processes and structures which play large parts in any reconstruction of how phonological systems evolve. Those processes and features we'll look at here are *splits* and *mergers* (10.2) together with *vowel (a)symmetries* (10.3). In 10.3 we'll begin to say something about what many handbooks on the history of English call the *Great Vowel Shift*, and will also notice that the concepts of *symmetry* and (chain-)*shift* might usefully be invoked in the context of analysing one recent synchronic change in RP (from /æ/ to /a/ in words such as *cat*) – see section 10.4. To conclude this chapter, we're going to return briefly to two topics we introduced, but didn't fully analyse, in chapters 8 and 9: the topic of word-final /ɪ/ (or /i/, or /iː/), as in words such as *happy*, which we'll look at in 10.5 with special reference to Northern varieties; and the topic of *rhoticity*, which we noted in chapter 9 and which will reappear here in 10.6.

10.1 Variation: synchrony and diachrony

The diagrams we've used to stylise where vowel phonemes are articulated, and the terminology we've developed to discuss vowel phonemes, certainly reveal the extent of the variations involved when vowel systems are analysed, and the last two chapters have given you some insight into what entities like 'long' and 'short' vowels are, and reveal how symmetrical or asymmetrical vowel systems may be. They have also given you some diagnostic tools by means of which you'll now be able confidently to classify a particular vowel as *front* or *back*, *high* or *low* and so on.

From another point of view, though, the work we've done in the preceding two chapters is unsatisfactory. For instance, we've observed that there is *variation* across the accents of contemporary English, but we've said nothing so far about *where such variation comes from*. This last matter is often of great interest to students beginning to analyse sound structure: '*Why* is his/her accent different from mine?'; '*Why* do I say [baθ] while she says [bɑːθ]?'; '*Why* was *house* once pronounced [huːs]?'; '*Why* is *house* still pronounced [huːs] in some parts of Scotland?'; '*Why* do so many Canadians say [əbəʊt] for *about* (/əbaʊt/)?' and so forth.

The answers to these questions are often more complicated (and interesting) than the enquirer might imagine. As a first step on the way to answering such questions, it's necessary to say something general about how linguistic systems work (or are perceived to work).

When we analyse our own language, or start to analyse the variations in our own speech, we're essentially unaware of the *history* that has brought that language, and many of its variations, into being. For example, somewhere in your exposure to English you, like me, learned that 'the plural of *foot* is *feet*'. You also realised that changing the vowel of the root of a word was a fairly unusual way of making plurals. The normative way of forming plurals in present-day English is 'to add an *s*' (or, more properly, to add /s/, /z/ or /ɪz/ depending on the nature of any preceding consonant!). Since you learned early on the 'add an *s*' method of pluralising nouns, then you, again like me, probably made the mistake of using **foots* and, if you were lucky, someone would correct you ('It's not *foots*, it's *feet*.').

You added the *foot–feet* alternation to your knowledge of the English you speak, and probably didn't think about it further. What you weren't aware of, and probably what nobody told you, is that this alternation is a product of linguistic *history*. 1500 years ago, in fact, there was an entire group of nouns which formed their plurals quite regularly in this way. This group included words such as *book* (whose plural 1500 years ago would have been spelled <bēc> and would have sounded something like /beːʧ/).

This group of nouns wasn't arrived at *accidentally* (it is itself a product of linguistic history), nor did the relevant vowel alternation take place *randomly*. As time progressed, however, so powerful (regular, transferable, generalisable, easy to learn ...) was the 'add an *s*' method of forming English plurals that many of the nouns which had previously formed their plurals by vowel alternation began to pattern with all the other 'add an *s*' nouns. *Book* is a good example of such a noun: its present-day English plural is invariably *book+s*. However, *foot* did *not* begin to pattern with the 'add an *s*' group. It didn't participate in the widespread analogical reformation that was going on. It got left behind, as it were, by historical change. Today, we say (if we think about it at all), '*foot–feet* is an exception'. And indeed, *today*, it is. But it was not in any way 'an exception' 1500 years ago. On the contrary, it behaved quite regularly with respect to its plural formation.

The crucial point is that when a speaker of English in the twenty-first century learns the *foot–feet* alternation, he or she is usually entirely unaware of the history that caused this alternation in the first place. Nevertheless, the fact that such alternation has (in the case of *foot–feet*) to be *learned* is one token of the utter unavoidability of linguistic history. History speaks into the present. It's almost impossible to understand some aspects of the linguistic present – including variation across English accents – without knowing something about the linguistic past. Equally, studying the linguistic present sometimes can give us vital clues as to what was going on in the linguistic past.

Think of your own linguistic awareness. It comprises your use of your own language; your knowledge of other varieties of English (and you'll be exposed to dozens of such varieties every day); your awareness of what is a *prestige* use of language and what is not; your knowledge of appropriacy, of register, of genre, of other languages ... and much else besides.

All this knowledge, and all your use of that knowledge, takes place within a particular slice of time that is coextensive with your lifetime – a three-generational slice (around 75 years, if we take 'one generation' to span 25 years). Linguists call such knowledge **synchronic**. When we study language *synchronically* we study the structures of a particular variety of a particular language as these are manifest at *one particular time*. (Notice that it's not just the present-day slice of time that can or should be studied. It's perfectly possible to analyse the structures of, say, early eleventh century late West Saxon *synchronically*. Similarly, it's entirely possible to study your particular variety of English *as its structures have been manifest in the past five years*. This, too, would be a synchronic study.)

As we've established above, though, any variety of English has a *history*. Some linguists use a metaphor to describe that history, and claim that varieties of English *evolved*. 'Linguistic evolution' must, obviously, take place in time, and often over rather long stretches of time. When linguists study languages and varieties of language as these evolve over time, and start to reconstruct *how* and *why* linguistic change takes place as it seems to, then they're studying language **diachrony**.

It's difficult to reconstruct the linguistic history that lies behind your deployment of the structures of your own variety of English, although we'll be doing some work later in this chapter that will make some aspects of that history manifest. On the other hand, there are two exercises you can do which can reveal something of the *synchronic* pressures on your own English. These pressures can lead to variation, even within your own accent.

First, get hold of a dictaphone or other recording device and record a stretch of your own connected speech. It helps if you record yourself in two different situations, e.g. reading aloud, then in informal conversation. Listen to the playback. (It's customary to be nervously self-conscious, even horrified, at this stage.) Is your accent what you think it is? If it is, how would you characterise that accent, and why? If your accent is different from what you think it is, what are the principal differences? (My hunch would be that the answer to this last question will focus on, but need not be entirely restricted to, your implementation of long vowels.)

Second, consider the synchronic pressures on your phonology. The easiest way to reveal those pressures is again to record yourself speaking in two different linguistic environments, the one formal, the other informal. How does your accent differ in each environment? (*Does* it differ?) If it does differ, why might that be?

Since many students find the distinction between synchrony and diachrony hard to grasp, it's worthwhile spending a moment longer on the topic. Below, you'll find a diagram. This diagram has been adapted from a similar figure found in Saussure (1983: 80), who was the first to make the distinction between the terms and ideas *synchronic* and *diachronic* clear and systematic.

The ellipse in the diagram represents you, as you are as a language user at this moment. This area represents not only all you implicitly or explicitly know about your own variety of English, but also all the ways in which you actualise that knowledge. The solid lines within the figure represent two different things: the horizontal line represents what you actually *do*, as a speaker of English; the vertical line represents your own *linguistic history* ('what you have actually *done*').

The two axes on the diagram, therefore, represent *synchrony* (horizontal) and *diachrony* (vertical) respectively. The ellipse – you – represents their moment of intersection.

Lying behind you in history, however, are all the structures of the entire history of English. Had these structures not existed in the way they did exist then you would not be able to use English in the way you do. Therefore we might represent that history with a continuation of a solid line which points backwards in time.

Lying in front of you, as it were, is your linguistic future. Since this future hasn't happened yet, we can represent it with a dotted line, a continuation of your own (and the language's) history. Lying around you, as it were, is not only your own synchrony but all the other synchronies of all the other users of English with whom you intersect. We can represent these other synchronies by extending the solid line on the horizontal axis into dotted continuations.

(1)   **Synchrony** and **diachrony**

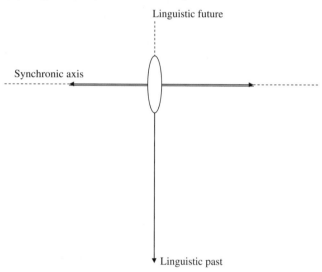

On the synchronic axis lie all the linguistic pressures that bear on you, the language user, at this moment. These pressures include things like prestige, appropriacy, 'correctness', and many others. These can be thought of as a set of simultaneous *states*.

On the diachronic axis lie all the changes that have taken place in the English language that underlie your present synchrony. These can be thought of as a set of *processes*.

- Linguistic synchrony, therefore, can be thought of as the analysis of simultaneous *states*, whether these states exist in the early twenty-first century or, say, in the early eleventh.
- Linguistic diachrony, therefore, can be thought of as a reconstruction of those successive *processes* by which language gradually evolves.

As far as the sound structure of English is concerned, then it wouldn't be too much of a simplification to say that you, like me, inherit and deploy a phonological system filled with what the linguist Roger Lass has vividly called 'the debris left behind by historical change' (1984: 36).

The word 'debris' suggests that when languages change, those changes are very seldom wholesale (languages don't change overnight), and further implies that language change can be messy and rarely seems to 'know where it's going' (language change isn't *teleological*). Language change, that is, seems to happen to discrete subparts of the total linguistic system, which changes then seem to have a greater or lesser impact on the system as a whole. Saussure made the same point: '[T]he language system *as such* [my italics: McC] is never directly altered. It is in itself unchangeable. Only certain elements change, but without regard to the connexions which integrate them as part of the whole. It is as if one of the planets circling the sun underwent a change of dimensions and weight: this isolated event would have general consequences for the whole solar system, and disturb its equilibrium' (1983: 84).

In the next two sections of this chapter we're going to look at two kinds of change to the system of English vowels as this system is considered as a set of successive *processes*. The analysis that follows is therefore *diachronic*. It will help to explain some (though of course by no means all) of the variation encountered in the synchronic vowel systems of present-day varieties of English.

It's helpful at this point to introduce ourselves to the *general character* of many diachronic changes in sound systems. Some of the changes are instances of **phonemic splits**, some are instances of **phonemic mergers**, and others are examples of **gap-filling**. These notions are going to be important in what follows.

10.2 Historical variation in short vowel systems: splits and mergers

We saw that there's a particular kind of variation in present-day Englishes which concerns the vowels different varieties have in words such as *bath*, *grass* and *path*. So far we've only noted the existence of this variation. We haven't yet explained it. Let's attempt that explanation now.

One of the major diagnostics of the difference between very broadly 'Northern' and equally broadly 'Southern' varieties of the English still spoken within the UK is the variation between Northern [a] and Southern [ɑ:]. In terms of the geography involved, many speakers born north of a line running roughly from the Wash (in the east) to Hereford (in the west) have the short vowel [a] in *grass*, *bath*, *chaff*, while many speakers born south of that boundary have [ɑ:] (see Wakelin 1977: 87).

One interesting fact about this variation is that it developed relatively recently. In the Middle English phase of the evolution of the language, for instance, that variation simply didn't seem to exist: *all* speakers of English had some low front short vowel – pronounced either [a] or [æ] – in words such as *grass, chaff* and *path* as well as in words such as *cat, ham* and *lash*. Speakers of Northern British English *retained* that vowel, while speakers of Southern British English *retained it* **except** *in words such as* grass, path *and* chaff.

What do the words *grass, path* and *chaff* have in common, in terms of their phonology?

In each case, an originally short vowel, associated with the nucleus of a stressed syllable, is followed by the single consonant /s/, /f/ or /θ/. That last piece of information is an important clue: the consonants whose symbols we've just given *are all voiceless fricatives*.

It looks, then, as if speakers of Southern British English were deploying a particular kind of change: where original /a/ was followed by a voiceless fricative in the coda of a stressed syllable, then it had the variant [ɑː]. Using the terminology we developed in the first three chapters of this book, we could perhaps say that at this stage, [ɑː] might be analysed an *allophone* of underlying /a/, since it had a particular environment reserved for it. Where that environment wasn't provided, then of course Southern British English speakers continued to use the short vowel [a] (in words such as *cat, ham, bad*).

The chronology of this change is somewhat uncertain, but it seems as if the change was underway by the eighteenth century and complete by the nineteenth (Wakelin 1977: 86; Wells 1982: 232). Significantly, speakers of GA or Antipodean Englishes do *not* have the same variation: this was a change that seemed to take place only within the geographical boundaries of the British Isles.

From our point of view the very significant thing is that we *may* be looking at an example of a **phonemic split**. In such splits, a single, historically prior phoneme develops two allophones. Thereafter, each of the two allophones becomes a phoneme in its own right.

A graphic illustration of phonemic split can be found in e.g. Lass (1984: 318), and we could certainly adapt that diagram to illustrate the apparent facts we've sketched in the preceding paragraphs:

(2)   **Phonemic splits (I):** *grass, path, chaff*

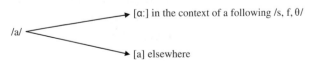

/a/ → [ɑː] in the context of a following /s, f, θ/

/a/ → [a] elsewhere

Once this split is accomplished, then the respective allophones *may* become phonemes in their own right. On the other hand, if they *do* become phonemes then there's also the theoretical possibility that the 'new' phonemes might *merge* with vowel phonemes that already exist. (We'll discuss that notion below.)

One problem with introducing the notion of *phonemic split* like this is that at present it seems to be merely a one-off piece of explanation designed to explain what is merely a one-off piece of phonological change. To give a more valid character to the notion of phonemic split we'd have to enquire whether there's evidence for such splits elsewhere in the evolution of the sound structure of English.

Fortunately, there's plenty of such evidence available to us. One such classic split can in fact be found in the evolution of the *consonant* system of English.

Consider the following data, and suggest what had occurred, in terms of **phonemic split, to account for the present-day English spellings. Words are given in their *alphabetic* forms, but in each line of example I have indicated which present-day consonant needs some kind of explanation, and this last I have transcribed phonemically.**

Old English (OE)	Present-day English	
fæder	*father*	/f/
fæst	*fast ('firm, fixed')*	/f/
æfter	*after*	/f/
clif	*cliff*	/f/
heofon	*heaven*	/v/
seolfor	*silver*	/v/

Even these very limited data suggest that in OE there was *one* phoneme /f/ which had *two allophones*, respectively [f] and [v]. [f] seems to have occurred syllable-initially and -finally, but the exclusive place reserved for the allophone [v] seems to have been the position *between two voiced phonemes*, as attested by the examples *heofon* and *seolfor*. Here, in a 'voiced' environment, /f/ turns up as the allophone [v].

So /f/ *splits*, and is now associated with *two allophones*. Eventually, those two allophones become phonemes in their own right. If and when they do so, then of course those writing in English will feel a new pressure to represent the now-distinct new phonemes graphically. That seems to happen during the thirteenth and fourteenth centuries (Strang 1970: 227–8). The letter shape <v> is then introduced – but it is a Continental innovation, and is by no means 'native' to the early English alphabets. (An Anglo-Saxon scribe would have

155

had no idea what such a written symbol might mean. For such a person, the *phonemic pair* /f/ and /v/ simply didn't exist – only /f/ did – and therefore there wasn't a phonemic distinction that needed to be captured in alphabetic terms.)

There is good evidence, then, that phonemic splits do indeed take place. In terms of the [a] – [ɑ:] distinction in some present-day English accents, though – *is* this in fact an example of a 'split'?

It would definitely be a split *if* two entirely new phonemes had been created, and *if* that split was the *sole* source of the new phonemes in question. However, the picture is complicated by a further phonemic change, and by chronology.

Present-day English /ɑ:/ has more than one source. The [a] – [ɑ:] split is indeed one of them, but further sets of words provide evidence for yet other sources of /ɑ:/. For instance, speakers of several present-day varieties have /ɑ:/ in words such as *palm, calm, alm* as well as in *arm farm, art.*

If /ɑ:/ evolves in e.g. the *palm, calm* words before it evolves in the *grass, path* words, then clearly the /ɑ:/ developed in that last change must **merge** with the /ɑ:/ that already existed as a result of the changes to the *palm, calm* set.

Does this happen? 'Insofar as it occurs in native English words,' writes Wells (1982: 143), 'the PALM vowel derives from Middle English /au/ or /a/ with lengthening. The lengthening is essentially the same as that in BATH words ... '

That doesn't help us much in terms of chronology. However, we do know from Wells and other reliable commentators that the *bath* split was taking place through the eighteenth century. If the development of /ɑ:/ in *palm* preceded the *bath* split, then the *bath* split would have the character of *both* a split *and* a merger, since the /ɑ:/ yielded as a result of the *bath* split would merge with the *palm* vowel.

Strang (1970: 111) suggests that the Middle English diphthong /aʊ/ was becoming a monophthong during the sixteenth–seventeenth centuries. Since /aʊ/ was one of the sources of the vowel in *palm* words (see above), then tentatively we could suggest that the *palm* words were developing a pronunciation in /ɑ:/ *before* the *bath* words developed their own phoneme /ɑ:/. If we're right, then the *grass, bath* developments begin life as a **split**, but subsequently acquire the character of a **merger**. What we are left with, as a relic of the historical process, are two new vowel phonemes, /a/ and /ɑ:/ – consider the minimal pair which for many speakers of British English obtains in the words *pat* and *part.*

Let's conclude this section by looking at another split. This is the split that occurs in *strut* words. It's well attested that speakers of southern varieties of British English have the phoneme /ʌ/ in words like *strut, butt* and *lump,* whereas speakers of many northern varieties have /ʊ/ in the same words. However, speakers of those southern English varieties who have /ʌ/ in *strut, cut, butt* and *lump* do have the phoneme /ʊ/ in words such as *bush* and *put.* The usual observation is that speakers of northern varieties of English do not have a /ʊ/ – /ʌ/ split, whereas speakers of southern varieties do. The geographical limits of the non-split varieties have a southern boundary that runs from the Severn in the west to the Wash in the east (see Wakelin 1977: 87 and Wells 1982: 351 for the relevant details).

Where and how does this split originate? It is definitely, of course, a split: these days, speakers of southern varieties have two distinct phonemes in words such as *put* and *putt* (a handy minimal pair).

In the Middle English phase of the development of English, *all* accents appear to have had the phoneme /ʊ/ in words such as *bush* and *put*. Northern English varieties – particularly what Wells calls 'more local, less overtly prestigious' varieties of Northern English (1982: 351) – simply retain the original phoneme. In southern varieties, however, a completely new phoneme /ʌ/ was introduced. This is strange, because the introduction of a new vowel phoneme into an already existing system and set of contrasts is relatively rare (Strang 1970: 112 calls the introduction of /ʌ/ 'one of the most unaccountable things that has happened in the history of English').

What seems to have happened is that original /ʊ/ lost its lip-rounding and started to drift downwards. This change didn't happen in all words: speakers of varieties which today have the /ʌ/ – /ʊ/ split retain the old phoneme in words such as *bush*, *bull*, *push*, *put*, *pull*.

> **Can you work out the environment which might suggest how and why /ʊ/ was retained in words such as *bush* and *pull*, but drifted to /ʌ/ in words such as *cut* and *strut*?**

The answer seems to be that in southern varieties /ʊ/ unrounded and usually drifted towards /ʌ/, *except where it was preceded by a bilabial consonant* (such as /b/ or /p/). That observation would help to account for the fact that speakers of southern British Englishes typically have /bʊʃ/ 'bush' alongside e.g. /nʌt/ 'nut'.

This in turn suggests that the relevant split has a similar character to the /a/ – /ɑ:/ split, and begins by the development of an allophone:

(3) **Phonemic splits (II): *bush* and *cut***

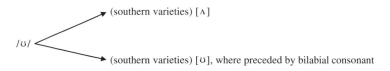

In the early twenty-first century, in southern varieties, /ʊ/ and /ʌ/ have become discrete vowel phonemes, but it also seems as if the wandering behaviour of /ʌ/ is not yet complete (words pronounced with /ʌ/ are still subject to great speaker-specific variation) and, furthermore, even those accents that might be expected to retain original /ʊ/ are subject to pressures from prestige accents which may result in either the development of a vowel phoneme distinct from either /ʊ/ or /ʌ/ (see Wells 1982: 352), or in **hypercorrection**, as in the spontaneous pronunciation of [ʃʌgə] for 'sugar'.

10.3 Historical variation in long vowel systems: vowel (a)symmetries

Turning now to long vowels, there is one much studied, and still controversial, set of changes which seems radically to have affected the system of English long vowels and diphthongs over a period of around 400 years, beginning (in traditional terms) around the first decades of the fifteenth century. This spectacular set of changes is somewhat quaintly known as the *Great Vowel Shift* (GVS).

There are two helpful pieces of information that can help us to reconstruct the GVS. The first is a vowel trapezium which stylises the long vowel system of Chaucer's London English, as this might have been spoken in the last decades of the fourteenth century (thus before the GVS took place). Barber (1993) and many other scholars have analysed Chaucer's long-vowel system as follows:

(4)   **The long-vowel system of Chaucer's London English, late fourteenth century**

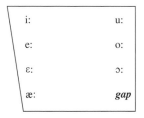

Notice how *symmetrical* this system is – four long front vowels and three back ones. There's a significant gap in the system, though, in position 5, the low back position. This gap is eventually filled (speakers now have /ɑː/ in words such as *aunt*, *palm* and *farm*, whereas Chaucer and his contemporaries apparently did not).

The point about *symmetry* might be a hint as to how vowels behave when one vowel starts, for whatever reason, to drift. Suppose, for example, that the vowel /uː/ for some reason (any reason!) begins to diphthongise. Such a diphthongisation would leave a gap in position 8, the high back slot. In order to maintain the contrasts on which such a vowel system depends, the natural tendency would be to *fill the gap* by allowing the nearest adjacent long vowel phoneme to move into it. The nearest adjacent vowel phoneme would in this instance be /o:/. And once /o:/ had raised to fill the gap left by the diphthongisation of /u:/, then of course there'd be another gap left by the raising of /o:/ … which in turn might be filled by the raising of the nearest vowel phoneme adjacent to /o:/, which in this instance would be /ɔ:/. That is, given a relatively symmetrical system of long vowels, change in one term of the system *is likely to result in a chain reaction which will cause all the other long vowels in the system to change in quality too,* **in order to maintain the phonemic contrasts on which the system depends**.

The second piece of helpful information is less theoretical, and allows us to align the vowel phonemes of the diagram in (4) with actual data. Interestingly, the *spellings* of the words from Chaucer's London English contain good clues as to the fourteenth-century pronunciation of the words in question. When Chaucer and his contemporaries spell the word *green*, for example, as <grene>, <greene> or <green>, the spellings seem to be an attempt to capture the fact that at that time the relevant vowel was pronounced as [e:]. Similarly, when these same writers spell e.g. *moon* as <mone>, <moone> or <moon>, then those spellings strongly suggest that the vowel of this word was pronounced as [o:]. Since Chaucer and his contemporaries were writing at a time when there was no national written standard, then it's entirely reasonable to suppose that people attempted as far as possible *to spell as they thought they spoke*. Such spelling evidence is, then, a vital clue to the historical pronunciation of varieties of English.

With that in mind, let's explore some evidence. What follows is a table of words and spellings. Against each word I have given the present-day spelling together with Chaucer's pronunciation, Shakespeare's pronunciation (London/SE Midlands, late sixteenth century), and that in relatively standard varieties of today:[1]

(5)	Spellings and underlying forms, GVS			
	Spellings		**Underlying forms**	
	ME	Modern	Chaucer[1]	Shakespeare	PDE ('standard' varieties)
	bite	bite	/bi:t/	/bəɪt/	/baɪt/
	bete	beet (sugar beet)	/be:t/	/bi:t/	/bi:t/
	bete	beat	/bɛ:t/	/be:t/	/bi:t/
	abate	abate	/əba:t/	/əbɛ:t/	/əbeɪt/
	foul	foul	/fu:l/	/fəʊl/	/faʊl/
	fol	fool	/fo:l/	/fu:l/	/fu:l/
	fole	foal	/fɔ:l/	/fo:l/	/fəʊl/

> Using the table in (5) above, and the diagram in (4), try to reconstruct
> where and how the long vowels changed in quality during the GVS.
> For instance, it seems the long vowel associated with position 1, /iː/,
> began to diphthongise, having the quality /əɪ/ in Shakespeare's English.
> Accordingly, and in terms of what we've been discussing in this section, it
> seems likely that the nearest adjacent long vowel would change in
> quality, filling the gap left by the diphthongisation of /iː/. Does this
> happen? And if that does happen, what is its consequence likely to be?
> Does something similar appear to occur in the set of back vowels?

The answer seems to be that we are indeed looking at a 400-year set of qualitative changes – a set of chain reactions. Once /iː/ begins to diphthongise, then /eː/ raises to fill the gap (*green* – /eː/ > /iː/, though today's *spelling*, the alphabetic form <green>, is based on the old quality of the vowel). And once /eː/ raises, /ɛː/ is also likely to raise, again to fill the gap left by /eː/ (*beat* – /ɛː/ > /eː/ in Shakespeare's English). And once /ɛː/ has raised, then once again, the nearest adjacent vowel – here represented as /aː/, though in some varieties of ME it will already have had the quality /æː/ – will raise to fill the gap left by /ɛː/ (*abate* – /aː/ > /ɛː/ in Shakespeare's English).

The GVS has been much studied, and readers can find standard accounts of the changes in many of the standard histories of English (Strang 1970: 170–4 offers a wonderfully compressed account; see also Barber 1993: 191ff. and Baugh and Cable 1993: 232–4. These accounts should be contrasted with the thought-provoking analysis offered by Lass 1984: 126–9). Our purpose here, however, is not so much to describe the details and chronology of the changes – such an account might occupy a further book – but to ask whether, in principle, such a change is likely to happen in the first place. *Do* speech sounds – phonemes – undergo qualitative changes that may be described in terms of chain shifts? Does gap-filling occur in the phonemic systems of other languages? What are the consequences, in terms of linguistic variation, of symmetrical, or near-symmetrical, vowel systems? What evidence can be found that phonemes (both consonants and vowels) do behave pair-wise, and/or step-wise?

Fortunately, answers to these questions are readily available, and these answers shed some light on the behaviour of phonological systems in general.

First, consider some diachronic evidence from *consonant* systems which suggests that phonemes do indeed change in a step-wise fashion. The evidence we need here, which is adapted from the fine account in Aitchison (1991: 155–6), comes from a set of changes known as the *High German Consonant Shift* (since the changes, which began in the sixth century, took place in the Germanic language known as Old High German, the ancestor of present-day German). In this change, the voiceless stops – /p, t, k/ – developed fricated allophones when they occurred initially in stressed syllables. So /p/ developed the allophone [pf] (Modern German *Pfeffer*, 'pepper', *Pferd*, 'horse', cf. Modern Dutch *peper, paard*), /t/ developed the allophone [ts] (Modern German *Zunge*, 'tongue', cf. Modern Dutch *tong*), and /k/ developed the allophone [kx] (or [x], Modern German *brechen*, 'to break', cf. Modern Dutch *breken*). However, these developments left gaps. Not all gaps were filled, since as Aitchison puts it 'the change appears to have petered out before completing itself' (1991: 156), but the gap left by /t/, for instance, was later filled by its voiced partner, /d/ (Modern German *tun*, 'to do', cf. Modern Dutch *doen*). Then the gap left by /d/ was filled by the nearest available consonant, /θ/ (Modern German *drei*, English *three*). This strongly suggests that phonemic gap-filling in turn depends on the concepts of *classes of sound* (phonemes with something in common, e.g. the class of voiced/voiceless stops, or the class of long front/back vowels) and *adjacency within a class* (voiced/voiceless pairings, alveolar/dental/denti-alveolar shifts, vowels filling adjacent slots as these slots are defined in the vowel trapezium, and so forth).

Second, there's further evidence that vowels behave, in terms of shift, both pair-wise and symmetrically. Aitchison (1991: 143–5) considers evidence from the early history of the Romance languages. Italian and Sardinian, for example, make use of the historically underlying vowels of provincial Latin (the language from which both were descended) in different ways. You'll see how in the following table:

Provincial Latin		Italian	Sardinian	Gloss
[ɪ]	*pira*	[pera]	[pira]	'pear'
[ʊ]	*gula*	[gola]	[gula]	'throat'
[ɛ]	*mele*	[miɛle]	[mele]	'honey'
[ɔ]	*dolo*	[duɔlo]	[dolo]	'grief'

The crucial observation is that in Italian, the historically prior higher vowels were *lowered symmetrically*, while the lower vowels [ɛ] and [ɔ] were diphthongised (probably to avoid a potential merger with the lowering of [i] to [e]). In Sardinian, the opposite happened: the short high vowels were moved to an even closer position (i.e. they raised as far as they could go), and (consequently) [ɛ] and [ɔ] also experienced pressure to raise.

These data help us to understand several things about the way phonological systems behave:

- Sound changes tend to be non-random.
- Phonology critically concerns the establishment and maintenance of contrasts (we noted this in our work on minimal pairs in chapters 1–2).

- Where symmetry exists in vowel systems (i.e. between front and back systems) then that symmetry is likely to be maintained. If, for example, a change occurs such that the quality or quantity of /i:/ is affected, the corresponding quality or quantity of /u:/ is likely to be affected.
- Both vowels and consonants have a preference for occurring in pairs (e.g. voiced/voiceless consonants, such as /p, b/, /t, d/ and so on; or front paired with back vowels, e.g. /i:/ and /u:/, /e:/ and /o:/).
- Real novelty – i.e. the introduction or development of entirely 'new' phonemes – is, therefore, rare in any phonological system, a view which accords very closely with the traditional insight of Saussure already cited ('The language system as such is never directly altered … ').

When we study diachronic variation, therefore, then of course we can and do study 'what has changed' … But even as the *terms* of a linguistic system are subject to the pressures for change, the system itself, as revealed in the contrasts that sustain it, remains very much the same.

10.4 Synchronic variation: the case of /a/ and /ʌ/

The previous section suggests that real novelty in linguistic systems is vanishingly rare. Nevertheless, novelty – or what appears to be novelty – is occasionally manifest. Two changes, for example, have taken place within British English in my lifetime (in two generations, fifty years), and it seems to me that these changes are not yet complete. We've mentioned one such change already, and that is the introduction of /ʌ/ in some varieties in words such as *strut* and *cut*. The other change involves the short low front vowel which in prestige accents of even twenty years ago was pronounced [æ], but which now, certainly in my variety, and observably even in today's prestige varieties, is pronounced with a more open, slightly more retracted variant, [a]. In what follows we'll consider these examples of synchronic change in turn, beginning with the change – if it is indeed a change – from /æ/ to /a/.

How can we reconstruct recent change, and gather data which will enable us to study synchronic variation as this manifests itself in English phonology? One resource is, obviously, reference texts such as Wells (1982), whose magisterial survey has featured before in this book (and whose analyses have been explicitly adopted in some cases). However, even given the accuracy and range of Wells (1982), there's a problem: the introductory volume of Wells' *Accents of English* was published in 1982, a generation ago, and there will certainly have been changes in English accents since then; and further, Wells exists as a *written* source, and a source, moreover, that sometimes uses non-standard symbols for the transcription of certain features of certain accents (we noted Wells' use of one non-standard vowel symbol in the last chapter). There's no place we can go, apparently, to hear for ourselves the kind of extensive spoken data to which Wells had access (and to which he did so much justice). Or is there?

A work mentioned before in this book – and mentioned in properly glowing terms – is Schneider *et al.* (2004), *A handbook of varieties of English*. This monumental work is in two volumes, with the first being devoted to phonology, and the second to morphology and syntax. There's also a most useful accompanying CD, which, interestingly for our purposes, is fully searchable, so that, for instance, by clicking on an appropriate vowel phoneme you have instant access to how that phoneme is pronounced in different English accents. The scope of the work is enormous and spans virtually *all* varieties of spoken English, from the UK, through American varieties, through Caribbean, Pacific, Australasian, African, and South and South-east Asian varieties.

Volume 1, on phonology, comprises chapters written by specialists on different varieties of English. Here we'll look just at two parts of the chapter on Received Pronunciation (by Clive Upton, pp. 217–30 of vol. 1).

In the present book we've already noticed that some features of RP are what we've called 'old-fashioned'. In that respect it's interesting to look at how the label 'RP' arose. Ultimately, as Upton shows, the concept (that there indeed *was* such a prestige accent as RP) came about because the eminent phonetician Daniel Jones, whose *English Pronouncing Dictionary* first appeared in 1917, defined a 'model' English accent as follows:

RP is an accent of English …

… most usually heard in everyday speech in the families of Southern English persons whose men-folk have been educated at the great public boarding-schools [these are private, fee-paying schools: McC]. This pronunciation is also used by a considerable proportion of those who do not come from the South of England, but who have been educated at these schools. The pronunciation may also be heard, to an extent which is considerable though difficult to specify, from persons of education in the South of England who have not been educated at these schools. It is probably accurate to say that a majority of those members of London society who have had a university education, use either this pronunciation or a pronunciation not differing very greatly from it. ([Jones 1917: viii] cited by Upton in Schneider *et al.* 2004: 217)

Like it or not, approve of it or not, Jones's definition rests on assumptions built on education, and (consequently) on class, and on the concept of fashionable society (e.g. the invocation of 'London society'). Jones, however, was (as Upton shows) much more open-minded about the boundaries of this prestigious, 'model' accent than superficial charges of elitism might imply, and moreover, Jones did not invent the term Received Pronunciation. That honour probably (in a British English context) goes to the philologist A. J. Ellis, writing in 1869. 'Received' meant 'generally adopted, accepted, approved as true or good', and it's no accident that the *Oxford English Dictionary* (OED, 2nd edition) defines 'Received Pronunciation' as 'the pronunciation of that variety of British English widely considered to be least regional, being originally that used by educated speakers in southern England' (in the OED, see *received* ppl [past participle], a. [adjective], sense 1b. 'Of language or pronunciation').

The term 'Received' extends further, and the phrase 'Received Standard' can these days refer to *any* spoken variety of English which is widely accepted as a standard. Therefore, there's a sense in which we might think of GA as a Received Standard in the US (a *national standard*) or of 'Tyneside English' as a Received Standard in Tyneside (a *local standard*).

Still, within the British Isles RP is summoned into life in order to describe (some features of) the speech of privately educated males who were either born or educated in the south of England. These voices are the first generation of the voices of BBC radio broadcasts; the sons (usually, the sons) of these voices are the voices we can still hear in old newsreel footage from the 1930s–1950s, or in radio broadcasts from the Second World War. It is precisely this variety of RP that now, in the early twenty-first century, sounds so old-fashioned. In my lifetime I have only rarely heard speakers my age use this form of spoken English – and when I did so, I could be fairly certain that these voices came from old-established southern English families, and had usually been educated at one of the old-established public (private, fee-paying) schools.

> Try to get hold of a recording of an RP speaker of English, preferably as his or her variety was recorded in the period 1920–40. (Such recordings can sometimes be downloaded from the Internet. Try searching on e.g. *Gaumont news*.) In what follows, I'm going to describe a mere *one* feature of (conservative, old-fashioned) RP, and that is its system of short front vowels, but there will be other features of the phonology that will have changed. What are they?

What features does this variety of English have which now make it sound so old-fashioned? One key feature is its system of short vowels. Old-fashioned RP had three short front vowels – /ɪ/ (*pit*), /e/ (*pet*) and /æ/ (*pat*). Speakers of advanced RP, or perhaps better, of Standard Southern (British) English, these days have lower (and/or retracted) variants of /e/ and /æ/, and are much more likely to have the phonemes /ɛ/ and /a/ in the same words. Diagrammatically:

Conservative RP	'Advanced' RP/Standard Southern (British) English
/ɪ/	/ɪ/
/e/	/ɛ/
/æ/	/a/

Notice that the 'conservative' vowels have either lowered (/e/ moves from a relatively mid-high position, to mid-low, position 3 in the vowel trapezium) or lowered and retracted (/æ/ retracts and lowers from its relatively raised position to such an extent that many speakers of Standard Southern (British) are likely confuse it with /ʌ/, see here Upton, in Schneider *et al.*, p. 222).

The intriguing thing here is that we might again be looking at *chain shift*. In old-fashioned RP, /æ/ was almost as fronted and raised as /ɛ/ (hence crude satire of 'the ket set on the met' type), but, perhaps as /e/ lowers to /ɛ/, /æ/ must also lower and retract, to keep its distance. Perhaps we are looking at a mini vowel shift – one, moreover, which has taken place in living memory, and which is still ongoing?

If so, we'd also expect /ɪ/ to be moving (i.e. to be lowering). Is there any evidence that this might be the case? There's some. Upton notes that /ɪ/ has a closer variant 'among older speakers', while younger speakers have a vowel that is 'half-close and retracted' (p. 221), while he also remarks that the /e/ > /ɛ/ movement 'is apparently part of a general lowering of the short front vowels' (p. 222). (Upton also notes specifically that RP /æ/ > /a/ is not only a change that has taken place 'among younger speakers' but is also '[a]ssociated with the general tendency of the modern RP front vowels to lower articulation' (p. 222).)

Certainly, the distinctions between advanced RP and Standard Southern English are not easy to describe (and on the notion of 'advanced RP', together with U-RP, adoptive RP and Near-RP, see Wells 1982: 279), but it seems significant that both middle- and working-class varieties of Standard Southern (British) English have varieties of /ɪ/ that are either lowered and/or retracted (see here the survey of Williams and Kerswill 1999, summarised in Upton's contribution to Schneider *et al.* 2004: 187–92). Therefore, we seem to be in a position where we might tentatively claim that if we detect synchronic variation in the set of short front vowels (as these are deployed in some varieties of Southern British English) then we do indeed seem to be observing another chain reaction … And further, if our work in this chapter is correct, then change in the front vowels is rather likely to be paralleled by similar changes in the set of short back vowels.

Here we might with advantage consider the wanderings of /ʌ/ once again. Here, you'll recall first that the historical underlier of /ʌ/ was /ʊ/ (at one time, *all* spoken varieties of English had /ʊ/ in words such as *strut* and *cut*), and second, that the synchronic distribution of this phoneme may be regarded as part of a very general north–south diagnostic: /ʊ/ in *putt* and *strut* is clearly a Northern feature, while /ʌ/ in such words is clearly a feature associated with South(-east) and 'general RP' varieties. Yet /ʌ/ is, historically, a most anomalous vowel phoneme, and for original /ʊ/ to drift in this way is unparalleled. And yet drift it does.

If the possible lowerings and retractions in the short front vowel set are to be paralleled in the set of short back vowels, then (as with the data from Italian and Sardinian considered above) it would seem that a pre-condition of such a spectacularly symmetrical set of changes must be that each front vowel affected by a change of quality must ideally be paired by a back vowel. Yet we've already established that for a speaker of RP (or Standard Southern British English) the system of short back vowels is *not* as symmetrical as the front set *precisely because of the prior wandering of /ʊ/.* That is, a speaker of those accents is likely to have the following front and back short-vowel distributions (I ignore schwa here):

(5) **Asymmetrical distribution of short vowels in twenty-first century Southern British English/RP**

In this diagram, original /æ/ is represented as having retracted and lowered to /a/; /ɪ/ is represented in position ɪ (but seems in many varieties to be retracting or lowering), although its 'back partner', here represented as [ʊ], can now be regarded as allophonic (see above); historical /ʊ/ has here been represented as having moved (lowered and retracted) to /ʌ/; and the short back vowel /ɒ/ (*dock*, *cot* etc) has lowered slightly from its original historical position (Gimson 1994: 109 mentions that this short vowel was probably closer in OE and ME, and reached its current 'more open' articulation at some point in the eighteenth or nineteenth centuries). Therefore, although generally speaking we *can* observe lowering in the set of short back vowels, these lowerings don't seem, in any tidy or obvious sense, to be caused by prior change in their front equivalents. Further, the early wandering of /ʊ/ (to /ʌ/ in some varieties) makes it unlikely that pair-wise, step-wise change could ever take place neatly in the short-vowel system considered as a whole. Nevertheless, there does seem to be good reason to suppose that the system of short front vowels is currently changing, and there the concepts of gap-filling, avoidance of mergers and distance-keeping supply us with an interesting conceptual framework within which to analyse the relevant changes, and compare them with other changes in vowel sets, whether these are found in the varieties of English or in other languages.

10.5 Synchronic variation: *happY*-tensing

We've already touched on the topic of how speakers of English realise word-final unstressed /ɪ/ as this occurs in words such as *happy* or *city*. In 8.2 we noted that although it's very plausible to transcribe words such as *happy*, *city* and *busy* with an underlying word-final /ɪ/ (i.e. an unambiguously short vowel), many speakers feel uncomfortable with such a transcription, and sometimes claim to use a longer allophone of /ɪ/ in that specific position. To handle that unease, so far I've suggested a fudge. Here's what we said in 8.2:

What I'm going to do here is follow in the spirit if not the letter of Roach (1991). I'm going to maintain the use of the symbol … /ɪ/ for the underlying short vowel, *but* I'm going to assume that there is a surface representation of underlying /ɪ/ which in syllable-final position can be symbolised as [i] (the same symbol as that used for /iː/, but without the length marks). In using this symbol, and in hinting that this surface vowel is 'neither long nor short', I'm aware that I'm storing up problems for us (not least, problems relating to how to match such a vowel with X-slots in a syllabic nucleus). However, if we regard the *underlying* vowel – the phoneme – as unambiguously short, then this also allows us for the moment to analyse variation in the pronunciation of (the final syllable of) *busy* as primarily a matter belonging to phonetics.

It seems to be an accurate observation, and helps to explain the typical allophony of underlying, unstressed, word-final /ɪ/ as this is found in some varieties of English, as in the following:

167

Word-final unstressed /ɪ/: some observations on its allophones		
Conservative RP	– markedly lowered and/or centralised ([ë]) realisation of /ɪ/	{ [ë] { [ɛ]
Advanced RP	– 'normal' realisation	[ɪ]
Standard Southern British English	– lengthened/tensed allophone	[i]
GA, Canada	– lengthened/tensed allophone	[i]

Nevertheless, the use of the symbol [i] is a fudge, since throughout our work on English vowel systems we've strongly implied that 'pure' vowels are either short or long, and equally, that in terms of their distribution within syllabic nuclei they are either one X (short) or two X (long). There's no easy way in which a vowel that is neither short nor long (i.e. the vowel symbolised by [i]) can 'fit' into the X-slots of syllabic nuclei as we've developed them here. Nor will it quite do to say: 'Yes, but this kind of problem belongs firmly to the domain of speaker-specific variation, and to phonetics and allophony, and therefore not to the analytical suppositions of phonology.' As we'll see in chapter 10, at least one model of contemporary phonological theory makes our classical conceptions of 'underlying structure' moot, and takes the *distribution of surface forms* (rather than underlying ones) as the starting point for its evaluations: there, as elsewhere in the theoretical consideration of sound structure, phonology simply cannot do without phonetics. And so it would be unwise to make arbitrary statements such as '[i] belongs in the domain of phonetics' without puzzling about them further.

Matters are made even more interesting if we briefly consider one variety where word-final unstressed /ɪ/ has, indubitably, a long(er) realisation (in [i(ː)]). This is Tyneside English. Wells (1982: 257–8) coins the term '*happ*Y-tensing' to describe the process by which English varieties arrive with allophones in [i] (or [iː]) in words such as *happy* or *city*, and the term itself suggests that what's going on here is more than just 'short vs long', since the word 'tensing' is used in the definition. It's worth reading what Wells has to say (1982: 257–8):

*happ*Y-tensing (1)

What we have called the *happy* vowel … was between the seventeenth century and 1950 regularly analysed by phoneticians as [ɪ] and implicitly assigned to the KIT phoneme. Latterly, though, there has been an increasing tendency throughout the English-speaking world to use a closer quality, [i(ː)], and for speakers to feel intuitively that *happy* belongs with FLEECE rather than KIT.

Where and when the [i] pronunciation arose is not certain. It has probably been in use in provincial and vulgar speech for centuries …

Beal, writing in Schneider *et al.* (2004: 126), supplies more detail, and specifically invokes Northern varieties of British English, among them Tyneside English, where a long (or tense) variety of *happY* has not only been around for two centuries, but has also become a prestige marker in some accents:

---

happY-tensing (2)

The unstressed vowel … varies between tense and lax realisations in northern dialects. Dialects with [*happY*-tensing] include those of the North-east, Liverpool and Hull. Elsewhere in the North, lax realisations of this vowel as [ɪ] or [ɛ] are heard. In the happY-tensing areas, the realisation may be [i] or even long [i:]. Perhaps because the tense vowel is found throughout the South and Midlands and in RP … Wells (1982: 258) describe[s] this as a southern feature, which has spread to certain urban areas in the North. However, a closer examination of 18th century sources reveals that the tense vowel was found both in the North-east and in London, suggesting that this is not such a recent innovation in these dialects (Beal 2000). In all the northern happY-tensing areas, the lax vowel is a shibboleth of the neighbouring dialects: it marks the difference between Teesside and Yorkshire, Humberside and West Yorkshire, and Liverpool and Lancashire. In every case, it is the lax variant which is stigmatised. For example, young middle-class women in Sheffield, which is on the border of the North and the Midlands, are increasingly using either a more tense variant or a compromise diphthong [eɪ], perhaps in order to avoid the stigmatised Yorkshire [ɛ].

And so *happY*-tensing proves to be an interesting example of change in progress – synchronic change. Attendant on the change are several issues concerning *attitude* – whether certain pronunciations are 'stigmatised', whether certain others are prestige; whether change relates to gender (note Beal's specific invocation of 'middle-class *women*'), and/or age ('*young* middle-class women') and/or status ('young *middle-class* women' … see here also Altendorff and Watt's contribution on 'The dialects of the South of England' in Schneider *et al.* 2004: 187). These matters are of course of great interest to those interested in the role of language in society, to sociolinguists.

Does your variety of English have *happY*-tensing? If so, is this feature of your speech high prestige, low prestige, or neither? How conscious are you of it (or of its absence from your speech)? How do you regard it – as prestigious, non-prestigious, neutral – when you come across *happY*-tensing in others?

However, there's also a theoretical point to consider, and that is the matter of vowel *length*, since each writer on *happY*-tensing invokes not so much 'length' but *tenseness* (and 'laxness') in his or her description. Perhaps what we've so far thought of as 'vowel length' – suggesting that length involves a simple distinction between long and short – could possibly, and with advantage, be reconceived of as a contrast between *tense vowels* ('long' pure vowels) and *lax vowels* ('short' pure vowels)?

What we might suppose is that speech sounds in general (and not just vowels) have certain **features**, certain 'internal properties', associated with them. These features are subparts of each phoneme, parts of its internal composition. We've already hinted as much when we analysed e.g. the feature of *voice*: all consonants, for instance, have the feature [voice], which feature could be switched on ([+voice]) or off ([-voice]). It seems plausible to assume that these features, themselves abstract, are binary – that is, they're either '+' or '–' (it would be difficult to think of a consonant phoneme which was *both* voiced *and* voiceless, for instance).

For vowels, so far we've talked of them as 'long' (occupying two X-slots within the syllabic nucleus) or 'short' (occupying one X-slot). We could possibly assume there was a feature [long] associated with vowels, such that those vowels spanning two X-slots would have the feature [+long], and those spanning one X-slot the feature [-long]. *And* we could assume that vowels also had the feature [tense].

'Tenseness' is notoriously hard to describe. /iː/ would be an example of a tense vowel, as would /uː/, whereas /ɪ/ and /ʊ/ would be examples of lax ([-tense]) vowels. Giegerich (1992: 98) writes that: 'In general, tense vowels are said to have greater force of constriction than their lax counterparts … [and] tense vowels have a tendency in many languages to be longer than lax vowels.' He goes on to define tense vowels as 'produced with a deliberate, accurate, maximally distinct gesture that involves considerable muscular effort'.

If this is on the right lines, we now have *two* possible features that might be properties of vowels, [long] and [tense]. However, to retain *both* features in the phonological model would risk redundancy, particularly since we already have a way of representing vowel length in the model (i.e. X-slots), and it's our task as phonologists to be as economical as possible with both our descriptions and the principles we use to construct them. Therefore, let's suppose (and see here Giegerich 1992: 144 for further argumentation) we should retain just the feature [tense], and at the same time construct a principle whereby the following happens:

[+tense] vowels fill two X-slots
[-tense] vowels fill one X-slot

This principle means that /iː/ would be associated with two X-slots, and /ɪ/ with one. That seems childishly simple, but in fact what we're doing here is complex, in that we're beginning to supply some *principles* that lie behind how certain phonemes pattern and behave. To that extent, the idea that phonemes are the expression of one or more *features* is a new one, and will in chapter 11 turn out to be crucially important. However, let's return to *happY*-tensing, and ask whether the new information about features (specifically, about [tense]) can help us understand the phenomenon more clearly.

Historically, *all* the word-final unstressed vowels in the *happY*-tensing set derive from a lax one, /ɪ/. We've seen that some varieties lengthen this to [i] (a sort of 'half-long' variant), to [iː] (a fully lengthened variant, though the handbooks are both inconsistent and interestingly reticent about transcribing [i] or [iː]) or, astonishingly, to a diphthong [eɪ]. One key problem is how to represent these variants in terms of syllable structure. Of course, where /ɪ/ is realised as [ɪ] that's straightforward. It's the allophone [i] or [iː] that seems so difficult to represent in a syllable tree: (i) [i] is neither fully long nor fully short, merely 'tensed' (or in the process of tensing), and (ii) tense vowels (such as /iː)/, or diphthongs (such as /eɪ/), have so far been associated with fully *stressed* syllables, which obligatorily contain a minimum of two Xs in their rhymes. And yet, whatever *happY*-tensing might be, its working is very clearly restricted to *unstressed* syllables.

Below I'm going to construct two diagrams. The first is a straightforward representation of how we might analyse non-tense /ɪ/ in varieties of English that don't have *happY*-tensing. The second is more interesting, and suggests a way of representing [+tense] but unstressed vowels (specifically, [i]) in a syllable tree, while remaining consistent with the principle '[+tense] vowels fill two X-slots' that we noted above.

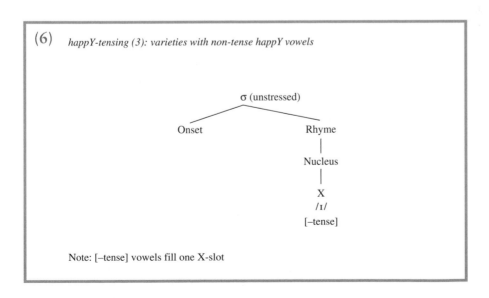

(6)   *happY-tensing (3): varieties with non-tense happY vowels*

σ (unstressed)

Onset   Rhyme
                                           |
                                        Nucleus
                                           |
                                           X
                                          /ɪ/
                                        [–tense]

Note: [–tense] vowels fill one X-slot

(7)   *happY-tensing (4): varieties with tensing to [i]*

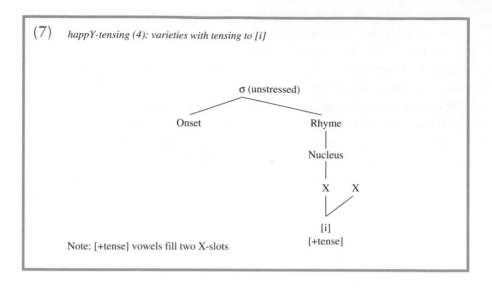

Note: [+tense] vowels fill two X-slots

One significant thing about the bottom diagram is that tensing has taken place, but we still can't analyse the tensed vowel allophone as eligible for the description 'heavy syllable'. Since the two Xs in question are aligned only with the *segment*, and not with the nucleus (which contains only one X), then the syllable *remains light* (and unstressed) even though the underlying vowel has tensed, and (therefore) has acquired an extra X.

Perhaps this is a means of making sense of just some of the data and principles involved in *happY*-tensing. At the very least, the preceding section has suggested one thought-provoking way of analysing the internal properties of phonemes themselves, to the extent that we're beginning to see them as having *features* – what are usually called **distinctive features** such as [tense] – attached to them. We shall be developing that feature-based analysis in chapter 11, and seeing what else it can do for us in terms of describing phonological structure. To conclude this chapter, however, we need briefly to look at one matter left hanging in 9.5, and that is the topic of *rhoticity*.

10.6 Long vowels, short vowels, and the problem of rhoticity

We touched on the problem of *rhoticity* in chapter 9.5. Accents of English in which /r/ may occupy post-vocalic positions within the syllable are known as *rhotic accents* (including Irish Englishes, varieties of SW British English, many prestige types of American Englishes, and Scottish English), while accents that do not have post-vocalic /r/ in such positions are *non-rhotic* (including all forms of RP, Northern forms of English and Antipodean Englishes). It's worth stressing that two hundred years (and more) ago, most if not all accents of English had rhoticity. Today, however, some accents appear to have lost rhoticity, and therefore rhotic and non-rhotic accents display the following kinds of structure in words such as *car*, *fear* and *hammer*:

	Rhotic accents	Non-rhotic accents
<car>	/kar/, /kɑːr/	/kɑː/, /kæː/
<fear>	/fɪr/, /fɪər/	/fɪə/
<hammer>	/hamər/, /hamr/	/hamə/

A note on symbolising 'r'

Throughout this book we've been using the symbol /r/ – familiar from the normal alphabet – to represent our post-alveolar approximant. Many textbooks (Geigerich 1992, Harris 1994) do the same. But if we strive, as we should, for *absolute* transcriptional accuracy, then simply using the symbol /r/ as a cover, as it were, for all possible varieties of /r/ (and there are many) needs a moment's further thought. Simply in terms of using the IPA accurately, for instance, our use of the cover symbol /r/ might be construed as inaccurate: in the IPA, the symbol /r/ stands for '[r]olled **r** as in Scottish English, Italian, Spanish, Russian. The letter is also used whenever possible to denote flapped **r** … fricative **r** … lingual frictionless continuant **r** … uvular rolled **r** … uvular fricative **r** … or the uvular frictionless continuant …' (*Principles of the IPA*, p. 11). Although this list sounds like something from a Gilbert and Sullivan operetta, note that our cover symbol /r/ is used 'wherever possible' precisely as a cover symbol, so we've not been *entirely* (or wilfully) inaccurate. However, we should observe that one very common realisation of 'r' is neither flapped, rolled, nor uvular, but is a 'voiced retroflex approximant, [ɹ], which is produced with the tip of the tongue curled back slightly from the alveolar ridge; this is the most common realisation of /r/ for speakers of Southern Standard British English and General American' (McMahon 2002: 32). That is in fact my variety of /r/, and therefore if I wished to transcribe the word *bread* as this occurs in my accent, I would be very accurate indeed if I were to make the phonemic transcription /bɹɛd/.

One significant problem with rhoticity concerns the occurrence of /r/ in accents known to be *non*-rhotic. In chapter 9, for instance, you were set an exercise which is adapted (and extended) here:

Transcribe the *phrases* below as these would be pronounced by the speaker of purportedly *non-rhotic* accents:

Word	Transcription	Phrase	Transcription
fear	/fɪə/	*fear is*	...
near	/nɪə/	*near enough*	...
air	/eə/	*air is*	...
hammer	/hamə/	*hammer is*	...

You should find that in your transcription of the *phrases*, /r/ appears, e.g.:

fear is   /fɪər ɪz/
hammer is   /hamər ɪz/

Where it appears in these contexts in non-rhotic accents, /r/ is known as **linking** 'r', since one of its functions is precisely to link a syllable-final vowel with the vowel of a following syllable (in a different word). Therefore, the appearance of /r/ in these contexts can be seen as an aspect of transition, of connected speech. The technical term we need here is *liaison*. Two other observations are pertinent:

(i)   where /r/ appears in these specific contexts then the syllable to which it relates *appears in a word which definitely has /r/ historically*. Indeed, one might well think of the structure of centring diphthongs, as these appear in non-rhotic varieties, as closely connected with former rhoticity: transcriptions such as /ɪə/ for *ear*, or /ɛə/ for *air*, seem to contain a historical trace of what was once /r/ (Giegerich 1992: 281 calls this 'some residue of historic rhyme-r'), and

(ii)   non-rhotic accents have a constraint whereby /r/ may appear in syllable onsets, but not in codas.

This last observation bears not only on how we conceive liaison, but also on the form of the transcriptions we can make. In the above exercise, we transcribed e.g. /fɪər ɪz/ and /hamər ɪz/, implying that /r/ was part of the coda of the final syllable of the relevant words. But if observation (ii) is true, then /r/ can't be part of the coda: it must be part of the onset of a following syllable. That follows from, among other things, the *Principle of Maximal Onsets* we began to discuss in chapter 6.4, where we discussed syllabification. Therefore, if we wish to syllabify strings of words such as *fear is*, or to represent the position of /r/ in single words such as *hammering*, then the relevant syllabifications would be as follows:

(recall that /m/ is ambisyllabic here)

I've been cagey, and have made narrow phonetic transcriptions (as indicated by the '[…]' brackets), implying that liaison of this kind is part of the phonetics of connected speech. But in fact since liaison is governed by general *phonological* principles – and specifically, by the PMO – then we would have been quite justified in making phonemic transcriptions such as /haməɪŋ/. Yet if we did *that*, then we'd also be claiming that the *underlying* form of e.g. *hammer* in *non-rhotic* accents is /hamər/.

> **If their underlying phonology contains precisely those post-vocalic 'r's which we'd unhesitatingly say were parts of the phonology of rhotic accents, then how 'non-rhotic' are 'non-rhotic' accents?**

One usual answer is to claim that there is an /r/-deletion rule – a **phonological rule** – operative in non-rhotic accents, such that underlying /r/ is deleted in certain environments (in this context, rhyme-finally). Such a rule simply would not apply in rhotic accents. However, if this claim is right then we are now looking at a major change in how we think of 'English phonology' (in fact, of phonology in general), since we're hinting that:

(a)   there are underlying forms, as these may be rendered in phonological transcriptions, and then

(b)   a rule or set of rules, which operate on the underlying forms, converting them into

(c)   a set of surface forms, as these might be rendered in phonetic (allophonic) transcriptions.

We'll be looking in more detail at the issue of phonological rules and representations in the next chapter, but before leaving the subject of liaison I'd like to close with some more data, again from non-rhotic accents, and again relating to /r/.

> Study the following data. The data relate again to non-rhotic accents, although the phenomenon also occurs in rhotic ones. First, phonemically transcribe the words in the left-hand column. Next, phonemically transcribe the phrases in the right-hand column. Last, consider liaison: what transitional phenomena can you observe in your pronunciation and transcription of the *phrases*? I've done the first example for you.
>
> | Word | Transcription | Phrase | Transcription |
> |------|---------------|--------|---------------|
> | <law> | /lɔː/ | <law and order> | ?/lɔːrənɔːdə/ |
> | <cinema> | | <cinema is> | |
> | <Crimea> | | <Crimea is> | |
> | <spa> | | <spa is> | |

I've queried the transcription of *law and order* because although a transitional /r/ may fairly readily appear between *law* and *and*, such an occurrence of 'r' is sometimes stigmatised. In fact, so stigmatised by prescriptivists is the appearance of 'r' in these contexts that the whiff of disapproval carries over into the term descriptive linguists use to describe this particular phenomenon: **intrusive 'r'**. That is, /r/ intrudes into contexts where it *never* appeared historically: unlike in words such as *car*, *farm*, *hear*, /r/ was *never* part of the pronunciation of the final syllables of *law* (*/lɔːr/) or *cinema* (*/sɪnəmər/).

Where does intrusive 'r' come from? Is it part of the underlying representation of words? And if not, how else might we account for its appearance and distribution in these contexts? (You'll find more work on this topic at the end of chapter 11, section 11.6.)

The previous two sections of text have examined merely some interesting aspects of English synchronic phonology. These are 'interesting' aspects precisely because they oblige us to think of the relationship that there is between history and the present (diachrony and synchrony). As our work in this chapter has suggested, and as the data on linking 'r' seem to prove, speakers of *all* varieties of present-day Engish are unavoidably interfered with, as it were, by linguistic history. But our work in this chapter, and specifically in the last section of text, has also obliged us to reconsider the nature of the concept 'underlying', and thus the nature of phonological representations themselves. We've also invoked two further, and important, ideas: first, that there may be distinctive features attached to each phoneme (a phoneme being the expression of the sum of those features); and second, that there may be such things as phonological rules which work on underlying representations, converting them to surface (phonetic) forms. The next chapter – the final chapter in this book – examines these ideas in more detail, and in doing so, introduces you to two current, and very influential, ways of thinking not only about the phonology of English, but about the principles that lie behind the phonology of all languages.

Exercises

Since we've just done a great deal of theoretical work in chapter 10, I'm going to confine exercises 10a–b to the construction of different kinds of transcription. In each exercise I'll indicate which parts of each transcription seem particularly significant, tricky, or thought-provoking. Some of the transcriptions you'll undertake anticipate work we'll be doing in chapter 11, but even if you get stuck (which you shouldn't), persevere with thinking through the theoretical questions that constructing the transcriptions implies.

Exercise 10a — Make simple phonemic transcriptions of the following words, as these transcriptions reflect your own variety of English, paying particular attention – based on the transcriptions you make – to whether or not you speak a rhotic or non-rhotic variety:

    <robe>, <prop>, <brown>, <torpedo>, <rip>, <part>, <appear>, <par>, <supermarket>, <Europa>

Exercise 10b — First, make simple phonemic transcriptions of each word, and then consider how each word would be syllabified. The data contain segments which may be ambisyllabic, or which are in other ways problematic or provoking in terms of their syllabification:

    <ample>, <implying>, <tunnel>, <tunnelling>, <care>, <caring>, <cough>, <coffin>, <summer>, <summery>, <summary>, <extraordinary>

Exercise 10c — In chapter 10 we said that a word such as *fear*, as this might be broadly transcribed in the underlying form of a non-rhotic accent, might be /fiːr/. Then we suggested that non-rhotic accents may have a rule of /r/-deletion. But even if /r/-deletion is assumed to operate on this example, how would you account for the form /fɪə/? Hint: you might need another rule – but what might that rule look like, and would it apply before or after the /r/-deletion rule?

Exercise 10d — We've suggested that phonemes may be the expression of the sum of their distinctive features. In chapter 10, for example, we specified possible features such as [tense] and [voice] that might be relevant for the classification of English vowels – and may help to explain the behaviour of vowels. Looking back at the work we've done in this book, and specifically at chapters 3–5, what kind of distinctive features might it be reasonable to propose as belonging to English consonants? Hint (1): a good idea would be to begin with a feature such as [voice]. Hint (2): what sort of distinctive feature might account for the difference between /s/ and /p/, /z/ and /k/, /m/ and /t/?

Key terms introduced in this chapter
diachrony
distinctive features
gap-filling
happY-tensing
hypercorrection

intrusive 'r'

liaison

linking 'r'

phonemic merger

phonemic split

phonological rule

synchrony

Notes

1. Although conservative speakers of Chaucer's variety of English appear to have had word-final schwa in words such as 'bite', 'bete', 'abate' and 'fole' – that is, the word-final <e> was still pronounced – in the table I haven't represented this word-final vowel because the most important changes are those occurring in the stressed vowels of the words in question.

Further reading

Many of the references from which the work in this chapter was developed are standard, widely available histories of English such as Baugh and Cable, and/or Strang; introductory handbooks such as Aitchison (or Wakelin, on some historical features of English dialects); widely used reference sources such as Gimson; or influential textbooks such as Giegerich:

Aitchison, Jean. 1991. *Language change: progress or decay?* 2nd edition. Cambridge University Press.

Barber, Charles. 1993. *The English language: a historical introduction*. Cambridge University Press.

Baugh, A. C. and Thomas Cable. 1993. *A history of the English language*. 4th edition. London: Routledge.

Giegerich, Heinz. 1992. *English phonology: an introduction*. Cambridge University Press.

Gimson, A. C. 1994. *Gimson's pronunciation of English*. 5th edition, revised by Alan Cruttenden. London: Arnold.

Lass, Roger. 1984. *Phonology: an introduction to basic concepts*. Cambridge University Press.

Strang, Barbara M. H. 1970. *A history of English*. London: Methuen.

Wakelin, M. 1977. *English dialects: an introduction*. Revised edition. London: The Athlone Press.

Wells, J. C. 1982. *Accents of English*. [Three vols. Vol. 1: *Accents of English 1: an introduction*. Vol. 2: *Accents of English 2: the British Isles*. Vol. 3: *Accents of English 3: beyond the British Isles*.] Cambridge University Press.

Some of the analyses of individual varieties, or details and transcriptions relating to those varieties, have been taken from Wells (1982, particularly volumes 1 and 2, though volume 3 should be consulted for details of varieties of English beyond the British Isles; see the entry above) and, as will have been readily apparent, from Schneider *et al.* (2004). The full reference to this text is as follows:

Schneider, Edgar W., Kate Burridge, Bernd Kortmann, Rajend Mesthrie and Clive Upton. eds. 2004. *A handbook of varieties of English. Volume 1: Phonology.* [Multimedia. Two vols plus CD-ROM.] Berlin and New York: Mouton de Gruyter.

It will pay you to familiarise yourself with the layout of this last work, including the layout of the CD that accompanies the hard text – particularly since the CD includes full bibliographic details of the major book resources the authors contributing to Schneider *et al.* used to construct *their* analyses. Particularly important to our work in the last chapter were the analyses of Clive Upton (pp. 217–30) and Joan Beal (pp. 113–33). Further useful references are the following:

Beal, Joan. 2000. 'HappY-tensing: a recent innovation?' In Ricardo Bermúdez-Otero, David Denison, Richard M. Hogg and Christopher B. McCully. eds. *Generative theory and corpus studies: a dialogue from 10 ICEHL.* Berlin and New York: Mouton de Gruyter, 483–97.

Foulkes, Paul and Gerard Docherty. eds. 1999. *Urban voices: accent studies in the British Isles.* London: Arnold.

Williams, Ann and Paul Kerswill. 1999. 'Dialect levelling: change and continuity in Milton Keynes, Reading and Hull'. In Foulkes and Docherty. eds. 141–62.

It's worth stressing, perhaps, that comparative *synchronic* analyses of the phonology of English varieties, particularly those varieties used outside the British Isles and North America, are in their infancy and much work remains to be done. In this chapter I have merely looked at one or two well-known features of two or three well-studied varieties, largely because those features are interesting (or controversial, or theoretically significant) in their own right, but also in the hope that work of this kind, undertaken even in a textbook, can serve as a stimulus for the more wide-ranging *comparative* work that urgently needs to be done on the synchronic phonology of English varieties. Since Wells and Schneider (and his editors) have published their surveys, the frameworks are there. All it takes now is persistence, accuracy, time – and a willingness to be surprised.

CHAPTER **11**

Problems, theories and representations

In this chapter …

In the last chapter we began to see that phonemes (which from another, and quite proper, point of view should be regarded as the *smallest meaningful units of speech*) can be conceived as expressions of their sum of *distinctive features*. So far in this book we've hinted at the existence of three such features – [voice], [long] and [tense] – but we've not yet done any systematic, thorough work on what a feature inventory might be. How many features are there? How do they work? How, if at all, are they patterned? How can they help us make our analyses more cogent, economical and elegant? Part of chapter 11 (11.1–11.2), therefore, is devoted to looking at distinctive features in more detail. At the same time, such detail can serve as an introduction to *distinctive feature theory* – a theory from which many more advanced textbooks start, and of which some prior knowledge is often assumed (see e.g. Durand 1990, Harris 1994 among many others). This theory is sometimes called classical generative phonology. (I'm using the adjective 'classical' here to distinguish the brand of phonology which developed distinctive features from later kinds of phonology that also have a claim to be called 'generative'.) Such a theory, based on work accomplished in the second half of the last century, has remained very influential, and in 11.3 in particular we examine some of the theory's apparent strengths as these apply to basic issues of syllable structure. Yet the theory isn't without problems, and more recently another model of phonology has come to the fore. This is Optimality Theory (OT – see Archangeli and Langendoen 1997, Kager 1999). This is still, broadly speaking, a generative model of phonology, but works rather differently from its theoretical predecessor. In the concluding sections of this chapter we'll look at some of the central claims and ideas of OT, and put them to work in three small case studies.

11.1 Syllabic codas and distinctive feature theory

In chapter 3.1 we looked at an aspect of the production of English consonants which we called 'voice'. Voice, in this sense, relates to the vibration which occurs in the vocal folds when a given consonant is produced, and we saw that consonants typically, though by no means invariably, fall into voiced/voiceless pairs such as /d/ (voiced) and /t/ (voiceless), /g/ and /k/, and so on. Given our work in later chapters, this strongly suggests that perhaps there is a **distinctive feature**, voice, written formally as [voice]. (The square brackets mean that the term 'voice' is here given a *theoretical* meaning.) In chapter 10, too, we considered two other possible features, [long] – a feature whose existence we rejected – and [tense].

If these features are indeed part of the underlying make-up of each phoneme, then it appears that they must be either switched on (and have the value '+') or off (value '–'). For instance, although it's entirely possible to conceive of certain allophones as being e.g. 'partially devoiced' (we came across such allophones in chapter 4, particularly in the context of work on voiceless stops and their allophones), it's almost impossible to conceive of *phonemes* as being 'neither voiced or voiceless' or 'just a bit devoiced'. Therefore it's customary, and right, to think of features having the following expanded form: a given consonant might be specified for [±voice], or a given vowel for [±tense]. Distinctive features, that is, are *binary*.

The problem is that we've now opened the phonologist's version of Pandora's box. If we admit the existence of distinctive features, how many features are there? What do they do?

To illustrate the answer to these questions we're going to look again at syllable structure, and specifically at the codas of English syllables. What we're going to suggest is that the last position in a maximally filled coda isn't filled randomly, but with consonants that have a certain property in common. Distinctive feature theory can help to explain what that property is.

As always, data first.

Study the following list of syllables. Next, transcribe them as they would occur in your variety of English. Next, draw the appropriate syllable tree for the *rhyme* of each syllable. Last, look carefully at the last position in their codas (i.e. the syllable-final position). What consonants occur there – and which consonants might *never* occur in that position of the syllable? Because today I'm feeling more than usually charitable I've done the first example for you.

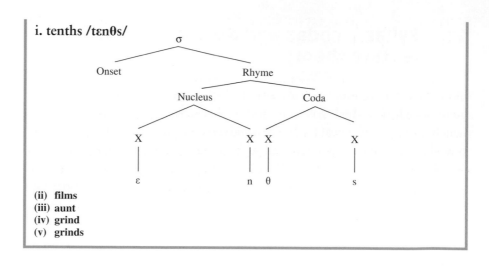

i. tenths /tɛnθs/

(ii)   **films**
(iii) **aunt**
(iv) **grind**
(v) **grinds**

You'll have found that *films* has a similar representation to *tenths*, except that in *films* the coda-final consonant is /z/. *aunt* is trickier. In my English, as in many forms of British English, *aunt* has a tense vowel (what in earlier chapters we unhesitatingly called a long vowel), while /n/ followed by /t/ belong firmly in the coda. In other forms of English, though, *aunt* has a non-tense vowel, and if so, it is followed by /n/ in the nucleus, while /t/ occupies the first position of the coda (i.e. in such pronunciations, the coda isn't maximally filled, although consider e.g. the pronunciation of *aunts* in the same accents). *grind* is less problematic: the nucleus is filled by a diphthong, /n/ occupies the first coda position, and /d/ the second. Yet there's still *grinds* to consider. Here, the rhyme itself is maximally filled, and the syllable-final /s/ seems to be some sort of extra, or appendix. In fact, /s/ here is an inflectional ending, part of the word's morphology that gives us the information 'third person present tense indicative'. It's *not* part of the basic syllabification of the word, but an extra piece of grammatical information. Nevertheless, we have to consider such extras, since they occur (if infrequently) at the end of maximally syllabified rhymes – *sixth+s* (/sɪksθ+s/) is another, often cited example.

On the face of it, those consonants that can fill maximally syllabified rhymes, together with those consonants that can occur, as an extra or appendix, after such rhymes, look ill assorted: /s/ (*tenths*), /t/ (*aunt*, in my variety), /d/ (*grind*) and /z/ (as an extra or appendix, as in *grinds*).

Some of these consonants are stops, some are non-stops (continuants, see 11.2); some are voiced, others voiceless. It doesn't therefore look as if these consonants can have anything in common. Of course, we could always resort to the brutal tactic of simply *listing* those consonants that are allowed to fill the last coda slot, but there's a more elegant way of handling coda structure.

The elegance is provided by distinctive feature theory, which shows that after all, /s, t, d/ and /z/ have something in common – specifically, they are all [+coronal] consonants.

The feature [±coronal] refers to a particular place of articulation. Coronals are produced with the blade of the tongue raised from its neutral position (Clark and Yallop, 1990: 431) and are articulatorily correlated with production using the tip and/or blade of the tongue. Several types of consonants, but in particular alveolar and dental consonants, share this feature, and this shared feature helps to explain why it is that such consonants behave phonologically as a single class. Therefore although /t/ and /θ/ (for example) have different specific places of articulation, they both share the feature of coronality.

Therefore it seems as if there's a constraint on structure relating to the second position of codas within maximally filled rhymes. If that slot is filled, it *must* be filled by a [+coronal] consonant. If we adopt this position, then *one* statement replaces what would be a brute list ('if that slot is filled, it can only be filled by /s, z, d, t/ … '). It's exactly the feature [±coronal] that can help us put this constraint more elegantly.

11.2 A first look at distinctive features and phonological rules

In fact we can do more than this. Using distinctive features, we can specify the underlying composition of consonant phonemes with accuracy, to the extent that we can regard each phoneme as being the expression of a set of features (what's sometimes referred to informally as a 'feature bundle' or more formally as a 'feature matrix').

Suppose, for instance, that there's a feature that distinguishes stops from non-stops. We could call this feature [±continuant], since, after all, one feature of continuant sounds (like e.g. /s/) is that there is no complete occlusion in the oral cavity (unlike with stops, where the complete closure of the articulators, however briefly, causes a complete obstruction to the airflow). We already have the feature [±voice]. And let's suppose that there's a further feature that distinguishes labial from non-labial sounds – transparently, this feature would be [±labial].

> Study the following list of consonant phonemes, and then using the features you've already found in this section of text, attach feature specifications to each one. You should find that each phoneme has a different feature specification (i.e. that the phonemes are distinguishable

precisely by their different feature specifications). I have done the first example for you:

/s/	[−voice], [+continuant], [−labial], [+coronal]
/z/	?
/t/	?
/d/	?
/b/	?
/p/	?

There's a further distinctive feature we might notice. How would you use features to distinguish, say, /d/ (in the list above) from /n/? /n/, too, is a stop (i.e. it's [−continuant], [+voice], [−labial], sharing those features with /d/). One way of making the distinction would be to claim there's a further feature, [±nasal]. /d/ would be [−nasal], /n/ – like /m/ and /ŋ/ – would be [+nasal].

Distinctive features aren't just a property of consonants. Vowels, too, may be distinguished if we see them as expressions of different feature bundles.

Suppose there are distinctive features of the following kind: [±high], [±low], [±back], [±round]. [±round] can be taken to mean 'produced with lip-rounding'. Now consider the following list of vowels (for the sake of simplicity, ignore whether a particular vowel is [±tense]). Assign features to each vowel. Your list should assign different feature specifications to each vowel. I've done the first example for you.

/iː/	[+high], [−low], [−back], [−round]
/e/	?
/æ/	?
/oː/	?
/uː/	?

One possible problem is whether we need both features [±high] and [±low]. After all, if a vowel is [+high] then clearly it's also [−low]. However, as you'll have found in trying to assign feature specifications to /e/ and /oː/, there are vowels which are neither [+high] nor [+low]: these are the mid-vowels. Notice two things: first, if we'd allowed /e/ to have the feature specification [+high] then it would have been indistinguishable from /iː/ (this implies that we also need the feature [±low]); and second, that /e/ and /oː/ alike have the feature specifications [−high, −low]. Nevertheless, the two vowels are differentiated by the features [back] and [round]: /e/ is [−back, −round], and /oː/ is [+back, +round].

184

We can now begin to analyse how certain phonological processes work, and to detail that working using distinctive features. There are very many such phonological processes. Let's begin with just one such process, a very simple phenomenon which occurs in many of the world's languages. This is the phenomenon of *nasalisation of vowels*.

> Study the following list of forms. I've given a short list of words – all monosyllables – and have given the phonemic and phonetic transcriptions of the first example. In the phonetic transcription of <can> I've shown that the vowel is (or has become) nasalised. To indicate nasality I've used the standard diacritic [~] over the vowel. Your job is twofold: first, transcribe the other words in the list both phonemically *and* phonetically; and second, suggest why it is that vowels become nasalised.
>
> | Word | Phonemic transcription | Phonetic transcription |
> |------|------------------------|------------------------|
> | <can> | /kan/ | [kʰæ̃n] |
> | <lamp> | | |
> | <hen> | | |
> | <hand> | | |
> | <hang> | | |

What seems to happen is that a vowel phoneme acquires nasality in a specific environment, namely *when that vowel is followed by a consonant segment which is itself a nasal stop*. It doesn't matter whether the nasal is alveolar (/n/), bilabial (/m/) or velar (/ŋ/). What matters is precisely that those consonants are alike [+nasal]. It's this feature that the preceding vowel seems to acquire. Another way of looking at this is to claim that the vowel **assimilates** to part of the feature specification of the following segment.

Assimilation is very widespread in languages. It's widespread because it seems to be a natural human tendency to *anticipate* 'what comes next' in any string of speech. Accordingly, we can find different forms of this anticipatory tendency. Here are some further examples, illustrating different kinds of assimilation:

(i) Phrase	Phonemic transcription	Phonetic transcription
<that pen>	/ðat pɛn/	[ðapˀ pʰɛ̃n]

Description: underlying /t/ of *that* acquires the labiality of a following [+labial] C = assimilation of *place*.

(ii) Phrase	Phonemic transcription	Phonetic transcription
<in Paris>	/ɪn paɹɪs/	[ɪm pʰaɹɪs]

185

Description: underlying /n/ of *in* acquires the labiality of a following [+labial]
C = assimilation of *place*.

In both cases, since it's a following segment that is anticipated by a
preceding one, we can speak of *regressive assimilation*. That is, some feature
(in the examples above it is a place feature) spreads backwards, and is
anticipated by a preceding segment. This can be graphically illustrated as
follows:

Regressive assimilation (assimilation of place)

<in Paris> /ɪn ⟵ paɹɪs/ ⟶ output [ɪm pʰaɹɪs]
⟵ [+labial]

Another example of regressive assimilation, this time of *manner* rather than
place, would be precisely nasalisation, which we noticed above:

Regressive assimilation (assimilation of manner)

<hand> /ha ⟵ nd/ ⟶ output [hãnd]
⟵ [+nasal]

Though it's very frequent, regressive assimilation isn't the only kind of
assimilation. We also find *progressive* assimilation, where a following segment takes on features of a preceding one. We've already seen several
examples of this. For instance, we noticed that some voiced consonants
have a devoiced allophone when they follow voiceless stops:

Progressive assimilation (assimilation of voice)

<play> /p leɪ/ ⟶ output [pʰl̥eɪ]
[–voice] ⟶

You'll have noticed that to the narrow phonetic transcriptions at the right
hand of each example I've ascribed the term 'output'. By this I mean that the
surface form – the phonetic form – is the product of, an output of, a
structured process. Schane (1973: 49) describes such processes well: 'In
assimilatory processes a segment takes on features from a neighboring segment. A consonant may pick up features from a vowel, a vowel may take on
features of a consonant, one consonant may influence another, or one vowel
may have an effect on another.'

One way of describing such processes is to think of them as being expres-
sible in **rules** – called **phonological rules** to distinguish them from the other
kinds of rules (morphological, syntactic) that may be operative in language.
Before we look at such a rule it's worth pausing for a moment to consider the
theoretical model in which phonological rules of this kind are assumed to
work.

- First, there's phonological structure, which of its very nature is abstract and underlying.
- Next, such underlying structure is converted into a surface (i.e. a phonetic) representation by means of the application of one or more rules.
- The result is a well-formed output, a phonetic representation.

Classical generative phonology: a graphic model

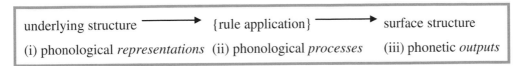

underlying structure → {rule application} → surface structure

(i) phonological *representations* (ii) phonological *processes* (iii) phonetic *outputs*

In such a model, rules mediate between the abstractness of underlying representations and their surface, phonetic forms. An example of such a rule might be precisely a rule for *nasalisation* that we began to consider above.

Recall that in nasalisation, vowels assimilate to the nasality of a following consonant. We may construct just the first part of a rule to show this process as follows:

V → [+nasal]

'V' stands for any vowel segment; notice that when one constructs phonological rules, only one element may stand at the left of the rightward-pointing arrow (= **what** *is affected*). The rightward-pointing arrow symbolises the application of the relevant rule, and the piece of structure immediately to the right of the arrow indicates the feature acquired (= **how** *the process takes place, and what is acquired during it*).

We've specified the *what?* and the *how?* – but if we leave it as it stands, our proto-rule would claim that *all* vowels become nasalised, in *every* conceivable linguistic environment. Clearly, that doesn't happen: it's only vowel segments preceding nasal consonants that acquire nasality. Therefore, alongside *what?* and *how?* we also need to say *where?* – *Where, in what environment, does this rule apply?*

It's customary for linguists to use shorthand in this context. One piece of shorthand is the deployment of the oblique slash, '/'. This stands for 'in the environment ... ' Then, as in the example below, to the immediate right of the oblique slash, there's a piece of underlining; this symbolises the *position* of the segment that is affected by the rule; that position is followed by (in the example of nasalisation) 'C [+nasal]'.

That sounds much more complicated than it is, as you'll see by looking at the relevant rule, here written in appropriate (and commonplace) shorthand:

Nasalisation of vowels in English, a first description

V ⟶ [+nasal] / _____ C
                                    [+nasal]

Longhand: 'A vowel segment acquires the feature [+nasal] when that vowel segment immediately precedes a [+nasal] consonant'.

Since they're so important it's worth spending just a moment longer on the formulation of phonological rules. As we've said, rules show *what?* (*what changes?*), *how?* (*how does it change?*) and *where?* (*in what environment does the change take place?*). Since it's common in all languages for segments to acquire features regressively from following segments, then many rules which show this kind of assimilation will have the following general form:

(1)   The form of a phonological rule (1)

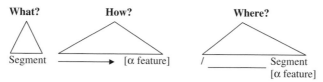

'[α feature]' refers to whatever feature is acquired, where 'α' can range over a number of different features e.g. [±nasal], [±voice] etc.

In the case of segments which assimilate to *preceding* segments, then the *where?* part of the rule must obviously precede the underline, which indicates where the segment affected by the rule is positioned:

(2)   The form of a phonological rule (2)

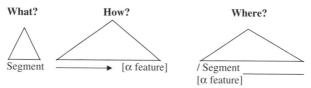

To conclude this section of text you should complete a two-part exercise. The first part relates to the *assimilation of place* that we touched on above. In part (1) of the exercise you'll find the example *in Paris* repeated. Try to think of four or five similar examples, i.e. examples where two-word phrases show regressive assimilation of place (e.g. *sad boys*; *good bloke* …). Then construct an appropriate rule which will specify *what* changes, *how* it changes, and *where* the change takes place.

Part (2) of the exercise relates to the (progressive) assimilation of *voice* we've examined in e.g. /pleɪ/. Again, try to think of four or five similar examples. Then construct a phonological rule which will specify *what* changes, *how* it changes, and *where* the change takes place.

> **(1) Consider the following:**
> *Regressive assimilation (assimilation of place)*
>
> | Phrase | Phonemic transcription | Phonetic transcription |
> |--------|------------------------|------------------------|
> | <in Paris> | /ɪn paɹɪs/ | [ɪm pʰaɹɪs] |
>
> **Find four or five similar examples and construct an appropriate phonological rule which will uniquely specify the relationship between the underlying and surface forms of your examples.**
>
> **(2) Consider the following:**
> *Progressive assimilation (assimilation of voice)*
>
> <play>   /p   leɪ/   ⟶ output [pʰl̥eɪ]
>   [–voice] ⟶
>
> **Find four or five similar examples and construct an appropriate phonological rule.**

Note: the astute reader will have noticed that the two rules introduced by this last exercise have subtly different characters. In the first rule, a segment acquires something – a property (in this instance, labiality) which it didn't have in its underlying feature specification. In the second rule, a segment acquires a feature (in this instance, voicing) which threatens to 'cancel out' a feature already ascribed to that consonant. I'm not going to comment directly on this problem here, though you'll find further commentary on the website which accompanies this book.

Distinctive features, together with phonological rules, seem to be a powerful descriptive and analytical tool, and the analyses we've begun to develop seem relatively elegant. Of course, we haven't even begun to construct an extended list of distinctive features as this might apply to the varieties of English – but this isn't a book about classical generative phonology, and you'll find other first-level works which begin from the point we've just reached. What is worth emphasising, though, is that the material we've looked at in 11.2 relates to the *internal* properties of segments, as these might be expressed in a set of some distinctive features. We should also look at how distinctive feature theory analyses larger-scale features – e.g. how vowel segments differ from consonants, or how certain consonants (such as /n/) can in certain contexts be syllabic. Because they involve larger-scale matters, as well as the inner composition of segments, the features classical generative theory uses to handle issues of vowel vs consonant, or syllabicity, are called ***major class* features**, and it's to these we now turn.

11.3 A first look at major class features

Distinctive features should help us make major distinctions between vowels and consonants, and the theory certainly provides a means to do so. For instance, several textbooks suggest that there is a feature [±consonantal] such that /p/, /f/, /ŋ/ etc would be [+consonantal], while /iː/ etc would be [−consonantal]. Specifically, this feature 'refers to a *narrowed constriction* in the *oral cavity* – either total occlusion [i.e. stops: McC] or frication' (Schane 1973: 26; Schane's emphasis). That leaves a problem with segments like /j/ and /w/, of course – segments which some handbooks tellingly refer to as 'semi-vowels'. But in fact since such segments do not have occlusion or frication, then, rather like the vowels, they're simply [-consonantal].

Another widely accepted major class feature is [±sonorant]. 'Sonorant' here refers to the resonant quality of a sound, such that vowels, liquids (/l/), approximants (including /r/) and nasals are always [+sonorant], while e.g. oral stops and fricatives are [−sonorant]. This feature helps us make sense of a constraint on syllable structure we looked at earlier: in general, the second segment of a well-formed, binary onset is a [+sonorant] segment.

Then there's the feature [±syllabic]. This feature is, as we'll see, much more controversial. Defined as a feature which 'characterizes the role a segment plays in the structure of the syllable' (Schane 1973: 26), then on the face of it vowels (but not semi-vowels) would be [+syllabic], as would consonant segments such as /l/, /r/ (in rhotic accents), /m/ and /n/. Such an assumption is still made, implicitly or explicitly, in recent introductory handbooks (e.g. Tserdanelis and Wong 2004, who define such segments without further ado as 'syllabic consonants', p. 46).

Ascribe major class features (and only those features, i.e. [±consonantal], [±sonorant] and [±syllabic]) to the following segments: /t/, /l/, /s/, /j/ and /uː/. I have done the first example for you:

/t/	[+consonantal], [−sonorant], [−syllabic]
/l/	?
/s/	?
/j/	?
/uː/	?

In terms of *major class features* you'll find that /t/ and /s/ have identical feature specifications. How can you use distinctive features to further differentiate these two consonants? (Hint: you'll find the answer in your work in the previous question, in section 11.2)

These three major class features of classical generative phonology actually help us towards a solution for one of the problems we left dangling earlier in this book. That problem is the role of /s/ in syllable structure, and specifically, in syllable onsets.

You'll recall from chapter 7, and particularly from 7.1, that /s/ poses a real problem for the theory of the syllable which we have developed in this textbook. First, it's only sC clusters that show increasing 'strength' (roughly, decreasing sonority) in syllable onsets; second, in that environment /s/ behaves unlike other voiceless fricatives (such as /f/), since it can co-occur with other alveolar consonants (e.g. /s/ and /t/ are both alveolar, and /st/ is a perfectly well-formed onset, cf. */fw/, where /f/ and /w/ are both labial); and third, it's only /s/ that may be followed by a further two consonants in the onset – /str/, /spr/ are well formed.

Major class features can be used to help us out here. In a classic paper published in 1982 (and reprinted in e.g. Goldsmith 1999), Selkirk proposes a general template for English syllables using major class features as labels. In the diagram below, the major class features are abbreviated (e.g. [+syllabic] becomes [+syll]), and the parentheses ( ) indicate a piece of structure that is optionally present. Here's Selkirk's template, to which I've added a phonemic transcription of *grind* for clarity:

(3)   A syllable template for English (from Selkirk 1982)

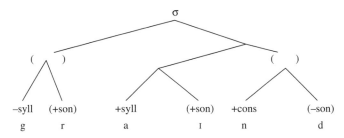

Such a template claims that what we've called onsets are optional; that what we've called codas are optional; that a minimal syllable consists just of a single [+syllabic] segment (a vowel or syllabic consonant), and that a maximal syllable consists of a branching onset, nucleus and coda, the terminal nodes of each having appropriate constraining feature specifications attached. So far, so good – in fact, very elegant. But Selkirk shows we can also use major class features to handle those problematic sC clusters, including those clusters of three consonants such as /str/, /spr/ and so on.

Look again at the very first position of the onset in (3). This slot *must* be filled by a segment that is [–syllabic]. What Selkirk proposes is that an *auxiliary template* may attach to this position such that /s/ plus a following consonant 'may here qualify as a single obstruent in English' (Selkirk 1999:

336). The auxiliary template, which again uses major class features, looks as follows:

(4)   sC clusters, major class features and the auxiliary template

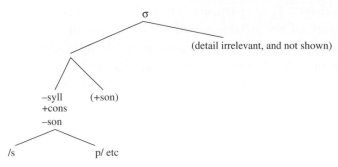

Under this analysis, /sp/, st/ and /sk/ are slotted, via the auxiliary template, into the first position of the onset, while the second position of the onset must continue to contain a [+sonorant] consonant. That means /spl/, /str/, /stj/, /skr/ are in these terms well formed, since /l, r, j/ are all [+sonorant], while e.g. */spw/ and */stl/ are ruled out by very general well-formedness principles such that two adjacent onset segments (where 'segment' now covers /st/ etc) are the better formed, the less they share a place of articulation.

Such an auxiliary template also (as Selkirk shows) helps to explain /st/ coda structures, e.g. as in /nɛkst/. Here, too, /st/ can qualify as a single position within the coda. This would in any case be necessary in Selkirk's 1982 theory, since that model would be obliged to cast the /k/ of /nɛkst/ into the coda, precisely because template (3) requires the second element of a branching nucleus to be [+son]. If, therefore, /k/ occupies the leftmost branch of the coda, that leaves the problem cluster /st/ to be syllabified – which would be neatly accomplished using the auxiliary template (4).

11.4 Some problems with features and rules

Before we look at some of the problems arising from a phonological theory which uses distinctive features and rules, it's worth emphasising what the advantages of such a theory are, and what such a theory can do.

First, as we've seen, the theory is *principled*: individual phonemes are the expressions of feature matrices. Many of the features within a matrix have a distinctly phonetic character. That is again fine in principle. In the earlier chapters of this book, for instance, we spent some time examining the linked natures of phonology and phonetics, and noted that for Saussure (and many others) phonology and phonetics are as indivisible as two sides of a single sheet of paper.

Second, the theory can help us make sense of some of the work we undertook in chapter 7 about the sequencing of consonants within syllabic onsets. There, you'll recall, we sorted the consonants of English into groups, such that a well-formed maximal onset, consisting of two segments, contained consonants belonging to different groups. The list of groups we used in chapter 7 is here repeated for convenience:

Groupings of English consonants with respect to their role in syllable structure

Class 1	plosives
Class 2	affricates
Class 3	fricatives
Class 4	nasal stops
Class 5	approximants

What seems to happen in well-formed onsets is that if a two-segment onset begins with a plosive (class 1) then any following consonant must ideally belong to class 5: /pr/, pj/, /tj/, /tw/ are all well formed, for instance, while */pʧ/ (plosive + affricate) or */tf/ (plosive + fricative) are not. In chapter 7 we developed this idea in order to try and make it as widely applicable as possible. Nevertheless, there remains the suspicion that the work we did in chapter 7 is in some ways a quick fix. We constructed these 'classes', for example, largely in order to address an apparent sequencing problem within the syllable – but we said little in chapter 7 about how such 'classes' could be motivated, nor detailed exactly what properties the members of each 'class' had in common. The list above, that is, looks rather (and merely) *stipulative*.

Distinctive feature theory can help us think about such apparent classes more accurately. If plosives are indeed a class, for instance, then it should logically be the case that they can be distinguished *as a class because all consonants belonging to that class have features in common.* Do they share such common features? Indeed they appear to do so: all plosives (i.e. all oral stops) are [+consonantal], [−continuant], [−syllabic], [−sonorant]. They may be distinguished in a principled way from affricates: although affricates share features with both oral stops and fricatives, they are themselves distinguished by the feature [±anterior]. (You haven't come across this feature yet.) Consonants showing constriction at the forward parts of the mouth (e.g. the alveolar ridge) are anterior, while if the relevant constriction is more retracted (e.g. palatal or velar) then those consonants are non-anterior (and see Schane 1973: 29–30). /t/, an *alveolar* plosive, would therefore be [+anterior], while /ʧ/ would be non-anterior. The following feature contrasts might help to make this distinction clear:

193

Feature contrasts, /t/, /ʧ/ and /ʃ/

/t/	/ʧ/	/ʃ/
+cons	+cons	+cons
−son	−son	−son
−continuant	−continuant	+continuant
+coronal	+coronal	−coronal
+anterior	−anterior	−anterior

And similarly with what chapter 6 here dubbed 'class 3' consonants – fricatives. Although fricatives have some features in common with affricates, one observable production mechanism of affricates is that they are [−continuant]. We can use distinctive features, therefore, to specify the distinction between fricatives and affricates, and in doing so motivate what we called, in chapter 7, 'class 3' segments:

Feature contrasts, /s/ and /ʧ/

/s/	/ʧ/
+cons	+cons
−son	−son
+coronal	+coronal
+anterior	−anterior
+ strident	+strident
+continuant	−continuant

And with what chapter 7 called 'class 4' – the nasal stops? Here we can simply make use of the feature [±nasal]. And for what we called 'class 5' segments – the group of approximants? Here, too, we're looking at an apparent class whose individual members have distinctive features in common: *all* the approximants, for instance – even the vowel-like consonants /w/ and /j/ – share the feature [+sonorant].

Therefore, we can use distinctive feature theory to *motivate* what would otherwise look like random groupings of sounds. That is very much to the credit of distinctive feature theory.

A third plus of distinctive feature theory is that it provides a natural-seeming solution to some real problems concerning syllable structure – and particularly, the role of /s/ in a description of the English syllable. This solution arose from the assumption that there were *major class features*. Major class features don't just help us with /s/, they also provide an interesting explanation of how and why segments such as /r/ or /n/ may under certain circumstances function as syllabic.

These are powerful theoretical advantages. Nevertheless, there are some significant problems associated with distinctive feature theory. The difficulties aren't merely technical. They go to the heart of what phonology *is*, what it *does*, and *how* it does what it does. In what follows I'll use bullet points to note just *some* of the difficulties with the classical generative model:

- **Distinctive features**

  When distinctive feature theory was first developed, during the first half of the twentieth century, some linguists proposed that features were *language-specific*. Trubetzkoy, for example, who was one of the founders of what came to be known as the Prague School of linguistics, wrote that 'It is the task of phonology to study which differences in sound are related to differences in meaning *in a given language* …' (1939: 10, cited in Hyman 1975: 2; my emphasis: McC). As the theory of distinctive features developed, and particularly after the theory received major revisions by Jakobson and Halle (1956) and by Chomsky and Halle (1968), the theory – now under the influence of the generative programme developed by Chomsky in the later 1950s and into the 1960s (and beyond) – became ever more *universalist* in character. That is, as well as to account for the phonemic oppositions which may exist in a given language, it has increasingly been seen as the task of a phonologist to determine distinctive features as these occur in *all* the world's languages – and therefore, to find **universals** of linguistic structure. (One example of such a linguistic universal would be the fact that *all* languages have a low, unround vowel phonemically /a/.)

  To my knowledge there are no linguists working today who would seriously propose that linguistic universals *don't* exist, nor who would question the universalist context of phonological enquiry. Still, the relationship between the language-specific (i.e. those features which are used in the description of a given language) and the universal is worth thinking about further: if the features operative at a given time in a given language (call it 'Language X') are merely a subset of all possible features as these may occur in all the world's languages, then does Language X contain *all* the features of *all* other languages, only somehow fail to use them or switch them on? That is, if languages in principle contain universal sets – in this case, of distinctive features – how and why are only some features used, and not others? Where – in what conceptual or mental place – are the features which don't happen at that moment to be switched on?

  That problem concerns the nature of linguistic universals, and their relationship with language-particular structures. Bound up in that problem, too, there's the issue of the *mental reality* of phonology. To what extent are our descriptions cognitively valid? How do we know?

- **Phonological rules**

  The kinds of rules we began to look at in 11.1–11.2 are powerful devices, and they imply a model of processing: underlying representations are converted into surface representations by means of rules.

195

Rules are stipulative. I'm not here using the term 'stipulative' in a pejorative sense. I mean merely that rules *stipulate* in the sense that they 'demand or specify' (*New Oxford Dictionary of English*). They say *what* changes, *how* it changes, and *specify the environment* in which the change takes place. Still, there are many examples of rules so powerful that their working has to be constrained in some way.

One of the ways phonologists handle the power of rules is to *order* them. Suppose there are two such rules, both working to convert one underlying representation into a well-formed output (a phonetic form). You've already begun to think about some relevant phenomena, as a matter of fact: in the last chapter, recall that we looked at *rhoticity*. In section 10.6, for instance, we supposed that so-called non-rhotic accents may indeed have post-vocalic /r/ as part of their phonology. If so, then clearly (since that /r/ never surfaces) a rule has applied at some point which deletes /r/. A further relevant observation, however, would be in that in words such as (RP) [hɪə] 'hear' or (GA) [hɪər] a [–low] vowel preceding post-vocalic /r/ surfaces as a diphthong, while the underlying form of that vowel is plausibly /iː/. That means that the underlying structure of 'hear' would be /hiːr/ – *both in RP (non-rhotic) and GA (rhotic).* To derive the correct surface forms – the one non-rhotic, the other rhotic – we'd be obliged to apply *two* rules: a rule that changed the vowel from /iː/ to /ɪə/ (which would apply to both varieties of English, but only in environments which were followed by post-vocalic /r/), and a rule which deleted post-vocalic /r/ (which would apply only in RP and other non-rhotic varieties). But crucially, we'd have to *order those two rules.*

Here are radically simplified versions of the two rules in question ('#' indicates merely 'the end of the root of a word'):

Rule A: /iː/ > /ɪə/ / ___/r/   (vowel change)
Rule B: /r/ > Ø / rhyme ___# (/r/-deletion)

To derive surface [hɪə] from underlying /hiːr/ then of course rule A must apply before rule B. Were rule B to apply first, then rule A could never apply, since the environment of rule A specifically states 'this rule applies where the relevant vowel is followed by /r/'.

Therefore, once we have phonological rules in the model their power must be constrained, and one way of constraining them is by ordering them. But who decides on the ordering of the rules? Phonologists? Speakers? Both? Neither? And further – how *real* are these rules? Do the users of language carry a whole battery of these rules around in their heads, applying them unwittingly? How do those unwitting speakers (including you and me) learn to order the rules?

The problem of rhoticity we've just looked at is in truth even more complicated than I've made out. Giegerich (1992: 302–3) suggests that the process of vowel change is tripartite, involving (i) insertion of /ə/, (ii) /iːə/ becoming /ɪə/ (a process he calls *laxing*), and then (iii) in non-rhotic accents, /r/-deletion. To which – as to many apparently rule-governed, rule-ordered phonological processes – students have sometimes retorted 'Overkill!'

How many rules are there? Are phonological rules, like distinctive features, universal or language-specific? Or, as with distinctive features, could all languages in principle have the same set of rules, selecting only those which were necessary at a particular place and/or time? Who decides which rules are necessary, and/or on how they're ordered? If rules become non-applicable (and we've seen some few examples of phonological change in e.g. chapter 10), where, as it were, do they go? Are they still a part of a language user's mental equipment? If so, where in the brain are these old, or dead, or never-yet-used rules stored?

Major class features

What I've here called classical generative phonology makes use of major class features ([±consonantal], [±syllabic], [±sonorant]). Of these features I'm going to pick out just one for special notice. That is the feature [±syllabic].

Although there are some distinguished exceptions (e.g. Fudge 1969, Vennemann 1972), until the late 1970s relatively few phonologists gave much attention to the structure of the syllable. Perhaps it was thought that the syllabicity (or otherwise) of particular segments could be handled simply by the feature [±syllabic] working in conjunction with other major class features. Following the publication of Liberman and Prince (LP, 1977), however, there was a veritable explosion of theoretical and practical work on syllable structure in the world's languages, and the development of many, often competing, non-linear representations of the syllable. Among other things, LP had drawn attention to some of the theoretical problems of classical generative theory, particularly as that had been modified by Chomsky and Halle (1968), and had suggested some brilliant new ways of thinking about phonological structures, particularly the structure of word and phrase stress. Although LP's ground-breaking paper didn't specifically concern syllables, it directly stimulated research into non-linear representations of the syllable, such that by the mid-1980s Selkirk (whose prior work on syllable structure and major class features remains classic) published a major revision (Selkirk 1984) to her earlier view of the syllable. What's so significant about that revision is that it scraps the major class feature [±syllabic].

Clearly, if a theory of syllable structure specifies how segments behave with respect to their position within onsets and rhymes – and that's exactly the kind of work we were doing in chapters 5–7 – then if that theory is analytically strong it will automatically follow that segments with particular properties will align within well-formed constituents of the syllable. That is, providing constituents of the syllable have been identified, and conditions placed on what segments can occur where, then there doesn't seem to be any theoretical reason why one might suppose that [±syllabic] should remain as part of the feature make-up of any given segment.

'So what?' you might say. 'Just dump the feature.'

The problem is that if we junk the feature [±syllabic] then we've to some extent compromised distinctive feature theory. Suppose, for example, that we need to specify the distinction between syllabic and non-syllabic /l/, and syllabic and non-syllabic /n/, using some version of classical distinctive feature theory.

One way of making that distinction would be as follows:

A problem with [±syllabic]

/l/ (non-syllabic – *slip* etc)	/l/ (syllabic – *bottle* etc)	/n/ (non-syll)	/n/ (syll)
–syll	+syll	–syll	+syll
+son	+son	+son	+son
+cons	+cons	+cons	+cons

The problem's twofold. First, distinctive feature theory seems obliged to postulate two different feature matrices for /n/ and /l/ according to whether /n/ or /l/ is syllabic or non-syllabic. (Without any specific representation of the syllable, then of course that is all feature theory could perhaps do with the problem.) Second, if we simply junk [±syllabic] then in doing so we apparently lose the ability to distinguish between syllabic and non-syllabic consonantal sonorants.

As it happens, the loss of [±syllabic] needn't be altogether critical so long as we have a plausible representation of the syllable, together with a well-founded set of conditions specifying which segment can occur where, and/or co-occur with what. And one might well argue that [±sonorant] and [±consonantal] are independently needed in order to handle distinctions between segments quite unrelated to syllable structure. Nevertheless, the case of the feature [±syllabic] highlights the vulnerability of distinctive feature theory. How many features, after all, do we need?

11.5 **Optimality Theory (OT)**

The problems we've just listed concerning distinctive feature theory aren't in principle insoluble, and many ingenious attempts at solution have been made. It would be fair to say that over the past fifty years much attention has been paid, in different theoretical frameworks, to the *internal composition of segments*, as well as to *universal principles of phonological organisation* (including e.g. syllable structure and stress patterning). You will find some of these approaches – and indeed, phonological approaches offering radically thorough alternatives to distinctive feature theory – listed in the *Further reading* section at the end of this chapter. There's one further problem, though, concerning distinctive features and phonological rules which is particularly difficult for rule-based approaches to phonological structure, and that is the problem of **opacity**.

In the classical generative model, rules work, as we've seen, to change one particular segment (or one property of one segment) in a given, stated environment. In addition, one or more rules may apply, in an ordered fashion, so as to derive a surface output. There's no apparent limit as to how many rules may apply. But there lies our problem: as an underlying form is processed by rules, many intermediate stages of derivation are possible, and the linguistic forms produced by these stages may appear to have little relationship either to the underlying form (on which the rules are operating), or to the phonetic output (which the rules are operating to produce).

The following figure, adapted from Kager (1999: 58) makes this clear. Suppose there's an underlying form /XAY/ ('X', 'A' and 'Y' are merely labels for three consecutive segments; they're not transcriptions!), and suppose there's a surface form [XCZ] which is to be derived from the underlying form by application of a set of rules. The derivation might run like this:

(5)   **Rule application and opacity (Kager 1999: 58)**

Underlying form: /XAY/

Rule 1: A ⟶ B/X_____   Intermediate form   XBY
Rule 2: Y ⟶ Z/B_____   Intermediate form   XBZ
Rule 3: B ⟶ C/X_____Z   Intermediate form   XCZ

Surface form: [XCZ]

Note that the rules *have* to apply in the order given so that the correct surface form is derived. (How do the rules know how to order themselves? Can rules 'conspire'?) Our problem, however, is crucially that the intermediate form XBZ isn't immediately inferable from *either* the underlying *or* the surface form. That intermediate form is simply mechanically generated as an inevitable part of a process, and – since it has no easily inferable relationship to either underlying or surface forms – is said to be *opaque*.

A key question to ask at this point is this: *how can any speaker ever learn such opaque forms?* If they are 'true', these intermediate forms are certainly parts of the linguistic competence of a given speaker, but since it relies on *opacity*, then *how can such a system ever be learned?*

Optimality Theory (OT) supplies at least a partial answer to this question. Specifically, within OT 'no property of phonological forms depends on information that is not present in the output [i.e. the surface form: McC] – either in the output alone, or in the relation between the input and the output' (Kager 1999: 58).

OT works as follows. First, underlying forms are conceived as a set of *inputs*. The term 'input' implies that such forms are subsequently subjected to a set of processes, but within OT such processes are rarely 'rules'. Instead, and second, a set of *candidates* is generated – the GEN function of OT. Next, OT *evaluates* the set of *candidates* – the EVAL function of OT. The evaluation takes place via a set of **constraints**, which select *one* candidate as being 'the best' (the most well formed). Last, 'the best' candidate of the set is said to be the *optimal* candidate. The optimal candidate is the *output*. The following schema offers a graphic summary:

(6)   **Evaluation of forms in OT**

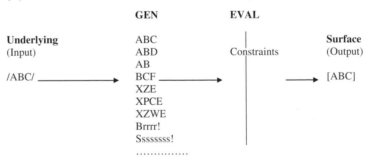

The forms listed under GEN can be **any** plausible kind of linguistic object. EVAL, a process formed by a ranked set of constraints, takes this candidate set and evaluates all of them. One form – the 'most harmonic', the most well formed – is selected as the output. In the schema above, it looks very much as if the candidate selected, [ABC], is the *closest* to the underlying form /ABC/: nothing has been changed – nothing added to, or deleted from, the underlying form. That is, the output is maximally *faithful* to the input. We might well infer from this that **faithfulness** ('in the evaluation input/output, keep everything as is') is a core constraint of OT. That's particularly important in view of the problem with which we began this section: because OT directly encodes (and favours) *transparency* in the relation between input and output, such a linguistic system is, and again in principle, *easier to learn*.

In principle, constraints are universal. But – and this is a very significant theoretical departure from rule-based phonology – *constraints are also, and in principle, violable*. Therefore, constraints differ fundamentally from rules in that the latter either exist for a language or they don't, whereas constraints exist universally in the phonology, but languages differ in terms of the constraints that they violate (or not) – i.e. languages can 'disobey' constraints. OT therefore deals with language-specific properties through the ranking of constraints, such that candidates are *the better formed, the fewer higher-ranked constraints they violate*.

These principles are better illustrated by putting a purely introductory (and very partial) version of OT to work in three small-scale case studies. In the following section of text you'll find that the first case study introduces a new phenomenon, that of **neutralisation** (and by no accident whatsoever, the detail here draws heavily on the introductory chapters of Kager's fine 1999 textbook), while the two following studies revisit work we've already undertaken.

11.6 Case studies in OT: (1) neutralisation; (2) onsets; (3) intrusive 'r'

(1) Neutralisation

Data first (cf. Kager 1999: 14ff.). In present-day Dutch, as in most varieties of German, obstruents are not voiced when they occur in coda-final position. Dutch and German do, of course, have a phonemic contrast between /d/ and /t/, /k/ and /g/ and so on, but these phonemes do not contrast on the surface when they occur syllable-finally. In that position (and *only* in that position) the voicing contrast between the pairs of obstruents is *neutralised*.

Consider the Dutch word *bed*, 'bed', when pronounced in isolation. Underlyingly, we might well assume that the underlying form of the word is /bɛd/. (Compare the Dutch plural form *bedden*, 'beds': /bɛdən/ (syllable division: /bɛ.dən/).) However, although the underlying form of the monosyllable is /bɛd/, the surface form is [bɛt].

One assumption we can make is that there is a universal constraint which is operative in Dutch and German such that 'obstruents must not be voiced in coda position'. A shorthand version of such a constraint might be *VOICED-CODA.

At the same time, there is a further universal constraint – in truth, a whole set of constraints – that requires surface forms (outputs) to be as close as possible to underlying forms (inputs). Ideally, nothing should be changed, nothing added or deleted. One of these constraints might run: 'preserve the identity of input–output correspondences' – a faithfulness constraint whose shorthand version is IDENT-IO. Where voicing is concerned, we would claim, in terms of faithfulness, that 'the specification for the feature [voice] of an input segment should be preserved in its output correspondent' (Kager 1999: 14) – thus IDENT-IO (VOICE).

We now have two constraints, one prohibiting voiced obstruents in codas, the other requiring input–output faithfulness. These two constraints are potentially in conflict. Within OT, that's fine: conflicting constraints are simply *ranked*. In the case of Dutch and German, we know that these same two constraints are going to evaluate a number of candidates, among them the forms [bɛd] and [bɛt]. Because we know independently, from our scrap of data, that [bɛt] is a 'better', 'more harmonic', candidate as an output than its rival, /bɛd/, then this strongly suggests that in Dutch and German, the constraint *VOICED-CODA is ranked above IDENT-IO (VOICE).

To show this, we can construct a graphic – the kind of graphic which is almost invariably, in this context, referred to as a **tableau**. The higher-ranked constraint is found in the left-hand column of the tableau. Candidates incurring violations of given constraints are marked with an asterisk, '*', in the relevant cell of the tableau, while candidates with *fatal violations* – the kind of violations that absolutely preclude them as possible outputs – are marked with '*!'. The candidate selected as the most harmonic output is indicated by '☞'.

(7)   OT tableau for neutralisation (Dutch) – cf. Kager (1999: 16).

Candidates (input: /bɛd/)	*VOICED-CODA	IDENT-IO (VOICE)
☞ [bɛt]		*
[bɛd]	*!	

One important feature of this tableau is the fact that the 'winning' candidate still violates a constraint (IDENT-IO (VOICE)). Nevertheless, that same candidate does not violate the higher-ranked constraint (*VOICED-CODA), whereas its competitor does – a fatal violation, as it turns out.

Compare the situation in English, where neutralisation of obstruents in codas does not take place. Exactly the same constraints occur in English – since constraints are universal, that's a given – but they are differently ranked, such that [bɛd] is, in English, always going to be evaluated as a better output to input /bɛd/ than its competitors:

(8)   OT tableau fragment for English – cf. Kager (1999: 17).

Candidates (input: /bɛd/)	IDENT-IO (VOICE)	*VOICED-CODA
[bɛt]	*!	
☞ [bɛd]		*

Another way of putting the respective ranking is as follows, where the symbol '>>' means 'is ranked higher than':

Respective rankings, Dutch and English (fragment):

Dutch: *VOICED-CODA >> IDENT-IO (VOICE)

English: IDENT-IO (VOICE) >> *VOICED-CODA

(2) Onsets

A second small-scale case study we can undertake using OT concerns the structure of onsets in English syllables. You'll recall that we've spent time in this textbook analysing how and why certain kinds of onset are well formed, why others aren't. In particular, we saw that there is a ranking of English consonants such that the least sonorous consonants tend to occur at the margins of syllables, while the more sonorous tend to occur non-marginally in complex onsets: /pr/, /tr/, /bl/ and so on are all fine, whereas */rp/, */lb/ are distinctly ill-formed onsets, since they violate a well-attested sonority-sequencing generalisation (cf. chapter 6.2). How might we handle this in OT?

Given the fact that constraints aspire to be universal, there are a number of factors an OT account of onsets has to take into account (these are developed, in an introductory fashion, in Archangeli and Langendoen 1997: 8ff., on which the following paragraph is based). First, does a language *require* syllables to begin with a consonant? This would be an ONSET constraint ('syllables begin with a consonant'). Second, does the language allow complex onsets – those with two (or more) consonant segments? Or does it require syllables to begin with one, and only one, consonant? We could formulate this constraint as *COMPLEX (ONSET) – 'syllables have at most one consonant at their (left) edge'. Third, does a language allow open syllables? We could formulate this constraint as NOCODA ('syllables end with a vowel'). And last, does a language require syllables to have vocalic peaks? If so, the relevant constraint might be conceived as PEAK ('syllables have a nucleus consisting of one or more vowel segments').

Since constraints are violable, it's no surprise to find that English violates some of these constraints: syllables have peaks, to be sure (although note again that there are syllabic peaks consisting of sonorant consonants, as well as those consisting of vowels), but English does not require syllables to end on a vowel (therefore NOCODA is systematically violated), nor does it require syllables to have exactly one consonant at their left edge (therefore *COMPLEX ONSET is systematically violated). Further, the constraint ONSET also appears to be violated, since there are many syllables (*edge, isle, egg, id, odd ...*) which appear to begin with a vowel.

On this last point it's worth very briefly revisiting a point we fudged earlier in this book. Recall that in chapter 6 we wondered whether lexical

203

monosyllables in English were *required* to begin with a filled onset. If so, then syllables such as *isle, egg, id, odd* etc might be analysed as beginning with a zero phoneme, /ø/. One fairly plausible allophone of that phoneme might be the glottal stop, [ʔ], so that a word such as *egg* would have the underlying representation /øeg/, and the phonetic representation [ʔeg].

From a universalist and typological perspective, though, that idea turns out to be simply wrong. It seems perverse to claim that English patterns with languages like e.g. Yawelmani, which do not tolerate violations of ONSET. And further, if we do persist with the notion that the zero phoneme is part of the underlying inventory of consonants in English, then this leads to further problems when we reconsider what the allophones of that phoneme might be. For instance, there's perhaps a case to be made that /ø/ might also underlie intrusive 'r' (*idea is*, /aɪdɪərɪz/) – but if so, /ø/ would then have two utterly ill-assorted allophones, [ʔ] and [r], which bore no articulatory resemblance to each other.

It's not merely 'perverse' to claim that English tolerates no violations of ONSET. From an OT perspective, such a claim would lead to entirely the wrong predictions – for example, that consonants would *always* have to be inserted into ostensibly onsetless syllables (so that ONSET would remain unviolated). That certainly doesn't happen in non-lexical words (e.g. the prepositions *in, at, of …*), and additionally, if ONSET is violated in English, we should ask what higher-ranked constraint might be fulfilled. The answer appears to be one or other of the *faithfulness* constraints, which require outputs to correspond as closely as possible to inputs, with nothing added, deleted or changed.

In sum, it appears that the critically important observations about English syllables, when these are glimpsed in an OT framework, are the following:

- Syllables have obligatory peaks (implying PEAK is highly ranked).
- Inputs are maximally faithful to outputs (implying *faithfulness* constraints are highly ranked).
- English syllables allow both optional and complex onsets and codas (implying ONSET, *COMPLEX (ONSET) and NOCODA are ranked low).

If the ordering PEAK >> *faithfulness* >> ONSET, *COMPLEX (ONSET) and NOCODA holds good for English, then we still need to account for sonority sequencing in onsets and codas. That is, our constraints still need to explain why /pr/, /pl/, /tr/ etc are well-formed onsets, and why */lb/ etc are not. Let's suppose there's a constraint called SONORITY, which requires that 'onsets must increase and codas decrease in sonority' (Hammond, in Archangeli and Langendoen 1997: 40). In English, such a constraint would be highly ranked:

PEAK, SONORITY >> *faithfulness* >> ONSET, *COMPLEX (ONSET) and NOCODA

In what follows I'm going to construct an OT tableau for the English syllable *imp*, using the above ranking together with the conventions introduced in this section. I'm radically simplifying the group of *faithfulness* constraints, of which so far we've seen only one specific manifestation, IDENT-IO, and here intending the cover term *faithfulness* to mean 'keep everything as it is in the input – don't add, delete, or change'. (For further work on these constraints, and specifically on their role in syllable structure, see Kager 1999, chapter 4.)

Where no particular ranking has yet been established between the constraints, I use a dotted vertical line.

Study this tableau carefully, and then construct a similar tableau to indicate the well-formedness of the syllable *grind* /graɪnd/. I have supplied a candidate set for you, so your task is merely to see in what ways the various candidates violate (*) or fatally violate (*!) each constraint.

PEAK, SONORITY **>>** *faithfulness* **>>** ONSET, *COMPLEX (ONSET) **and** NOCODA

OT tableau for *imp*, /ɪmp/

Candidates (/ɪmp /)	PEAK	SONORITY	*faithfulness*	ONSET	*COMPLEX (ONSET)	NOCODA
☞ [ɪmp]				*		*
[pɪmp]			*!			*
[ɪpm]		*!	*	*		*
[mɪp]			*!			

OT tableau for *grind*, /graɪnd/

Candidates (/graɪnd /)	PEAK	SONORITY	*faithfulness*	ONSET	*COMPLEX (ONSET)	NOCODA
☞ [graɪnd]						
[rgaɪdn]						
[gəraɪnd]						
[rgk]						

It's noticeable that although an OT analysis can indeed frame the gross features of well-formed syllables, some important details are missing from these admittedly simplified tableaux and analyses: for instance, what about the problematics of /s/?; what about the role of semi-vowels?

Such questions are well beyond the scope of an introductory textbook, but suggestions for further reading and study are given at the end of this chapter.

It's worth noting, though, that for some of these details we still need a phonological theory that includes a syllable template and distinctive features: OT can't (and nor should it) be expected to do everything. Nevertheless, because OT offers theoretical *transparency* and *learnability*, it seems to be an improvement over wholly rule-based analyses which cannot avoid the problems posed by opacity.

(3) Intrusive 'r'

A third and final case study we might conduct concerns intrusive 'r'. Recall that we specified the distinction between linking and intrusive 'r' in 10.6, where among other things you were offered the following exercise, here repeated for convenience:

Study the following data. The data relate to non-rhotic accents, although the phenomenon also occurs in rhotic ones. First, phonemically transcribe the words in the left-hand column. Next, phonemically transcribe the phrases in the right-hand column. Last, consider liaison: what transitional phenomena can you observe in your pronunciation and transcription of the *phrases*? I've done the first example for you.

Word	Transcription	Phrase	Transcription
<law>	/lɔ:/	<law and order>	?/lɔːrənɔːdə/
<cinema>		<cinema is>	
<Crimea>		<Crimea is>	
<spa>		<spa is>	

The problem is that /r/ appears here (specifically, between words) in contexts where it would *never* appear historically: there's no way we could postulate an underlying representation for e.g. *law* as */lɔ:r/. So where does /r/ come from, when it appears in these and similar contexts?

One thing to notice is that intrusive /r/ is *stigmatised* in some varieties: BBC newsreaders, for instance, used to be taught to avoid using intrusive /r/ (a fact which presupposes that intrusive /r/ occurred more or less readily in the *casual* speech of those users of English). A second thing to notice is the vocalic context in which intrusive /r/ occurs: it's invariably preceded by a [-high] vowel, and therefore doesn't seem to occur in the following phrases:

Non-occurrence of intrusive /r/

lay it	/leɪ ɪt/	*/leɪrɪt/
do it	/du: ɪt/	*/du:rɪt/
see it	/si: ɪt/	*/si:rɪt/

There seems, then, to be a phonological precondition for the occurrence of intrusive /r/: it only ever occurs following a [–high] vowel. But that precondition doesn't explain everything.

It's noticeable that in the examples above, although /r/ doesn't occur as transitional there are other phonemes that might:

Transitional phenomena in connected speech

lay it	/leɪ ɪt/	*/leɪrɪt/	?/leɪjɪt/
do it	/du: ɪt/	*/du:rɪt/	?/du:wɪt/
see it	/si: ɪt/	*/si:rɪt/	?/si:jɪt/

What seems to happen in connected speech is that where they immediately follow stressed syllables, *unstressed* monosyllables are the better formed *if they have onsets*. The precise form of such onsets seems to be governed by the feature specifications of the preceding vowel segment: /r/ follows [–high] segments, while /w/ follows [+high, +back] ones, and /j/ [+high, –back] ones. It's actually quite hard to see how such an observation could be built into our present OT-style analysis, since as we've developed it so far, it says that English syllables may have *optional* onsets. (The alternative would be to revisit our fudge concerning obligatory onsets and the zero phoneme – but we've already found good grounds for rejecting that.)

One possible solution might be to claim that there is a separate set of constraints which handle phenomena belonging just to connected speech. Such a (sub)set of constraints would be properly *post-lexical*, since feature specifications, basic syllabification and so forth would be part of a given word's lexical entry. It would only be transitional phenomena – and intonation? – that would form part of a post-lexical constraint set. And among that set, of course, it would be possible to set up a constraint that would favour onsets in unstressed monosyllables, where these occur in connected speech. To my knowledge, however, such a constraint has never been seriously proposed. Nor has the existence of separate constraint batteries been seriously entertained – largely because the existence of two discrete sets of constraints, lexical and post-lexical, would require given linguistic forms to shuttle between the two constraint batteries while they were checked for well-formedness at every stage of their lives. That would radically complicate the simplicity of OT grammars – and be uncomfortably reminiscent of some of the undesirable aspects of earlier, rule-based derivations.

Even given these observations, we've not found a reason why many educated speakers of non-rhotic varieties may consciously reject intrusive /r/ in phrases such as *spa is*, while freely allowing linking /r/ in phrases such as *hammer is*.

The answer proposed by Giegerich (1992: 283) is surprising. The only way, he claims, in which speakers can accept linking /r/, but reject intrusive /r/, is on the basis of that speaker's knowledge of the *spelling system* of English. In casual speech, conscious knowledge is at a discount: there, intrusive /r/ is, in the appropriate contexts, just as likely to occur in non-rhotic accents as linking /r/. But in the case of the conscious rejection of intrusive /r/, then the grounds for rejection are very possibly *non-phonological* – and therefore impossible to explain in any OT-style (and/or feature-based) analysis. Literate English speakers, it appears, are quite unconsciously influenced not only by history (a point we made in the last chapter), but also by what they understand of the spelling rules appertaining to their language.

OT, then, has limits – and has those limits in common with other theoretical frameworks. Yet, on the face of it, OT seems to offer a fairly new way of conceiving what speakers do when they produce well-formed English syllables, words and utterances. OT, after all, is *evaluative*, not *stipulative*. It suggests that speakers continually assess *possibilities*, rather than (or as well as?) undergo *rules*. It also provides a new framework in which linguists and others can ask the questions: 'What do we actually *do* when we learn a language? What does it mean, "to learn a language"? How can any language ever be learned?'

While OT seems to offer precisely 'a new way of ... ,' the theory is also in some respects surprisingly close to a very traditional, even classical view of the overall organisation of sound structure. Of particular interest here is the attention OT pays to outputs, and to the relationship between output and input (a relationship continually regulated by the requirements of *faithfulness*). Explicit abstraction is, in the OT model, at a discount: what counts is largely the evaluation of surface forms, and the transparency of their relationship to their inputs. In OT, phonology becomes more surface-driven, more susceptible to (and hospitable towards) surface-driven generalisations. To that extent the theory is remarkably close to the view of Saussure, for whom the relationship between phoneme and (allo)phone was indivisible. And so, perhaps, in our end here was also our beginning, way back there in chapter 1.

If this final chapter seems to have raised more questions than it's solved, then ... good. It was meant to do so. After all, it's a measure of the vitality of intellectual enquiry within linguistics that even after decades of serious and distinguished work on English phonology, much remains to be analysed, reanalysed and discovered. If this textbook has equipped you with merely some of the skills with which you can engage with further questions concerning the nature and use of sound structure, and has allowed you to specify analytical and procedural problems in English phonology with precision and rigour, then it will have achieved most of its initial objectives. Above all, this textbook has tried throughout to encourage you not only to understand but also to *enjoy* working with English sound structure – that intricate, challenging, much studied, historically rich and almost baffling thing.

Exercises

Exercise 11a   We've so far transcribed words such as *sing* as /sɪŋ/. For speakers of several present-day varieties of English, however – as well as for speakers of several historically attested varieties – the relevant transcription would be /sɪŋg/. Compare also *sink*, which is plausibly /sɪŋk/ cross-varietally. Given this data, consider whether /ŋ/ is a phoneme of English.

Exercise 11b   More on /ŋ/. In what was one of the founding texts of classical generative phonology, Chomsky and Halle (1968: 85) propose two rules to account for surface [ŋ]. The rules (adapted here from Hyman 1975: 75) are as follows:

1. /n/ ⟶ [ŋ]/_____ {k, g}
2. /g/ ⟶ ø/ [ŋ]____

Is such a rule-based account either adequate or necessary to account for the distribution of /ŋ/ or [ŋ]?

Exercise 11c   Given their apparent distribution, what grounds can you find for arguing that /ŋ/ and /h/ are *not* phonemes of English?

Exercise 11d   Consider the following forms:

at ease   a tease
an aim   a name
an ocean   a notion

It's difficult (if not impossible) to differentiate the phonetics of the respective forms. Consider how an OT-style analysis might begin to analyse the relevant distinctions. Note that you won't find 'a solution' anywhere in chapter 11, but you might like to consult this book's website for further suggestions.

Hint: think about how word edges are aligned (or not aligned) with the edges of syllables.

Exercise 11e   Consider the example *softness*, /sɒftnəs/. Suppose you were trying to construct a set of OT constraints which would evaluate the following candidate set (where '.' indicates a syllable division):

[sɒft.nəs]
[sɒf.tnəs]
[sɒftn.əs]
[sɒ.fə.tə.nəs]
[m.naargh]

What constraints would you use? How would you rank those constraints?

Once you have worked out what constraints you might use, attempt to construct the relevant OT tableau, showing how such a tableau encodes the most harmonic output.

Key terms introduced in this chapter
assimilation
classical generative phonology
constraints
distinctive features
faithfulness
major class features
neutralisation
opacity
Optimality Theory (OT)
phonological rules
tableau

Further reading

i. Distinctive features and phonological rules

There is a voluminous literature on classical generative phonology and distinctive features. The most influential treatment of classical generative phonology was that of Chomsky and Halle (1968 – a work standardly abbreviated to SPE):

Chomsky, Noam and Morris Halle. 1968. *The sound pattern of English*. New York: Harper and Row.

Textbooks by e.g. Hyman, Schane, and later, by Durand, and Clark and Yallop are strongly influenced by SPE. Indeed, many other textbooks are equally under the influence – but the ones noted above happen to be some of those I've used in constructing this chapter (and this book):

Clark, John and Colin Yallop. 1990. *An introduction to phonetics and phonology*. Oxford: Blackwell.

Durand, Jaques. 1990. *Generative and non-linear phonology*. Harlow, Essex and New York: Longman.

Hyman, Larry. 1975. *Phonology: theory and analysis*. New York: Holt, Rinehart and Winston.

Schane. Sanford A. 1973. *Generative phonology*. Englewood Cliffs, NJ: Prentice-Hall Inc.

A particularly valuable, more topical and rather more recent work, focussing specifically on English, is:

Harris, John. 1994. *English sound structure: an introduction*. Oxford: Blackwell.

Equally, Giegerich 1992 focusses specifically on English (chapters 5 and 6 are a good starting point), while of current introductory textbooks McMahon 2002 gives a particularly useful and concise introduction to features and rules as these are expressed in English consonant systems in chapter 4 of *An introduction to English phonology* (Edinburgh University Press).

ii. Other approaches to the internal organisation of segments

It would be quite wrong not to notice an important alternative (and still highly current) view of the internal organisation of segments (indeed, of sound systems in general). This is the view of *Dependency Phonology* (DP). The starting point for further enquiry should be the following textbook:

Anderson, John M. and Colin Ewen. 1987. *Principles of dependency phonology.* Cambridge University Press.

Further textbooks or monographs are:

Anderson, John M. and Jacques Durand. eds. 1987. *Explorations in dependency phonology.* Dordrecht: Foris.

Durand, Jacques. ed. 1986. *Dependency and non-linear phonology.* London: Croom Helm.

An introduction to DP (written by John Anderson), together with a comprehensive bibliography, can be found in the collection of DP papers held online by the University of Bremen:

http://www.fb10.uni-bremen.de/linguistik/dpng/dp/dp.htm.

iii. Optimality Theory

OT is represented in two current major textbooks:

Archangeli, Diana and Terence Langendoen. eds. 1997. *Optimality theory: an overview.* Oxford: Blackwell.

Kager, René. 1999. *Optimality theory.* Cambridge University Press.

What can be considered the founding documents of OT, however, are the following:

Prince, Alan and Paul Smolensky. 1993. *Optimality theory: constraint interaction in generative grammar.* Ms., Rutgers University Center for Cognitive Science Technical Report #2. (And see below.)

McCarthy, John and Alan Prince. 1993. 'Generalized alignment.' In G. E. Booij and J. van Marle. eds. 1993. *Yearbook of morphology.* Dordrecht: Kluwer, 79–153.

These and many other papers are collected, searchable and readable in an important online collection relating to OT held at Rutgers University. This is the Rutgers Optimality Archive (ROA): http://roa.rutgers.edu. It is searchable by author, topic, or document number. For example, Prince and Smolensky (1993) is available as document 537–0802. The reader should also consult John McCarthy and Alan Prince. 1993. *Prosodic morphology: constraint interaction and satisfaction*, ROA 482–1201.

Appendix: the IPA

THE INTERNATIONAL PHONETIC ALPHABET (revised to 2005)

CONSONANTS (PULMONIC)

© 2005 IPA

	Bilabial	Labiodental	Dental	Alveolar	Postalveolar	Retroflex	Palatal	Velar	Uvular	Pharyngeal	Glottal
Plosive	p b			t d		ʈ ɖ	c ɟ	k ɡ	q ɢ		ʔ
Nasal	m	ɱ		n		ɳ	ɲ	ŋ	N		
Trill	ʙ			r					R		
Tap or Flap		ⱱ		ɾ		ɽ					
Fricative	ɸ β	f v	θ ð	s z	ʃ ʒ	ʂ ʐ	ç ʝ	x ɣ	χ ʁ	ħ ʕ	h ɦ
Lateral fricative				ɬ ɮ							
Approximant		ʋ		ɹ		ɻ	j	ɰ			
Lateral approximant				l		ɭ	ʎ	ʟ			

Where symbols appear in pairs, the one to the right represents a voiced consonant. Shaded areas denote articulations judged impossible.

CONSONANTS (NON-PULMONIC)

Clicks		Voiced implosives		Ejectives	
ʘ	Bilabial	ɓ	Bilabial	’	Examples:
ǀ	Dental	ɗ	Dental/alveolar	p’	Bilabial
ǃ	(Post)alveolar	ʄ	Palatal	t’	Dental/alveolar
ǂ	Palatoalveolar	ɠ	Velar	k’	Velar
ǁ	Alveolar lateral	ʛ	Uvular	s’	Alveolar fricative

OTHER SYMBOLS

ʍ	Voiceless labial-velar fricative	ɕ ʑ	Alveolo-palatal fricatives
w	Voiced labial-velar approximant	ɺ	Voiced alveolar lateral flap
ɥ	Voiced labial-palatal approximant	ɧ	Simultaneous ʃ and x
ʜ	Voiceless epiglottal fricative		
ʢ	Voiced epiglottal fricative	Affricates and double articulations can be represented by two symbols joined by a tie bar if necessary.	
ʡ	Epiglottal plosive	k͡p t͡s	

DIACRITICS

Diacritics may be placed above a symbol with a descender, e.g. ŋ̊

̥	Voiceless	n̥ d̥	̤	Breathy voiced	b̤ a̤	̪	Dental	t̪ d̪
̬	Voiced	s̬ t̬	̰	Creaky voiced	b̰ a̰	̺	Apical	t̺ d̺
ʰ	Aspirated	tʰ dʰ	̼	Linguolabial	t̼ d̼	̻	Laminal	t̻ d̻
̹	More rounded	ɔ̹	ʷ	Labialized	tʷ dʷ	̃	Nasalized	ẽ
̜	Less rounded	ɔ̜	ʲ	Palatalized	tʲ dʲ	ⁿ	Nasal release	dⁿ
̟	Advanced	u̟	ˠ	Velarized	tˠ dˠ	ˡ	Lateral release	dˡ
̠	Retracted	e̠	ˤ	Pharyngealized	tˤ dˤ	̚	No audible release	d̚
̈	Centralized	ë	̴	Velarized or pharyngealized	ɫ			
̽	Mid-centralized	e̽	̝	Raised	e̝	(ɹ̝ = voiced alveolar fricative)		
̩	Syllabic	n̩	̞	Lowered	e̞	(β̞ = voiced bilabial approximant)		
̯	Non-syllabic	e̯	̘	Advanced Tongue Root	e̘			
˞	Rhoticity	ɚ a˞	̙	Retracted Tongue Root	e̙			

VOWELS

	Front		Central		Back
Close	i • y		ɨ • ʉ		ɯ • u
		ɪ ʏ		ʊ	
Close-mid	e • ø		ɘ • ɵ		ɤ • o
			ə		
Open-mid	ɛ • œ		ɜ • ɞ		ʌ • ɔ
		æ	ɐ		
Open		a • ɶ			ɑ • ɒ

Where symbols appear in pairs, the one to the right represents a rounded vowel.

SUPRASEGMENTALS

ˈ	Primary stress	
ˌ	Secondary stress	ˌfoʊnəˈtɪʃən
ː	Long	eː
ˑ	Half-long	eˑ
̆	Extra-short	ĕ
ǀ	Minor (foot) group	
‖	Major (intonation) group	
.	Syllable break	ɹi.ækt
‿	Linking (absence of a break)	

TONES AND WORD ACCENTS

LEVEL			CONTOUR		
e̋ or	˥	Extra high	ě or	˩˥	Rising
é	˦	High	ê	˥˩	Falling
ē	˧	Mid	e᷄	˦˥	High rising
è	˨	Low	e᷅	˩˨	Low rising
ȅ	˩	Extra low	e᷈	˧˦˧	Rising-falling
↓		Downstep	↗		Global rise
↑		Upstep	↘		Global fall

Glossary of key terms

accent   As we've been using it in this book, 'accent' refers to the spoken system (i.e. the manifestation of a given phonology) pertaining to a particular variety of English. *Accent*, in this sense, is distinct from *dialect*: *dialect* features of a variety will include syntactic, morphological and lexico-semantic materials as well as phonological ones. We may speak, therefore, of the *accents* of e.g. Northern Englishes, South African English, *General American* (GA), and so on.

affricate   A consonant phoneme whose production involves two manners of articulation: a *stop* component and a *fricative* release. Examples in English are /ʧ/ (<<u>ch</u>ur<u>ch</u>>) *and* /ʤ/ (<<u>j</u>u<u>dge</u>>). It's necessary to distinguish clearly between affricates such as /ʧ/ and fricatives such as /ʃ/. The *minimal pair* <chin> and <shin> is instructive here.

allophone   Allophones are surface (i.e. phonetic) realisations of underlying *phonemes*. They occur predictably in specified environments, and the predictability of their occurrence leads directly to the observation that the allophones of a given phoneme are in *complementary distribution*. An example would be an allophone which is the phonetic expression of underlying /p/: [pʰ]. This last occurs entirely predictably in (and only ever in) the *onset* of stressed syllables.

alveolar ridge   The bony ridge situated just behind the upper teeth. This is the *place of articulation* of many *consonants* in English (/t/, /s/, /d/, /z/, /n/).

approximant   Approximant consonants are phonemes which have articulatory features in common with *vowels*, and which may behave rather like vowels, e.g. may function themselves as syllabic peaks. Examples are /w/ and /j/, which have articulatory features in common with the vowels /u:/ and /i:/ respectively. /l/ and /ɹ/ may also be classified as approximants – notice these last phonemes may function as syllabic peaks in words such as <bottle> and <butter> (/bɒtl/, /bʌtɹ/).

articulation   The way in which a given speech sound is produced (phonetically realised) by the manipulation of the vocal apparatus is called its *articulation*. *Consonant phonemes* are generally described and classified in terms of (at least) three articulatory parameters: *voice; place* (of articulation); and *manner* (of articulation). *Vowel phonemes* are described and classified in terms of three articulatory parameters: height (high-mid-low, or sometimes close-mid-open is used instead); back-front; and roundness.

British English (BrE)   A cover term for a group of accents within the British Isles which do not have marked regional characteristics but which nevertheless appear to share all (or very large parts) of the same underlying phonological system. For practical purposes, BrE may be held to be spoken in large parts of the mainland UK, not including the extreme west and south-west, Scotland or Ireland.

(I acknowledge here the clumsiness of the term 'British'; the alternative would be to use an even clumsier and more potentially misleading cover term such as 'English English' – a variety whose prestige accent would until recently have been RP.) See also *General American*; *standard*.

Cardinal Vowels   The (Primary) Cardinal Vowels consist of 'eight basic vowels of known formation and acoustic qualities, which serve as a standard of measurement, and by reference to which other vowels can be described' (*The principles of the International Phonetic Association* 1949: 4). There are eight such reference points, four front and four back.

chain shift   *Chain shifts* may occur in phonological systems when one term (i.e. *phoneme*) in the system changes, causing consequent change in what are perceived to be neighbouring or adjacent terms in the same system. The most spectacular examples of such chain shifts occur in the system of vowels (the *Great Vowel Shift* in English is one such example of a major chain shift), but equally important chain shifts may also occur in consonant systems.

   Suppose, for example, that the vowel /iː/ starts (for whatever reason) to change in quality. That change leaves an empty 'slot' in the high, front vowel position. In a chain shift, an immediately adjacent vowel– i.e. the next lowest term in the front vowel set, /eː/– might be expected to raise in order to occupy the position just vacated by the change in /iː/.

class   Where *phonemes* appear to have several or most features in common (features which are most often given in articulatory terms), and where these phonemes appear to behave in the same ways in the same environments (something that may be deduced most clearly from the allophones related to those same underlying phonemes), then one may begin to suspect that one is analysing a 'class' (a *natural class*) of phonemes. An example would be the class of *voiceless stops* in English: /p, t, k/ are all strongly aspirated when they occur initially in a stressed syllable.

coda   A constituent within the syllable which contains syllable-final consonant phonemes. In the syllable <ground> for example, /nd/ would fall within the coda; in <groom>, /m/ would fall within the coda. Many of the world's languages, while having obligatory *onsets* and *nuclei* within well-formed syllables, do not tolerate filled codas.

complementary distribution   *Allophones* are said to be in complementary distribution since particular environments are reserved for the occurrence of distinct allophones related to one underlying phoneme. The allophones of /p/, for instance, include [pʰ] and [p]: 'initial in a stressed syllable' is the environment reserved for the aspirated allophone ([pʰleɪ], <play>) and 'after a stressed vowel and before an unstressed one' is the environment reserved for [p] ([sʌpə], <supper>). Since they occur predictably in specified but different environments, [pʰ] and [p] are in complementary distribution.

compound   A word consisting of minimally two, and occasionally more, lexical items. Of these items, the leftmost characteristically bears stronger *stress* than the rightmost. One syllable of the leftmost item is said to bear *primary stress*, while one syllable of the rightmost lexical item bears *secondary stress*. Examples of compounds are *bookcase, fairground, redcap* (a kind of bird) and *yellowhammer* (another kind of bird). Compounds are usually both structurally and audibly distinct from phrases, thus a *yellowhammer* (bird) is something quite different from a *yellow hammer* (a hammer coloured yellow).

consonant A phoneme whose articulation 'involves some audible obstruction in the oral cavity' (Giegerich 1992: 8).

constituent A structural part of a larger entity (in our context, a linguistic entity). The *onset*, *nucleus* and *coda* of a syllable, for instance, are *constituents* (but not the only constituents) functioning within the syllable. Constituents may be distinguished if two terms suspected to belong to the same possible constituent seem to have a structural relationship with each other. An example here would be the restrictive relationship between the first and second consonants in a well-formed English syllable: the second of the two consonants generally has to be more sonorant than the first (/pleɪ/ is well-formed, but */lpeɪ/ is not). This relationship seems to hold *only* between those two terms in the syllable, and therefore we suppose that those two terms function within a constituent of the syllable, i.e. the onset of the syllable.

constraint *Constraints* are key components of a linguistic model of language production and processing known as *Optimality Theory* (OT). In such a model, constraints are well-formedness conditions which evaluate possible output forms, rejecting some while privileging others – and decisively choosing, from among all conceivable competitors, in favour of the *optimal* candidate to emerge from the shuffle of constraint evaluation. Constraints are held to be universal (i.e. phonological systems of all languages will in principle contain all constraints), and are ranked language-specifically in such a way that some are more important than others. (Some low-ranked constraints, in fact, may not play any ostensible part in evaluating certain output forms, and a certain amount of apparent redundancy is built into OT.) All constraints are in principle violable, but where a constraint is violated, such violation is (only) permitted because some higher-ranked constraint within the set of constraints remains non-violated. This model is introduced and discussed in chapter 11. The few constraints we used in the case studies there are:

*COMPLEX (ONSET)
Syllables contain no more than one segment in their onsets
IDENT-IO
Keep the identity between input form and output candidate exact, i.e. change nothing. This constraint is one instantiation of a larger group of FAITHFULNESS constraints.
NOCODA
Syllables must end with a vowel
ONSET
Syllables must have onsets
PEAK
Syllables must have a nucleus containing one or more vowel segments
SONORITY
Onsets must increase and codas decrease in sonority

contrast A key principle of phonemic analysis. One *phoneme* within a system must show at least a minimal contrast with another phoneme within the same system. The consonant phonemes /b/ and /p/, for example, are both bilabial, and both are plosives, but they differ (minimally) in terms of voicing. That difference or contrast is also exemplified in the *minimal pair* /bɪn/ and /pɪn/. Since these items are different words (i.e. they have different meanings), the minimal contrast between /b/ and /p/ is sufficient to enable us to claim we have in that contrast identified a pair of phonemes.

contrastive distribution   Because of those principles sketched under *contrast* above, phonemes are said to be in *contrastive distribution*. *Distribution* means roughly and in this context 'place within the syllable', thus in a word like <pin>, /p/ occurs in ('is distributed in') syllable-initial position, and it is in that position that /p/ contrasts so meaningfully with /b/. (Note that *allophones* of phonemes are said to be in *complementary distribution*.)

dental   *Dental* consonants are those produced with an articulation involving the teeth: /θ/ (voiceless *dental* fricative) and /f/ (voiceless *labio-dental* fricative) are two instances of dental consonants.

derivational morphology   The process by which words are built through the compounding of component parts (morphemes). *Morphology* is the systematic study of the internal structure of words. Derivational morphology contrasts with *inflectional morphology* in that a derived form (contra inflected form) generally involves a change in either the meaning and/or the word class to the base form and derivation is said to occur at an earlier stage (or deeper level) than inflection.

diachronic variation   Languages, and varieties within languages, vary not only at one particular time, but vary (change) across time. *Diachrony* in the linguistic context means 'historical'. If a linguist is interested in reconstructing how one language (or variety of that language) has shown variation (changed) across time, then he or she is studying the diachronic variation exhibited by that language or variety.

dialect   A variety of a language which exhibits regional characteristics including syntactic, morphological, lexico-semantic and phonological forms. My little finger, for instance, might be your *pinkie*; her *fringe* might be another's *bangs*; my *boot* may be your *trunk*. *Pinkie*, *bangs* and *trunk* are lexical items occurring characteristically in the dialect 'American English'; *little finger*, *fringe* and *trunk* occur in the dialect 'British English'.

diphthong   A vowel phoneme whose quality changes during the pronunciation of the vowel. Examples would be /aʊ/ (*house*), /əʊ/ (*hose*) and /aɪ/ (*hide*). See also *vowel quality*.

distinctive features   Parts of the internal composition of phonemes. *Distinctive features* (informally, just 'features') are binary, i.e. they are switched on or off during speech production. That binarity is symbolised by +/- . The terms used for the distinctive features themselves are almost invariably set within square brackets, thus [coronal], [voice] etc. Here I shall confine myself just to those features discussed in chapter 11.

[±anterior]:   [+anterior] sounds are those produced with constriction occurring in the forward parts of the mouth (e.g. the alveolar ridge).
[±back]:   [+back] sounds are produced with the back of the body of the tongue retracted and/or raised. /u:/ is [+back]; /i:/ is [-back].
[±consonantal]:   [+consonantal] sounds are those produced with a radical constriction in the oral cavity.

[± continuant]: [+continuant] phonemes are produced with incomplete obstruction to the airstream in the oral cavity. [-continuant] phonemes are produced with maximal obstruction (i.e. the stops).

[±coronal]: [+coronal] consonants are produced with the blade of the tongue raised from its neutral position.

[+high]: [+high] sounds are produced with the blade and tip of the tongue markedly raised from neutral position.

[± labial]: [+labial] sounds are produced with an articulation involving one or both lips.

[±long]: [+long] vowels are associated with two X-slots within the nucleus of the syllable. (Note: precisely because there is a syllable-based generalisation available to us which accounts neatly for the structure of 'long' vowels, [+long] may well turn out to be redundant in English, and indeed was rejected here in chapter 10.)

[±low]: [+low] vowels are produced with tongue-lowering, i.e. there is a maximal distance between the body of the tongue and the hard palate.

[±nasal]: [+nasal] sounds are produced with a lowering of the velum and consequent nasal air-escape. [-nasal] sounds are produced with the velum raised.

[±round]: [+round] sounds are produced with marked lip-rounding. /u:/ is [+round]; /i:/ is [-round].

[±sonorant]: [+sonorant] sounds are highly resonant sounds produced with voicing.

[±strident]: [+strident] sounds are produced with a perceptible hiss.

[±syllabic]: [+syllabic] defines the role a segment might play in the structure of the syllable. Since it may occupy a syllabic nucleus in its own right, for example, [l] might be regarded as a [+syllabic] consonant (*bottle, nettle*).

[±tense]: [+tense] vowels are 'produced with a deliberate, accurate, maximally distinct gesture that involves considerable muscular effort; nontense sounds are produced rapidly and somewhat indistinctly' (Giegerich 1992: 98). /i:/ would be a [+tense] vowel, /ɪ/ would be [-tense].

[±voice]: [+voice] sounds are produced with vibration in the vocal folds.

A full discussion of distinctive features will be found in Giegerich (1992), especially chapters 5, 6 and 9.

In a view of phonology relying critically on distinctive features, an individual *phoneme* is itself the expression of all those features (and their +/- values) associated with that phone. See also *features*.

egressive (airstream) The airstream issuing from the lungs which we use for speaking is called *egressive* ('exiting'). The opposite term is *ingressive* – but it's very hard to speak using an ingressive airstream, i.e. when you're breathing in. (Try it.)

faithfulness, in OT See *constraints* (above), and within *constraints*, IDENT-IO. That last is only one example of a faithfulness constraint. For others, see Kager 1999.

factorial typology See *typology*.

feature bundle, feature matrix See *features* below.

features See *distinctive features*. Within generative and other types of phonology, a *phoneme* is held to be the expression of all those distinctive features (and their +/- values) associated with that phoneme. The assembly of features (and their +/- values) pertaining to the behaviour of a phoneme or class of phonemes is sometimes said to be a *feature bundle* or, more formally, a *feature matrix*.

fricative A sound produced with a continual air-escape and audible friction. See also *affricate*.

General American (GA) '… a cover term used for a group of accents in the United States that do not bear the marked regional characteristics of either the East (more precisely, Eastern New England and New York City) or the South (mainly ranging from Virginia, the Carolinas and Georgia to Louisiana and Texas' (Giegerich 1992: 47). It's worth repeating here that GA is 'one of (at least) three "standard" accents found in the United States; it is by far the most widespread one' (Giegerich 1992: 47). See also *British English*.

glottal An articulation involving the glottis. Within the English *consonant* system, /h/ appears to be the only glottal *phoneme* (a glottal fricative). See also *glottal stop* below.

glottal stop A relatively widespread phonetic realisation of /t/ in BrE – so widespread that '/t/-glottaling' may be used as a diagnostic for certain *accents*, notably Cockney. One particularly acute problem for phonemic analysis is the fact that the glottal stop may *also* be a realisation of /p/ and /k/ where these occur in syllable-final position – in which case, the glottal stop [ʔ] cannot be defined without further ado as an allophone of /t/.

grammar A rule-governed and/or *constraint*-based linguistic system.

graphology The system lying behind the production of written symbols.

Great Vowel Shift Usually held to be a *chain shift* involving long and (to some extent) short vowels, the Great Vowel Shift (GVS) is usually held to have begun as a chain shift in the late fourteenth century, either by the diphthongisation of /iː/ or by the earlier fronting and raising of /ɑː/. Barber (1993) gives a concise overview. A much studied set of changes – and still controversial.

hard palate The bony arch lying at the roof of the mouth, and extending from the soft palate at the rear to the alveolar ridge.

homophone Two – usually lexical – words having identical pronunciations but different meanings are called *homophones*. An example would be *new* and *knew*. Slightly more interesting examples are formed by pairs where the pronunciation of one of the two terms might be stigmatised, e.g. in BrE *picture* ([pɪtʃə], sometimes stigmatised) and *pitcher*.

hypercorrection '[T]he use of an erroneous word form or pronunciation based on a false analogy with a correct or prestigious form' (*New Oxford Dictionary of English*). From a formal perspective, hypercorrection can be viewed as the over-generalisation of a phonological rule: '… a Scotsman, for instance, trying to acquire RP, may well not be aware that in RP /əʊ/ cannot occur before /r/ within the same morpheme' (Wells 1982: 115). The same Scotsman will therefore consciously acquire /əʊ/ in words such as *goat*, *coat*, *snow* but might then begin to overapply the acquired /əʊ/ phoneme to words such as *four*, *course* – words which have never had the /əʊ/ pronunciation in RP. (Example drawn from Wells 1982:

115. Wells 1982, section 1.4.8, 'Altering one's accent' is most illuminating in the context of a discussion of hypercorrection.)

inflectional morphology   The study of the internal structure of words is known as *morphology*. Within morphology, one can look at how elements such as prefixes, suffixes and even other words combine with word roots to make new words (e.g. *happy*, *happy-clappy*, *unhappy*, *unhappily*). That is part of the analysis of a language's *derivational morphology* – how new words are derived. But one can also study how (most typically) single segments may be added to word roots in order to indicate grammatical information. An example would be the study of how English nouns might be made plural: normatively, some kind of 's' is suffixed to the root, and forms an *inflection* expressing plurality. What interests the phonologist in this example of inflectional morphology is that the form of the 's' depends on the voicing of the consonant (if any) final in the root. If that consonant is voiceless, then the plural inflection will be voiceless (/kat-s/, cats), whereas if the root-final consonant is voiced, then the inflection will also be voiced (/dɒg-z/, dogs).

intrusive 'r'   /r/ is said to be *intrusive* when it appears in speech (most characteristically, between vowels) where no underlying /r/ is present in the syllables and words being pronounced. A notorious example of intrusive /r/ often occurs in the phrase *law and order* (/lɔːrənɔːdə/– for a further discussion, see section 11.6 of this book, and compare the pronunciation of *law* when this is spoken in isolation).

inventory   An inventory is a collection; therefore *inventory*, in phonological terms, may refer to the entire set of *consonant* and *vowel phonemes* of a particular language variety ('the inventory of phonemes'); the term can also apply to the full collection of *distinctive features* pertaining to and defining those phonemes, thus 'the inventory of features' or 'feature inventory'.

labial   Labial consonants are those produced using one or both lips as the chief articulators (e.g. /b/ or /f/). The distinctive feature [±labial] is discussed above under *distinctive features*.

labio-dental   Labio-dental consonants in English are the *fricatives* /f/ and /v/, which involve articulation using the bottom lip and top teeth.

larynx   A term for the cartilaginous casing which protects the *vocal folds*. The front part of this casing can be felt at the top of the windpipe: it is the Adam's apple.

lateral   *Lateral* consonants are those where the articulation involves the airstream flowing laterally (i.e. around the sides of the tongue). An example in English is the lateral approximant /l/.

lexical monosyllable   *Lexical monosyllables* are semantically meaningful single-syllable words of a known minimal syllabic composition which includes a minimally two-X *rhyme*. Examples would be *egg*, *good*, *dog*, *watch*, *pen*, *cup* and so on. Such meaningful words may be usefully contrasted with non-lexical monosyllables such as *in*, *a*, *the*, *by* and so on: these last are not semantically meaningful, though they have important grammatical functions; they also do not fulfil the phonological criteria for lexical monosyllables, in that their rhymes may consist just of a single X-slot (e.g. *a*, /ə/)

lexical word   A *lexical word* is a word with meaningful content, usually belonging to the syntactic categories noun, verb or adjective/adverb. *Butter*, *happenstance*, *computer* and *unhappiness* are examples of lexical words.

lexicon   When a linguist refers to the *lexicon* he or she is referring to a speaker's total 'mental dictionary' of language together with those levels of structure into which that mental dictionary is organised, and comprising any operations relevant to the well-formedness, storage and retrieval of items within that mental dictionary. Such a lexicon would contain, for example, two entries for the words *atom* and *atomic*, and would also contain the principles whereby *atomic* could be derived from *atom*.

linking 'r'   The allophone [r] does not appear to be present syllable-finally in an RP speaker's utterance of a word such as <war>, [wɔː], but it is more certainly present in that same speaker's utterance of the phrase <war is>. Where [r] occurs in such words and environments (apparently between vowels) then it is said to be a *linking 'r'*. Parts of chapters 10 and 11 of this book, however, propose that in words such as *war* and *lore* an /r/ is *underlyingly* present even in apparently 'non-rhotic' accents, see e.g. sections 10.6 and 11.6.

long vowels   *Long vowels* are vowels associated with two X-slots within the syllabic nucleus. One significant characteristic of their composition is that such 'long' vowels are usually [+tense] (see *distinctive features*). Examples include /iː/ (/hiːd/, *heed*) and /ɔː/ (/hɔːl/, *hall*).

manner (of articulation)   The *manner of articulation* of a given segment is a concise statement of *how* that segment is pronounced, particularly with respect to the manner of modification to the airstream. The term *fricative*, for instance, is a statement of the manner of articulation: continuous airstream, but with occlusion in the oral cavity so that friction occurs such that the airstream is made turbulent.

merger   Vowels, in particular, may be subject to *mergers*, often for historical reasons. One example of a merger is discussed in section 10.2, and involves the merger of the /ɑː/ vowel of words such as *calm* with the /ɑː/ vowel which was later to be heard in words such as *grass* – which words had, historically, a short vowel. As the vowel in the *grass* words lengthened (in some varieties), it *merged* with the vowel already existing in the *calm* words.

minimal pair   Pairs of words contrasting minimally in one segment, such that the segmental *contrast* yields two meaningfully different words. Examples are *bad* and *mad* (where the contrast is between /b/ and /m/) and *neck* and *beck* (where the contrast is between /n/ and /b/). The analysis of such minimal pairs is a key discovery procedure in phonology, since it establishes the phonemic *inventory*.

monosyllable   A word containing only one syllabic *nucleus*.

morphology   The systematic study of the internal composition of words. Those studying morphology find it useful to make a distinction between *derivational morphology* and *inflectional morphology*.

nasal   A *nasal* consonant is produced by lowering of the *velum*, allowing the airstream to escape through the nasal cavity. English has the nasal consonants /n/, /m/ and /ŋ/.

natural class   Phonemes having some of the same articulatory characteristics may be said to form a *natural class*. A well-known example is the class of voiceless plosives: they are all [-voice]; they are all [-continuant]; they are all [-sonorant] … and all have the same range of *allophones* associated with them.

noun   A *lexical word* which may undergo known patterns of derivational affixation, and which may be inflected for plurality. See also *lexical monosyllable*.

nucleus   The *nucleus* of a syllable is that part of the syllable which is usually associated to vowel segments, but which may also be associated to so-called [+syllabic] consonants.

onset   The *onset* of a syllable is the leftmost internal constituent of the syllable, and in many of the world's languages it is obligatorily filled by one or more consonants.

opacity   *Opacity* may occur in ordered rule applications which are attempting to derive a phonetic output from a phonological input. Opaque forms are forms produced merely mechanistically, and whose existence cannot be inferred either from the phonological structure or from the form of the phonetic output. The question then arises as to how any speaker could ever learn such forms. Opacity is briefly discussed here in 11.4.

oral cavity   An *egressive airstream* flowing up through the *larynx* can then pass through (maximally) three cavities: the pharyngeal cavity, the oral cavity and the *nasal* cavity. English speech sounds are articulated most often with some sort of (modifying) constriction in the oral cavity, which contains the body and front part of the tongue.

palate   A rather over-general term for the roof of the mouth, though also, and more accurately, used to refer to the *hard palate*. The 'roof of the mouth' extends from the soft palate (or velum) forwards to the *hard palate*, and extends from there to the *alveolar ridge*.

palato-alveolar   Consonants whose articulation involves *alveolar* occlusion plus *fricative* release on the (hard) palate are said to be *palato-alveolar affricates*. There are two of them, /tʃ/ (*chur*ch) and /dʒ/ (*ju*dge).

phoneme   A sound segment whose existence is confirmed by phonological *contrast* within *minimal-pair* tests. Phonemes are parts of the sound system (phonology) of a given language, and are themselves abstract and underlying; the surface (phonetic) realisations of underlying phonemes are *allophones*. Phonemes are always transcribed within slant brackets, whereas allophones are always transcribed within square ones, thus the representation /pɪt/ 'pit' is a phonemic representation whereas [pʰɪʔ] is an allophonic one.

phonemic transcription   A phonemic transcription is a transcription of a string of *phonemes*, such as these occur in the variety of the language which the analyst is transcribing. Such transcriptions are enclosed within /.../ brackets placed at the beginning and end of the entire string of sound being transcribed. Usually, phonemic transcriptions will contain a minimal number of diacritic marks.

phonetics   The study of the physical production (articulation) and acoustic signal of speech sounds. While *phonetics* is indivisibly linked with *phonology*, phonetics may be said to focus on the manifest physical events, whereas phonology attempts to identify and describe the system lying behind the events comprising the acoustic signal.

phonological rule   A *phonological rule* regulates the relationship between underlying *phonemes* and their phones and *allophones* insofar as its application will derive, in as exceptionless a way as possible, surface forms from underlying sequences of phonemes.

phonology   The identification and description of the system underlying the events comprising the acoustic signal of speech in any given language.

phonotactics   Literally, 'sound-touching': the study of the principles governing what sounds can co-occur and lie directly adjacent to each other within the syllable. The observation that /pl/ is a well-formed *onset*, and that */lp/ is an ill-formed one, is a *phonotactic* observation.

place (of articulation)   A diagnostic feature of the production (and classification) of *consonants*. Such diagnostics include terms such as *alveolar*, *palatal* and so on.

plosive   A feature of the production of *consonants*, namely those whose articulation involves the brief stoppage of the airstream within the oral cavity, with a subsequent explosive (note the term: *ex+plosive*) release.

polysyllable   A word is *polysyllabic* when its root contains more than one syllable. Since one diagnostic of syllables is identity between the syllable and its *nucleus* (i.e. monosyllables will have one and only one nucleus), then polysyllables will have more than one nucleus. The term is usually applied to *lexical words*, but there are also many non-lexical words which are polysyllables: *under, over, between* are examples of these last.

post-vocalic   Occurring immediately after a *vowel* segment.

pre-vocalic   Occurring immediately before a *vowel* segment.

RP   An abbreviation for *Received Pronunciation*: 'In England ... there are some speakers who do not have a local accent. One can tell from their speech that they are British (and very probably English) but nothing else. This non-localisable accent of England is what phoneticians refer to as *Received Pronunication*' (Wells 1982: 10). RP now seems increasingly old-fashioned – see *standard*. I have heard the term 'received' explained by the observation that a speaker of RP was eligible to be 'received' at court, but a less decorative explanation is that 'received' here means 'widely accepted as authoritative'.

rhoticity   *Rhotic* accents of English are those with a surface manifestation of *post-vocalic* /r/. Accents having this characteristic are said to include *rhoticity* as a part of their phonology and phonetics, i.e. they are rhotic accents.

rhyme   As the term is used in this book, a *rhyme* is a constituent of the syllable. The rhyme of an English syllable obligatorily contains a filled *nucleus*, and may contain a filled *coda*.

rule   See *phonological rule*.

runic   The *runic* alphabet was employed in West, North and East Germanic, and pre-dates the Latin alphabet. The symbols of the runic alphabet were often carved into wood or stone, and were largely angular in shape (so that the cross-strokes stood out against the grain of the material into which the runes were being carved).

schwa   Also spelled *shwa*. A *vowel* associated with one X-slot within the *nucleus*, whose phonetic characteristics include centrality and lack of tenseness, i.e. the tongue is central and in a neutral position, neither markedly raised nor lowered. *Schwa* is associated with unstressed vowels, and forms one very perceptible and usually useful diagnostic in identifying such vowels.

segment   A *segment* is a unit within the sound structure of a language which may have a simple or complex internal composition. That is, all *phonemes* within a language are segments of that language, yet the segmental inventory of a language may also in principle include items such as '/ø/', which is not in itself contrastive. Simple segments are associated with one X-slot within the syllable in which they occur; complex segments may be associated with two X-slots.

short vowel   A *short vowel* is a simple (non-complex) vocalic segment occurring within the *nucleus* of a syllable.

soft palate   A less formal term for the *velum*, the perceptibly soft tissue at the rear of the roof of the mouth.

sonority   *Sonority* appears to be a scalar phenomenon in which the segments of a language are ranked with respect to their relative openness, relative lack of occlusion, and voicing. On a prototypical sonority scale, *vowels*, for example, are very highly sonorous (relatively open, relative lack of occlusion, always voiced), while *voiceless stops* lack sonority (airstream occluded, voiceless).

Sonority Sequencing Generalisation (SSG)   Because *sonority* plays an important role in the internal organisation of syllables, several attempts have been made to construct sonority scales from which generalisations may be made about what segments may precede/follow other segments within the internal constituents of the syllable. A longhand statement of one such generalisation, a *sonority sequencing generalisation*, might be something like: 'the least sonorous consonants fall at the extreme margins of the syllable; the most sonorous segments fall in the leftmost or only position within the nucleus'.

split   Just as there are *mergers* within the phonological system of a language, so are there *splits*. Like mergers, splits seem to occur most frequently in the *vowel* system. In this book, one particular example of a split is discussed in chapter 10.2. The discussion there focuses on the split of the /a/ vowel originally found in words such as *cat*, *cap*, *grass*, *chaff* and *bath*. Where this vowel preceded a voiceless continuant then in some varieties it developed a lengthened variant. In 10.2 this split is diagrammatised as follows:

Phonemic splits: *grass*, *path*, *chaff*

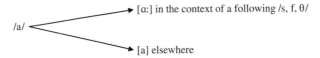

/a/ → [ɑː] in the context of a following /s, f, θ/

/a/ → [a] elsewhere

standard   Wells (1982: 34) defines a *standard accent* as follows: 'A standard accent is one which, at a given time and place, is generally considered correct: it is held up as a model of how one ought to speak, it is encouraged in the classroom, it is widely regarded as the most desirable accent for a person in a high-status profession to have.' Until relatively recently, RP was regarded as the standard accent for BrE, though it is now perhaps regarded as old-fashioned, particularly 'conservative RP', and has to some extent been replaced as a standard accent by Standard Southern British English – a standard which nevertheless contains some features of an originally 'Northern' character, such as /a/ in words like *hat*.

Note that there are also *regional standard* accents (Tyneside, Merseyside and several others within the British Isles; New York City and several others within North America). See also *RP*.

stop   A *stop* is a consonant whose production involves the brief stoppage of the airstream in the vocal tract, with a subsequent *plosive* release. Stops may be voiced or voiceless. Examples are /p, b, t, d, k, g/.

stress   A *stressed* syllable is one that is perceptibly more prominent, in terms of either duration, complexity or intensity (where 'intensity' includes loudness) than any immediately adjacent syllable (or, in the case of lexical monosyllables, silence). In English, stressed syllables often have a minimal syllabic composition, with two X-slots in their *rhymes*, meaning that stressed syllables effectively have either complex vowels (*long vowels* or *diphthongs*) or short vowels followed by at least one consonant.

It's worth noting here that stress in English is also sensitive to lexical and syntactic information, insofar as the stress pattern obtaining in most *compounds* is 'leftmost-strongest' (i.e. strongest relative stress falling on the leftmost lexical item within the compound), while the stress pattern obtaining in phrases is characteristically 'rightmost-strongest', i.e. the main perceptible stress of the entire phrase falls on the strongest syllable of the rightmost lexical item of that phrase.

Although they fall outside the scope of this book, the principles governing word- and phrase-stress assignment in English are well known, if often problematic. There is a very good discussion of those principles in Giegerich (1992: 179–207).

substitution frame   A frame into which segments may be inserted to make meaningful lexical monosyllables, thus helping to establish *minimal pairs* and therefore the existence of phonemic *contrasts*. An example of a *substitution frame* would be /_ at/, into which (among others) the consonants /p, k, h/ could be inserted at the relevant (underscored) space. Such a substitution frame would therefore strongly suggest that /p, k, h/ were *phonemes* of English.

syllable   A syllable is a constituent into which segments of a language are gathered under language-specific well-formedness principles whose form and nature it is the business of phonologists to discover. Syllables have obligatory *nuclei*, very often have obligatory *onsets*, and may include *codas*.

synchronic variation   Variation within a language, or variety of a language, which is observable and describable at a given moment in time. For example, the study of 'present-day English' would usually include the study of synchronic variation, as would e.g. the study of 'the phonology of present-day Tyneside English' or 'the phonology of Tyneside English, 1900–1950'. The term *synchronic* is often, and properly, contrasted with the term *diachronic*: diachronic linguistics studies variation *across* time, rather than *at* a particular time.

synchrony   A *linguistic synchrony* is that period of time chosen for the analysis of that linguistic structure and variation exhibited by a particular variety of a language. See *synchronic variation*.

tableau, in OT   Within Optimality-theoretic analyses the working of and ranking between a set of *constraints* is often set graphically in the form of a display or *tableau*. The more high-ranked constraints in the set are displayed at the left of such tableaux, while lower-ranked constraints are displayed at the right edge. Solid vertical lines separating the relevant constraints indicate that a constraint ranking has been established, while a dotted vertical line between constraints indicates that no ranking has (yet) been established. Optimal candidates are indicated within a tableau by a particular symbol, often a pointing hand. An example of such a tableau is the following, taken from chapter 11 in this book:

OT tableau for *imp*, /ɪmp/

Candidates (/ɪmp /)	PEAK	SONORITY	*faithfulness*	ONSET	*COMPLEX (ONSET)	NOCODA
☞ [ɪmp]				*		*
[pɪmp]			*!			*
[ɪpm]		*!	*	*		*
[mɪp]			*!			

tap   A *tap* is an allophone of /t/, produced with a very brief contact between the tongue and the alveolar ridge. The symbol for the alveolar tap is [ɾ]. Such a tap occurs intervocalically in words such as *latter*, [laɾɹ].

trill   In spoken varieties of English (particularly some varieties of Scottish English) the phoneme /r/ sometimes has surface realisations in an alveolar *trill* involving brief repeated contacts of the tip of the tongue with the rear of the alveolar ridge.

typology   *Typology* means 'classification according to general type' (*New Oxford Dictionary of English*). In a linguistic context, classifying by 'general type' isn't usually very helpful, though a typological approach to phonology would (and does) include methodological classification sufficient to distinguish vowels from consonants, stressed syllables from unstressed, major class features from other features, and so on.

More recently, the word *typology* has been used within OT alongside the adjective factorial: factorial typology. Within OT, that is, it is the job of the analyst to sort out those factors pertaining to a particular ranking of different (types of) *constraint*, and that task therefore means establishing a plausible factorial typology for a given set or subset of constraints.

universal   For the last forty or fifty years it has increasingly been seen as the task of linguistics to study, and thereby to establish, all that the world's languages have in common, including those principles obtaining in the construction of their ostensibly different *grammars*. A universalist approach to phonology would concentrate, for example, on the establishment of an apparently universal set of *distinctive features*, or of *constraints*, showing how a given language made use of all of, or a subset of, those universal features or constraints. 'The search for linguistic universals' is still underway. Much progress has been made – and there is still much to be discovered.

uvular   A *uvular* articulation involves contact between the (back of the body of the) tongue and the rearmost extremity of the velum, the *uvula*. In some varieties of BrE, notably those of the West Riding of Yorkshire and Tyneside, older speakers may have uvular 'r' (more properly, a uvular and fricative 'r') in words such as *brown*, [bʁaʊn].

velum The technical term for the *soft palate*.

vocal folds Also called the vocal cords – horizontal folds of tissue within the *larynx*. Although we are usually unconscious of these folds, they may be held closely together so that they vibrate when the airstream passes through them, or be held apart so that no vibration is caused. Vibration in the vocal folds results in *voiced* sounds, lack of vibration in *voiceless* sounds. The relevant (lack of) vibration may be felt by placing the fingers of the right hand lightly on either side of the larynx, and pronouncing 'ssssszzzz', switching from the voiceless to the voiced sound.

vocal tract A broad term for all those organs, articulatory muscles and other articulators used in the production of speech. It's useful to distinguish between the *subglottal vocal tract* (i.e. those organs lying geographically, as it were, below the larynx, including the trachea and the lungs) from the *supraglottal* vocal tract, a physical space which includes all the other articulatory organs.

voicing When the production of a sound involves vibration in the vocal folds that sound is said to be 'voiced'; when the production of a sound involves no such vibration it is said to be 'voiceless'. *Voicing* is a cover term for this phenomenon.

vowel A *vowel* is a segment within the sound structure of a language whose production is characterised by relative openness, i.e. relative lack of obstruction in the oral cavity. Vowels are described by reference to the relative height and front–back position of the tongue, and by (non-)rounding and further distinguished as long or short. See also *Cardinal Vowels*; *long vowel*; *short vowel*

vowel quality The *quality* of a given vowel refers to its relative height and position, as these last are established by the raising/lowering and fronting/retraction of the (blade and body of the) tongue.

vowel quantity The *quantity* of a given vowel refers to its length or shortness, where such length or shortness is correlated with the internal structure of the syllabic *nucleus* where that vowel occurs.

References

Aitchison, Jean. 1991. *Language change: progress or decay?* 2nd edition. Cambridge University Press.

Anderson, John M. and Colin Ewen. 1987. *Principles of dependency phonology.* Cambridge University Press.

Anderson, John M. and Jacques Durand. eds. 1987. *Explorations in dependency phonology.* Dordrecht: Foris.

Archangeli, Diana and Terence Langendoen. eds. 1997. *Optimality theory: an overview.* Oxford: Blackwell.

Barber, Charles. 1993. *The English language: a historical introduction.* Cambridge University Press.

Baugh, A. C. and Thomas Cable. 1993. *A history of the English language.* 4th edition. London: Routledge.

Beal, Joan. 2000. 'HappY-tensing: a recent innovation?' In Ricardo Bermúdez-Otero, David Denison, Richard M. Hogg and Christopher B. McCully. eds. *Generative theory and corpus studies: a dialogue from 10 ICEHL.* Berlin and New York: Mouton de Gruyter, 483–97.

Broselow, Ellen. 1995. 'Skeletal positions and moras'. In John Goldsmith. ed. *The handbook of phonological theory.* Oxford: Blackwell, 175–205.

Chomsky, Noam and Morris Halle. 1968. *The sound pattern of English.* New York: Harper and Row.

Clark, John and Colin Yallop. 1990. *An introduction to phonetics and phonology.* Oxford: Blackwell.

Crystal, David. 1991. *A dictionary of linguistics and phonetics.* 3rd edition. Oxford: Blackwell.

Crystal, David. 1995. *The Cambridge encyclopedia of the English language.* Cambridge University Press.

Durand, Jacques. ed. 1986. *Dependency and non-linear phonology.* London: Croom Helm.

Durand, Jacques. 1990. *Generative and non-linear phonology.* Harlow, Essex and New York: Longman.

Foulkes, Paul and Gerard Docherty. eds. 1999. *Urban voices: accent studies in the British Isles.* London: Arnold.

Fudge, Erik. 1969. 'Syllables'. *Journal of Linguistics* 5: 253–87.

Giegerich, Heinz. 1980. 'On stress-timing in English phonology'. *Lingua* 51: 187–221.

Giegerich, Heinz. 1983. 'On English sentence stress and the nature of metrical structure'. *Journal of Linguistics* 19: 1–28.

Giegerich, Heinz. 1985. *Metrical phonology and phonological structure: German and English*. Cambridge University Press.

Giegerich, Heinz. 1992. *English phonology: an introduction*. Cambridge University Press.

Gimson, A.C. 1994. *Gimson's pronunciation of English*. 5th edition, revised by Alan Cruttenden. London: Arnold.

Goldsmith, John. ed. 1995. *The handbook of phonological theory*. Oxford: Blackwell.

Goldsmith, John. ed. 1999. *Phonological theory: the essential readings*. Oxford: Blackwell.

Graddol, David, D. Leith and J. Swann. 1996. *English: history, diversity, change*. London: Routledge.

Harris, John. 1994. *English sound structure: an introduction*. Oxford: Blackwell.

Hulst, H. van der and Norval Smith. eds. 1982. *The structure of phonological representations*. Dordrecht: Foris.

Hyman, Larry. 1975. *Phonology: theory and analysis*. New York: Holt, Rinehart and Winston.

International Phonetic Association. 1949. *The principles of the International Phonetic Association*. [Contains the International Phonetic Alphabet (IPA).] University College, London.

Jakobson, Roman and Morris Halle. 1956. *Fundamentals of language*. The Hague: Mouton.

Jones, Daniel. 1917. *An English pronouncing dictionary*. London: Dent.

Kager, René. 1999. *Optimality theory*. Cambridge University Press.

Ladefoged, Peter and Ian Maddieson. 1996. *The sounds of the world's languages*. Oxford: Blackwell.

Lass, Roger. 1984. *Phonology: an introduction to basic concepts*. Cambridge University Press.

Liberman, Mark and Alan Prince. 1977. 'On stress and linguistic rhythm'. *Linguistic Inquiry* 8: 249–336.

McCarthy, John and Alan Prince. 1993. 'Generalized alignment'. In G.E. Booij and J. van Marle. eds. *Yearbook of morphology 1993*. Dordrecht: Kluwer, 79–153. (See also John McCarthy and Alan Prince. 1993. *Prosodic morphology: constraint interaction and satisfaction*. Rutgers Optimality Archive, ROA 482–1201.)

McMahon, April. 2002. *An introduction to English phonology*. Edinburgh University Press.

Prince, Alan and Paul Smolensky. 1993. *Optimality theory: constraint interaction in generative grammar*. Ms., Rutgers University Center for Cognitive Science Technical Report #2 (also Rutgers Optimality Archive, ROA 537–0802).

Roach, Peter. 1991. *English phonetics and phonology*. 2nd edition. Cambridge University Press.

Saussure, Ferdinand de. 1983. *Course in general linguistics*. Translated and annotated by Roy Harris. [First edition assembled after Saussure's death, and published in 1916 as *Cours de linguistique générale*.] London: Duckworth.

Schane, Sanford A. 1973. *Generative phonology*. Englewood Cliffs, NJ: Prentice-Hall Inc.

Schneider, Edgar W., Kate Burridge, Bernd Kortmann, Rajend Mesthrie and Clive Upton. eds. 2004. *A handbook of varieties of English. Volume 1: Phonology.* [Multimedia. Two vols plus CD-ROM.] Berlin and New York: Mouton de Gruyter.

Selkirk, Elisabeth. 1982. 'The syllable'. In H. van der Hulst and N. Smith. eds. *The structure of phonological representations* (Part II). Dordrecht: Foris, 337–83.

Selkirk, Elisabeth. 1984. 'On the major class features and syllable theory'. In Mark Aronoff and R.T. Oehrle. eds. *Language sound structure: studies in phonology presented to Morris Halle by his teacher and students.* Cambridge, MA: MIT Press, 107–36.

Strang, Barbara M.H. 1970. *A history of English.* London: Methuen.

Trubetzkoy, Nikolai. 1939. *Grundzüge der Phonologie.* Prague: Travaux du Cercle Linguistique de Prague, 7. Translated by Baltaxe, Christiane A.M. (1969) as *Principles of phonology.* Berkeley and Los Angeles: University of California Press.

Tserdanelis, Georgios and Wai Yi Peggy Wong. eds. 2004. *Language files: materials for an introduction to language and linguistics.* 9th edition. Colombus, OH: The Ohio State University Press.

Vennemann, Theo. 1972. 'On the theory of syllabic phonology'. *Linguistische Berichte* 18: 1–18.

Wakelin, M. 1977. *English dialects: an introduction.* Revised edition. London: The Athlone Press.

Wells, J.C. 1982. *Accents of English.* [Three vols. Vol. 1: *Accents of English 1: an introduction.* Vol. 2: *Accents of English 2: the British Isles.* Vol. 3: *Accents of English 3: beyond the British Isles.*] Cambridge University Press.

Williams, Ann and Paul Kerswill. 1999. 'Dialect levelling: change and continuity in Milton Keynes, Reading and Hull'. In Foulkes and Docherty. eds. 141–62.

Index of topics